WHAT I WAS LISTENING TO WHEN ...

A MEMOIR SET TO MUSIC

JACK L.B. GOHN

McHenry Press 2021

What I Was Listening To When ... : A Memoir Set to Music

First Hard Copy Edition

Published by McHenry Press, 743 McHenry St., Baltimore, MD 21230, USA

Cover by Vanessa Mendozzi

Book design by Michael Grossman

Photo of commencement used by permission of Robin Janiszewski

Screenshot of Adventure game, copied from Wikipedia, redistributed to the public under the GNU Free Documentation License

Picture of the author by Sandi Gohn, used with permission

Icons are in public domain or subject to public use licenses

All other images copyright Jack L.B. Gohn

Visit the author's website: www.jackgohn.com.

ISBN: 978-1-7342264-3-0

READ THIS FIRST

A MUSICAL PLAYLIST runs through the heart of this book. To read the book without at least sampling the music would be a waste. Almost all of the listed songs (with one or two little extras) have been assembled, in order, on an easily- and freely-available Spotify Playlist entitled "What I Was Listening To When..." Access it by that name or at **HTTPS://OPEN.SPOTIFY.COM/ PLAYLIST/5IPCzOnG0KSuDERQ4yUBFU?SI**, and drop in on it as you read, by clicking on the Playlist Tracks indicated at the head of almost every chapter.

Check out the Playlist now. I'll wait.

Then you can turn the page.

CONTENTS

INTRODUCTION

THE NOTED PHILOSOPHER Chris Rock postulated that: "Whatever music was playing when you started getting laid, you gonna love that music for the rest of your life." Rock's postulate is valid, but it's incomplete. Two other propositions need to be added. First: You are always going to love all the music you loved whenever anything important happened to you, including those things that hurt the worst. And second: You're going to love at least hearing some of the music you hated at memorable times and maybe still do, because it reminds you of the stuff you want to remember anyway.

The music evokes the moments and the moments evoke the music. And the way these things have connected for me is my subject.

I call the songs that trigger these sorts of memories Theme Songs, and I will often refer to them that way in this book.

So: Here's my life and many of the Theme Songs that went with it. And you can hear most of them by clicking this link below that takes you to my Spotify playlist of those Theme Songs, not surprisingly entitled "What I was Listening To When…" which you can also reach by its URL: HTTPS://OPEN.SPOTIFY.COM/PLAYLIST/5IPCzOnG0KSuDERq4yubfU?si. Spotify carries almost everything you need. I've had to make a few substitutions, but not many. In two instances (including the first selection, as it happens), there is no suitable substitute in Spotify's library. But mostly, you'll hear exactly what I heard. And in all but one of those rare exceptions, you'll hear something close to what I heard. I'd hoped to also include cover art for each of the musical pieces discussed here, but the copyright issues proved too complex for me to attempt this.

Music reaches us through many media, and each medium breeds a somewhat different experience. Playing a record on a turntable is different from hearing the same recording on a car radio, and each are different from a download played on a computer. There are icons at the head of each chapter indicating the medium by which I first experienced the selections in question there.

Hopefully, some of these stories will not only amuse you but strike a spark of recognition too. And maybe you'll be moved to share your own tales about these songs with me. I can be reached via the link on my website: jackgohn.com/. I look forward to hearing from you.

Happy reading, and happy listening!

1

THE SAFEST TIME

PUSSYCAT'S CHRISTMAS, BY M. W. BROWN, TOLD BY ALBERT GROBE,
FEATURING THE GENE LOWELL CHORUS (1949), ENCOUNTERED CA. 1950

NO PLAYLIST TRACK

I REMEMBER ONLY one record of my own from before my mother and my father went their separate ways. This was *Pussycat's Christmas*, a 78 rpm shellac which, in two short sides playable in about 5 minutes, depicts a cat exploring the sights, sounds and feel of Christmas in a happily-stereotyped snow-covered American town. In this safe and secure place, she is no stray but neither is she a fettered housecat; she is free to venture out and listen to carolers and the bells of a sleigh, secure that at any time she can also demand readmittance to the warmth of a fireside near a Christmas tree. There is no hint of competing religious or cultural traditions: here Christmas prevails uncontested and unquestioned. The world is stable and safe, and yet, in its wintry and holiday possibilities, it is thrilling.

This mirrored how I felt about my own world as I was coming to consciousness. I knew my parents loved me, and had no idea yet that anything else mattered. I did not know that there could be threats in this exciting place. If you had told me, for instance, that there had recently been powerful people who would have tried to kill me and my father just for who we were, I would have been incredulous. If you had told me that my situation would shortly change in all sorts of unsettling ways, I would have been equally stunned.

3

Often complacence like mine is justified; there is a permanence to a child's family and his or her place in it. Not in my case, however. Though I did not know it, my world was rigged to be blown away in a moment, and even the fact that I had a place in it for that moment owed to a set of unlikely circumstances.

I was an American child born into what amounted to a provisional and temporary marriage, living a high and pampered life in London, celebrating Christmas when it might with equal likelihood have been a Jewish feast or no feast at all.

Emile, my father, was the first-generation child of secular Jewish immigrants to the U.S. and New York, a grad student at Harvard when he met my mother. Louise, my mother, was then an undergrad at Radcliffe, in the midst of the Great Depression. He sat behind her in a class taught by philosopher Alfred North Whitehead, and the story goes that he was so struck by her beauty and brains that he immediately pursued her. As I'm sure became known to him on their first date (at a tea room on Harvard Square), they hailed from different worlds. Louise, a Bostonian, was nominally Catholic, although she was then beginning a period (it proved to be temporary) of disowning that identity. She had done formidably well as a scholar at the Boston Girls' Latin School, but she was as interested in English poetry as in the classics. They were married within a year of her 1935 graduation, as he was working on (and she was typing) his doctoral dissertation in sociology (since at that time Harvard reportedly would not allow persons of Jewish extraction to pursue a doctorate in his real field, economics).

Not only did they come from different places, but after a few years, it seemed clear they were going to different ones as well. I do not know precisely when they separated, but it is clear that during most of the World War Two years they were living apart. He had become a part of the New Deal Labor Department, and I believe had also worked in war production regulation. She was pursuing advanced degrees first at Cornell and then at the Johns Hopkins University. Even when they both resided in Washington, she was not living with him.

You would not have expected any child to have issued from such a marriage. But they maintained a lot of affection for each other, and they each wanted a child notwithstanding the absence of conventional marital bonds. In 1948, Emile was given the opportunity to join the State Department and run the Marshall Plan for England with the position of Economic Attaché at the U.S. Embassy in London. They worked out a deal; I don't know who asked whom. But the deal was that my mom would come with him, and they would try to have a child together, apparently without any expectation that they would stay together after a child was born. Louise signed on, even though by then she was "returning to Rome," becoming the fervent Catholic her mother had failed to make of her twenty years earlier.

I'm sure from my mother's perspective the deal was irresistible, even though there is some evidence that at that time she was already involved with her fellow-grad student Ernie, the man who later became my stepfather. To live in Europe for awhile, though, as the consort of one of the American viceroys ruling the continent amid the war's wreckage, in the land that had produced the literature and drama she loved the most, and to have a child during some of her last fertile years – I'm sure it wasn't a hard decision for her.

The photo albums tell the story of those three years in London, complete with ocean liner travel, excursions around England, and trips to the Continent (Eiffel Tower, Alps, Colosseum). Louise's diary reflects audiences with the King and Queen, shows on the West End, and diplomatic receptions. And then, to top it off, in mid-July  1949, there was me. Outwardly to many of their friends, and, most importantly, to me, they must have seemed like a happy and glamorous couple.

I assume the Pussycat record, that little bit of Americana, made its way into my mother's hands from the shelves at the PX, the Post Exchange in London where the U.S. occupiers, diplomatic and military, shopped, unhindered by the postwar rationing that created so much discontent for our neighbors. I remember hearing the record played for me at Christmastime at least once during my first four years, and, so long as our placid but precarious situation passed as normal, I felt exactly like the Pussycat.

2

NOSTALGIA AT A YOUNG AGE

SNAKE RAG, BY LOUIS ARMSTRONG AND KING OLIVER,
PERFORMED BY HUMPHREY LYTTELTON AND HIS BAND
(CA. 1950), ENCOUNTERED CA. 1954

PLAYLIST TRACK NO. 1

PICTURE A BOY of four or five standing by himself in an unfamiliar gift shop in an unfamiliar town in an unfamiliar country. It is a weekend morning before the store opens, and before anyone else has arisen. The boy stands before a lacquered wooden cabinet containing a device called a Victrola. He has figured out how to work it; he turns a knob, the big tubes glimpsed through a grille begin to glow, the front display lights up while a heavy piece of shellac drops from a record changer spindle to a platter, the tone arm drops a needle on the record, and the mechanism begins to play.

And that boy of course is me; I'm preparing to listen to a rarity, British hot jazz: Humphrey Lyttelton and his band performing the Louis Armstrong and King Oliver hit *Snake Rag*. My introduction to the Pussycat and her Christmas is already half a lifetime and half a world away.

Since then we have moved repeatedly. First, from London to Vienna, where my father took essentially the same job he had performed in London. In Vienna we have lived on the top floor of a mansion, with four bronze frogs large enough for me to sit upon guarding the pond in our garden, and I'm assigned a beloved nursemaid. My father, I later learn, has taken a girlfriend, his interpreter. My mother has grown more Catholic, and has become very accomplished in German.

Postwar domestic politics, far away and yet not far away enough, have witnessed the resurgence of an endemic anticommunist crusade. One of the victims of that crusade turns out to be my father, who (though he calls himself a Quaker now) is, we suspect, too Jewish for the anti-subversives and has a cousin who was at one time a bona fide communist. Also, my father has given a talk praising the notion of world government. In consequence, in late 1953 he has been ejected from the State Department, with no opportunity to defend himself or appeal. We see him off at the Vienna airport, and that is the effective end of his diplomatic career and of my parents' marriage.

My mother carries on serenely with the life of a diplomat's wife (parties and theater and receptions), until it is time to go. After a night ride to Genoa in the back of an Army jeep through guarded Cold War checkpoints, she and I sail to New York on a ship destined to go down in history because (on a later voyage) it is destined to go down, the Andrea Doria. Back in the States our travels continue. I watch my first television, the McCarthy hearings and Howdy Doody, at my grandparents' home in Boston. I get bitten by my aunt's mean dog in Colorado. We spend a month at a Carmelite nuns' monastery in Carmel, California. We pass the obligatory six weeks at an apartment house for divorcing spouses in Reno, Nevada. And on our way back, we stop at Helen Gohn's gift and antiques store in Chicago Heights, Illinois, called The Tudor Shop.

Helen is the mother of my mom's fellow grad-student Ernest Gohn, and has been something of a den mother to the graduate students in the English Literature program at the Johns Hopkins University in the mid-1940s when Ernest and Louise were students there. But my mother's approach has also caused Helen to tell Ernie that it's time for him to act on the torch she's known he's carried for Louise since they were students together. Ernie, now employed at the Air University in Montgomery, Alabama, drops everything, and drives through the night to intercept Louise at the Tudor Shop. On the night of May 29, he asks her to marry him and she accepts. And less than a month later than that, they are married in Montgomery.

Somewhere in all of this activity, I suspect between the night he proposes and our arrival at his new job at the University of Michigan in Ann Arbor on September 7, my mother's things, probably in storage or transit since Vienna, have arrived in Chicago Heights to be picked up. And among those things is the record of Humphrey Lyttelton and his band playing *Snake Rag*. I have no present recall of having laid claim to it, but I know it is my missing, and missed, father's record, and I want to hear it. I can remember Emile's enthusiasm for this kind of music; I've listened to it with him more than once, as he would puff on a cigar.

I have, and will never have, any certainty how this record, one that should by rights have stayed with my father's things in New York, has nonetheless found its way to Chicago Heights and to me. Perhaps my father knows I liked it, and has sent it along so I'd have it, or even so I'd not forget him. But I know I listen to it that day, standing next to the Victrola on the landing of the steps down to the store's side entrance, on a morning where the sunlight picks up the dust motes, and that as I listen I think of him.

At that point, of course, I have no musical sophistication yet, no "ear." I certainly do not know that British white guys aren't supposed to play jazz at all. I just know I like it a lot. I play it over and over, and the next thing I know I'm trying to whistle along. I've never whistled before, and I'm not very good at it, but I would have to be a virtuoso whistler to manage this very fast and very tricky song.

You have to know something about that song to understand why it so caught my ear. The song was developed as one of the great milestones in the partnership between King Oliver and Louis Armstrong at the very birth of jazz. The song comes in sections, and some of them are bound together by a break in which Oliver and Armstrong on cornets slide down about a chromatic octave in perfect synch, maintaining a third interval between them. They run down that octave as quickly and light-footedly as children scampering down stairs. At the bottom they are stopped by a trombone that does a three-note figure like an adult muttering a warning, and then the next section begins, as if ignoring the adult.

What distinguishes this song as Lyttelton and his mates play it is that every solo, whether presented through the cornets, the clarinet, or the trombone, furthers the central melodic development. There's no running in place, no mere showing off, with the solos.

To be fair, no matter who performs it, the song does contain a portion of the entire ensemble baying at the moon together, as it were, but not the solos, and especially not those two cornets sliding down the scale in dazzling, uncanny synch. In each of the two seminal Oliver/Armstrong recordings, however, those baying at the moon sections have a certain static quality, a huffing-and-puffing in place quality that contrasts with the solos, which are the place, the only place, where the music moves ahead.

When Humphrey Lyttelton comes to the song a quarter century later, he's spotted that flaw. So when his trumpet and that of some sideman I can't identify hit the bottom of that glorious slide, the three-note trombone figure that Honoré Dutry just made a transition for Armstrong and Oliver turns into a slingshot in the hands of Lyttelton's sideman Keith Christie, propelling the music right back into the driving rhythm of the main segment. And there is no standing still, no puffing in place. The nearly narrative drive that Armstrong and Oliver were reaching for and fell a little bit short of is pretty much achieved.

What I hear in *Snake Rag* in 1954 is a little more naive, of course. I like the sonorities, the trombone butting in and guiding things whenever the music seems to stop, the clarinet warbling, the trumpets blasting. In 1954 I would not be able to identify which instruments I'm listening to, but I understand they are not all the same, and that they do something magical by diving in and out of that structured cacophony like dolphins racing alongside a boat.

I don't need to be sophisticated about it yet. I'm hooked.

3

O FOR A WOODEN O

HENRY V: LONDON 1600, BY WILLIAM WALTON (1944),
PERFORMED BY THE PHILHARMONIA ORCHESTRA,
CONDUCTED BY MUIR MATHESON, ENCOUNTERED 1956

DEATH OF RICHARD AND FINALE, BY WILLIAM WALTON
(1955), PERFORMED BY THE PHILHARMONIA ORCHESTRA,
CONDUCTED BY MUIR MATHESON, ENCOUNTERED 1957

MOVEMENT 1: ALLEGRO ASSAI, SYMPHONY NO. 1 IN B
FLAT MINOR, BY WILLIAM WALTON, PERFORMED BY
THE LONDON PHILHARMONIC ORCHESTRA, CONDUCTED BY
ADRIAN BOULT (1956), ENCOUNTERED CA. 1957

PLAYLIST TRACKS NOS. 2, 3, 4

SHAKESPEARE WAS IN my blood from the first. While we were establishing divorce residency in Reno in early 1954, even before my fifth birthday, my mother took me to a movie house to see *Julius Caesar* with James Mason and Marlon Brando. The auditorium was hot. There was no air conditioning. But I insisted on sitting through it twice. I may not have understood that much of the language or the story, but I just loved the sight of the togaed men and women striding around and striking poses amidst ancient Roman columns. So when, a year or so later, after we'd moved to Ann Arbor, a University of Michigan film series brought in Laurence Olivier's *Henry V*, there was no question my mom and my stepdad would take me.

It's an extraordinarily impressive movie, given the film technology of 1944, and given that it was made under wartime conditions, but no doubt the thing that impressed me most was the music. I was delirious with composer William Walton's fustian.

I'm not sure if we acquired the record album, containing the soundtrack music and Olivier's performances of certain passages, before or after seeing the movie. The album itself was a series of 12-inch 78s in sleeves bound together with covers like a book (the style for record albums in those days). I can't even find a vintage copy listed today on e-Bay, but I believe the musical contents have been decanted to a British Composers CD, the relevant cut from which is linked to as Playlist Track No. 2. This music, which made a giant impression on me that night in the Art Department Auditorium at the University of Michigan, was the opening, *London 1600*.

A playbill flutters through a blue sky. When it drifts into focus (to the accompaniment of a complex flute arpeggio), it reveals that the Globe Theater is putting on "Henry the Fift" today, May 1, 1600. There follows an orchestral flourish.

Then suddenly we are looking down at the Tower of London, and embark on a pan something like a helicopter flight over the London of 1600, Shakespeare's London. The camera comes to rest over the Globe Theater, Shakespeare's "wooden O." Today, of course, that shot would be a riot of CGI, and "sold" with all kinds of tricks so one practically believed one was looking at a real city three hundred years before the invention of photography. The scale model Olivier must have relied on isn't nearly that good, though many of the chimneys actually smoke and some of the boats move on the Thames. But it certainly isn't laughable. In fact, it took my breath away. And all the while, Walton is at work, with an orchestral and choral crescendo that may have owed something to the dawn sequence from Ravel's *Daphnis and Chloe*, keying up our anticipations.

Then we catch a glimpse of a flag being hoisted above the Globe's tower, cutting to a closeup of the man in the tower raising the flag. After he secures it, he lifts a trumpet to his lips and sounds a summons (a Waltonian stately and rousing trumpet blast). This is a cue to the string and woodwind orchestra a story below him to play an overture, and we follow a long pan from the orchestra around the interior of the Globe as the theatergoers troop in.

London, 1600, indeed! I played that album over and over.

It was the same with Walton's music for *Richard III*, the soundtrack of which (including most of the movie's dialogue) I'm pretty sure was a Christmas gift for me after we'd all seen the 1955 movie.

I committed all six LP sides of the recording to my auditory memory, including all of the dialogue, but certainly my favorite cue was the last: *Death of Richard and Finale*. Evil Richard, mortally wounded in battle, grasps a sword, making stabbing motions as his expressive last actions, and the music closely follows the helpless thrusts. As he expires, dropping his sword, a solo violin skitters down the scale. His corpse is loaded upon a horse, and a sort of funeral march takes over for a few bars. But then the music shifts again; the minor-key funeral march is swept away for a triumphal major-key march celebrating, apparently, the crown itself.

And indeed the focus shifts to the crown. It has rolled away from Richard during the battle like Tolkien's Ring of Power deserting one owner for another. But as Richard's corpse vanishes over the brow of the hill, the Crown is suddenly discovered in a bush, and brought to Henry Tudor, Earl of Richmond, the man destined shortly to have it encircle his own head, making him Henry VII. It is held up to him. That image is succeeded by a disembodied crown suspended in the sky, which stands at the head of the end credits.

The message of that triumphal march was not lost on me. The Crown, as underlined by that gorgeous major key march, was a glorious thing worth all the fighting over it that the movie had just chronicled. No wonder Richard had lusted after it so. I wanted a crown too, with music just like that playing in the background.

Yes, I knew I was an American, now living in a land that does not brook royalty. But there was the very recent example of Grace Kelly marrying into royalty; maybe I could do that! When I asked, though, I learned that the only British princess remotely age-appropriate for me was Princess Anne. And with all due respect to the lady, at the age of seven I already sensed that I would not be her type, or she mine. Though I often returned to the theme, I always concluded that I had no shot at this. Reality triumphed, and my fantasy perished like Richard, stabbing away feebly.

Except that fantasies don't always stay dead long. Mine were revived by a gift from my parents, perhaps a year later, of Walton's marvelous *Symphony No. 1*, which is not like a soundtrack, exactly, but somehow conducive to such notions. The opening of the first movement, Allegro Assai, to this day conjures up for me a solitary knight riding a horse swiftly uphill under lowering skies in the direction of some danger. I wanted to be that knight.

A friend of the family gave me some King Arthur armor, and that helped too. I knew, from Sidney Lanier's *The Boy's King Arthur*, which also came into my possession around this period, that Arthur and his knights existed in a different and earlier narrative from those

of Shakespeare's combative Plantagenet kings. It didn't matter. I wanted to live in that whole world, the world of knights and battles, and all the noble stuff that you could see onstage and on the screen, even if it wasn't much in evidence in a Great Lakes college town.

Nor was it irrelevant that I'd started life in the country where all that noble stuff had actually taken place. It was not that I felt British, exactly. The trouble was that I didn't feel quite American. I'd come "home" without having ever heard of baseball, way behind the curve in knowing about Davy Crockett and the Mickey Mouse Club, and raised among people who didn't much resemble the other parochial school parents in lifestyle or convictions. The noble knight fantasies made a lot of sense to me.

4

ALL IN WHITE

ALL I NEED IS THE GIRL, BY STEPHEN SONDHEIM AND JULE STYNE,
PERFORMED BY PAUL WALLACE (1959), ENCOUNTERED CA. 1959

PLAYLIST TRACK NO. 5

LISTENING TO RECORDED music must have been more of a shared activity in the America of my youth. There were no iPods then with user-programmed playlists, and less solitude in which to enjoy music. Few record players were portable, and they tended to be situated in common areas within homes. About the only music one could carry off to a private space was, in fact, was the transistor radio and the car radio, and with both of those, you were still at the mercy of the DJ when it came to selection. So if one person was listening to a record, there was an excellent chance that everyone else in the house would be listening to it, or at least hearing it, too.

Of course, in practice this tended to mean that kids had to listen to a lot of the music their parents liked. Perhaps it was because of that communal consumption that as a child I was particularly likely to take for granted the subliminal attitudes and assumptions that the music communicated. Up to a certain moment, what a child's parents and their community believe is pretty automatically assumed by the child as well.

One place where this osmotic transfer of attitudes certainly happened for me was with my parents' penchant for original cast recordings of musicals. We had a lot of them, and I still possess them all in their banged-up jackets

14

and their scratched-up glory: *Call Me Madam*, *Carousel*, *South Pacific*, *My Fair Lady*, *Bells Are Ringing*, *The Boy Friend*, *A Funny Thing Happened on the Way to the Forum*, and on and on. They'd get played a lot, and I'd hear them a lot, especially on game nights. Clue, triple solitaire, Monopoly, Scrabble, and Flinch were the games I mostly remember us playing in the living room, maybe four or five nights a week. And while that was going on, musicals made up a lot of the background music.

And of course I'd talk to my parents about the musicals, asking for explanations of the lyrics, and comparing everyone's responses to the music. As I remember those conversations now, it seems to me that I was measuring what was possible in life against what the songs depicted. Of course I understood that King Arthur was a myth and that *Camelot* was not a true story. I knew that the stock stereotypes evoked by *A Funny Thing Happened on the Way to the Forum* were deliberately overblown. But I was later to realize that, even making allowances for such things, I had still placed too much faith, particularly in what all the musicals had to say, unchallenged by my parents, about romantic love and everything surrounding it.

This is about one of the things surrounding it. I'm sure my parents and I talked a lot about *Gypsy*, which I'm guessing arrived as a present from one of them to the other in 1959, the year it was recorded. *Gypsy*, considered by many the greatest musical of the mid-20th Century, tells the parallel tales of Louise, a lonesome girl trying to grow up in the world of vaudeville, and of Rose, a monstrous stage mother who has channeled all her aggressive aspirations into the mission of making Louise and her sister into stars. Rose succeeds with Louise, in unexpected fashion, as Louise, after many false starts in the collapsing world of vaudeville, becomes the superstar stripper Gypsy Rose Lee (1911-1970). The dramatic arcs of mother and daughter sort of go in opposite directions, in a fashion reminiscent of *A Star Is Born*.

You might think that the big discussion there would have concerned burlesque itself, which in some households, particularly of that era, might have been a fraught subject. But it really wasn't a big discussion. My folks simply took a just-the-facts-ma'am approach to what went on at a burlesque show. I was ready for the basic facts, even if as a 10-year-old I didn't need to think about the male gaze yet or its implications for me as the possessor of one. No, where I got misled was on the romance part.

And yes, if you're scratching your head over that, objecting that there's precious little romance in *Gypsy*, you're right, but still there's enough, if you know where to look. That place is hardly Mama Rose's abusive relationship with Mr. Goldstone. Nor will you find it in the standard numbers that the musical has bequeathed us (*Small World*, *Everything's Coming Up Roses*, *Let Me Entertain You*, *You'll Never Get Away From Me*), but in a novelty number that is a definite non-standard: *All I Need Is the Girl*.

There are lots of decent videos of this number on YouTube which you can check out. In the scene, late-teenaged Louise, isolated by her mother from almost all peer contact, is trying to build bridges with Tulsa, a personable young man who is part of her vaudeville troupe. She asks him to demonstrate a song-and-dance act he is working up as part of his own effort to strike out for freedom and autonomy. As he enthusiastically cooperates with the request, his routine evokes elegance and romance, ballroom, tap, and ballet, and Louise responds by trying to become part of the act in more than one sense, dancing along but also wishing she could romance along as well. But Tulsa is lost in his own world, dancing with an imaginary partner ("all in white!"), while Louise is stuck in part of a miserable animal costume from the vaudeville act her mother makes her do. They do touch and he allows her to share the flourish at the end, but the momentary sharing is only about the showbiz of it, not the romance. So the song, which sounds a bit as if Tulsa were seducing Louise, is really about Tulsa and Louise having their separate dreams side-by-side. It works for him, but not for her.

Louise's disappointment doesn't come across on the record, and my parents never took me to the actual show. So what I heard was what I got. And what I heard was something I couldn't even express yet. It's all there in the music, though. It's Jule Styne's music, nicely set off by Stephen Sondheim's lyrics. The lyrics tell the tale of a young man dressing for the romantic role he wants to play by upgrading his wardrobe: "Once my clothes were shabby./ Tailors called me cabbie./ So I took a vow:/ Said this bum'll be Beau Brummel." And he goes on to describe the "Paris silk" and "Harris tweed" he has acquired. And the hoped-for next acquisition is "the Girl." But the outfit is only the prerequisite; the real attraction is the young man's dancing. And so the dance number takes over, in which, in Tulsa's imagination, the girl "all in white" appears for a romantic pas-de-deux involving both waltzing and tap.

Styne meanwhile has been weaving in a sophisticated, jazzy little melody that creeps upwards by half steps, then retreats in a flurry of dance patter, only to come surging back, again and again. After the transition to the dream sequence with the girl in white, the melody returns in subtly different form, morphing from waltz to jazz, getting faster and more explosive as it reaches its climax – a word chosen advisedly. For this music is nothing if not sexual. And by that I don't mean salacious, I mean sexual, evocative of the emotions and rhythms of lovemaking itself. But it's all sublimated in the ritual of dance (the taps are audible on the recording).

At 10, I could hear this and respond to it. Sex, I was being taught, was about looking perfect, about the ability to do something incredibly beautiful and difficult in conjunction with another person without really even needing to rehearse. It was about feeling elated about oneself and one's athleticism and one's body, based on miraculously having that athleticism and that body. And all of it leading to sublime emotion.

Well, at 10 I wasn't ready for all that, and I knew it. But I filed it away. I filed it as the notion that love is moving in some effortless concord with another person. There was nothing in this notion about love being work, about the reality that no two lovers throughout history have ever been perfect in themselves or perfect for each other. I really believed that, if I held out for the realization of this perfect balletic dream, I could achieve it.

And when, later on, I began experiencing romance as we humans actually do experience it, I still maintained that notion, even as reality contradicted it. Bringing my ideas and my experience together took longer than it should have. Blame those beautiful misleading musicals!

5

A STATELY ROLL

WINDJAMMER (THE SHIP) BY MORTON GOULD (1958), ENCOUNTERED 1960

NO PLAYLIST TRACK

OF COURSE, ONE does not automatically snap back from the kinds of upheaval my life had gone through in my first few years. I've sometimes been guilty of overly happy talk about my feelings then, because it's undoubtedly true that all my birth parents and my stepparents were good and interesting people, and they all loved me. And that mattered a lot; I believe that my experience of what they called in that era a "broken home" was about as painless as it is ever possible for that experience to be. But still, losing one's geographical and social place, one's way of life, one's country, one's family structure, and even one's last name, as I did, and having to come to terms with different ones entirely, that takes work and time. Let me talk here about some music that I always associate intimately with the altered bond I now had with my father.

My mom, Louise, and stepfather, Ernie, were my custodial parents, and my home was with them in Ann Arbor, Michigan. My father, Emile, was back in New York; by 1960 he was a professor at Columbia. He found both professional and personal reasons to visit me often. And when he came out to Michigan, it was always with presents, and we always had good times together.

One can argue that a non-custodial parent who's all about gifts and treats is somehow doing it wrong. All I can say is, this was my father's way of showing love, and I unhesitatingly accepted them in that spirit. Plus, I loved the presents.

You might think, living only about 40 miles west of Detroit, I'd have gotten chances to go there on occasion, but for some reason my mom and stepdad never visited Detroit with me as a family. Hence it was with my dad, not my mom and stepdad, that I received most of my experiences of the car-making metropolis to the east.

For instance, on one Saturday in October of 1960, my father flew into Willow Run airport where I was waiting for him. From there we traveled into Detroit, staying at the large and swanky Park Shelton Hotel, and made an evening of it by going to the grand art deco Music Hall Theatre and seeing the movie *Windjammer*. This was the one and only feature movie made in Cinemiracle, a rival process to Cinerama. Neither name may mean much today, 60 years later, but they were sensations then. Each technology involved filming with three cameras and exhibiting with three projectors. With all that square footage of celluloid, the resulting image could be huge. The screen was designed to wrap around its audience (similar to IMAX today, but more so). The idea was to give the viewer the sense of being in the midst of the action.

Despite the technical imperfections of the processes (join lines where the pictures bordered being probably the worst), Cinerama/Cinemiracle did have the undeniable power of putting you in the middle of things. So far as I am aware, there was never a truly great movie made by either process, but the depiction of certain things like roller coaster rides or buffalo stampedes would be so awe-inspiring, no one was going to be carping at the mere absence of great art.

Windjammer, which had its U.S. premiere in April of 1958, follows the men and boys of the Christian Radich, a Norwegian tall ship used as a training vessel for that nation's merchant marine. They have adventures like riding out a squall in the Bay of Biscay, attending a private cello recital by Pablo Casals, riding basket sleds in Madeira, and experiencing the bright lights of New York City. I had a riotous time, and came out with my eleven year-old brain intoxicated by the wild spectacle. My father, who was always one to make the flavor last when he could, bought me the soundtrack LP from a lobby concession on the way out the door.

When I got back to Ann Arbor, that record promptly became one of my favorites, and not merely because of the associations I've mentioned.

I still have it. It is a musical potpourri doubtless designed to appeal to a wide variety of tastes: not only the aforementioned Casals track, but also some purpose-composed "easy listening" ballads allegedly sung spontaneously by the crewmen, a couple of dollops of Caribbean steel band, and regular film score music. The latter was composed by Morton Gould, a remarkable American composer comfortable as Leonard Bernstein writing in popular genres but just as clearly capable of working in the classical tradition. I think I recognized immediately the difference between the quality of the hackwork on the "spontaneous" songs of the crew and the haunting melodies and orchestration that emanated from Gould.

The gem of the album is Gould's composition for the ship's own theme song, Windjammer (The Ship), which somehow captures the stately roll of a powerful rigged vessel, and conveys a sense of the fitness for adventure which such a vessel offers its crew. While I did not, and could not realistically, see myself as a sea traveler anymore, a boy could dream, especially when his dad offered up the dreams and the theme music for them.

6

A KITSCHY GLIDE

CALCUTTA, BY HEINO GAZE, PERFORMED BY LAWRENCE WELK
AND HIS ORCHESTRA (1960), "ENCOUNTERED" 1959

PLAYLIST TRACK No. 6

NOT ALL GOOD music is sophisticated. Lawrence Welk's version of *Calcutta*, however intelligently constructed and played, is musical kitsch. Doesn't mean it's not good.

How kitschy? Try this: **HTTPS://WWW.YOUTUBE.COM/WATCH?V=2FCJC9TCEJW**, a video of the song from Lawrence Welk's show, which incidentally gives you the complete performance of the song with the exact orchestration of the 1961 hit. One's jaw hangs loose as one watches it, especially when one considers it was shot in 1971: the accordion-and-harpsichord orchestration, the dreadful clothing choices, the green jackets on the musicians, the female singers adorned with the helmet-coifs and the matching puce dresses clapping in time, the Geritol sign on the wall, the dancers, many of whom are unapologetically old and dowdy-looking, being watched by an even grayer audience – all of this captured in the same year that Jim Morrison died. And I haven't even gotten to the music yet.

There is also a very German kind of musical superficiality, honed by the polka and the drinking song, and this number is from that tradition. The melody, composed in 1958, is by Heino Gaze (1908-1967), a journeyman German film composer who also did a considerable business in drinking songs and cute little melodies. It pretty much defines Easy Listening, German Division. It conjures up a world of resolute cheeriness.

Could it be that there was something slightly deeper, something exotic, under the surface? After all, it's not called *Hamburg*. Well, for starters, title notwithstanding, it's not in any way evocative of Indian music. The propulsive rhythm, melody, chord structure, and orchestration are all cheerfully Western. Nor is there anything truly exotic in the English lyrics. (You can hear the lyrics as recorded by the Four Preps in a cover of the Welk version, which charted in February 1961, two months after Welk's.) Basically, it's all about how the lucky protagonist has kissed girls in Naples, Spain, and Par-ee, but prefers the way they kiss in Calcutta. (The same basic idea as *California Girls* (see Chapter 17), when you think of it.) One suspects that *Calcutta* was designated simply because it scanned properly. So no, when listeners hear no real hint of the Indian city now more correctly known as Kolkata, they're correctly not hearing what isn't there. The song's a *heimisch* confection that poses no challenge whatsoever to the musical taste buds. But for that very reason it's delightful as ice cream.

So what was my connection with all of this? That too inspires humility, because, though I can't be quite certain, it appears that somewhere in the recesses of my mind I've forged an association that has no real-life basis.

Let me explain.

My parochial school in Ann Arbor, Michigan, had, for at least one year of my youth, a summer recreation program. Now, I made a lot of good use of my summers as a kid, learning to type, to swim, and to play tennis, and doing advanced studies in Math and German. But at least during the summer of 1959, I took part in that rec program. I think that was the most summer fun I ever had. And most of it was pretty basic. We piled into buses and went to lakes to swim. We also took the buses to amusement parks. And we roller skated in the former school gym, which at a pinch also became the auditorium when folding seats were lined up there.

I loved the skating the best. And it was a remarkably unsophisticated pleasure. Just get yourself issued the old-fashioned 2X2 skates in your shoe size, strap them on, and go round and round on the green vinyl tiles.

Round and round, that is, while the easy listening music plays. In my mind, it's always *Calcutta*. Except it couldn't have been. If 1959 was my rec program summer, you hit an anachronism like a brick wall. *Calcutta* hadn't been recorded yet that summer. There was, I understand, a German version from 1958, but I can't imagine that we were playing that.

So the bottom line is my favorite association from the summer of 1959 is inextricably linked to a 1961 song.

Sometimes, when presented with the impossible, you just have to go with it. It's my story and I'm sticking to it. The song that always reminds me of those simple unsophisticated afternoons of skating lazily around in circles is a song I probably first heard two years later. The song is as square and kitschy, as reassuring that nothing will ever change for the worse, as the pleasure that will always come to mind when I hear it. In the song's lyrics, the singer's encounters with the women who kiss him all over the world don't entail any heartbreak or betrayal, any regrets, any chance of STDs. Music with any shadows in it, any exoticism even, would be all wrong. It's all a charming game, just like roller-skating on a Sunday afternoon. And that connection, I guess, will have to be enough.

7

DANCES FOR TOLKIEN

POLOVETSIAN DANCES BY ALEXANDER BORODIN
(WITH NIKOLAI RIMSKY-KORSAKOV AND ALEXANDER GLAZUNOV)
(1890), ENCOUNTERED CA. 1961

THE SORCERER'S APPRENTICE BY PAUL DUKAS
(1897), ENCOUNTERED CA. 1961

SUBSTITUTE PLAYLIST TRACKS NOS. 7, 8, 9, 10, 11, 12, 13, 14

I COME NOW to a record, indeed a kind of record, that seems to have disappeared, even from the electronic yard sale racks of e-Bay. It has disappeared so thoroughly I can't find an image to link to. Heaven only knows where my own copy disappeared to, probably four decades ago. I'm speaking of my grocery store classical music anthology.

Many people can remember grocery store encyclopedias, sold a volume a week. This was the same idea, but instead of volumes, the grocery store would sell classical records. Along with the first one, you got a leatherette binder about four inches thick, all in burgundy with black accents and gold lettering, with a title something like *The Treasury of the World's Great Music*. (One Raymond Tuttle has written about a similar product marketed the same way, *The Basic Library of the World's Greatest Music*. See HTTP://WWW.CLASSICAL.NET/MUSIC/RECS/REVIEWS/R/RED00110A.PHP.) Whatever the title of my own anthology was exactly, I know it suggested that once you bought and learned about all the pieces inside, you'd be a connoisseur. Well, I wanted to be that, so I persuaded my mom to pop for a dollar or so at the A&P on Huron Street each time one more piece of vinyl sophistication was issued.

As my parents were out to make a cultured intellectual, they took little persuading. They had their own quite extensive collection of classical music, but if I wanted a set for myself at a modest outlay, they'd see to it that I got one.

The arrival of each LP was an event. Each record came in a sleeve punched to fit in the binder. Accompanying it was a lavishly-illustrated (in black ink plus one extra color) leaflet, I think of eight pages, that told you all about the pieces on the record, and the life of the composer. I'd crack open the cellophane package, unscrew the binder, insert my leaflet and liner, rescrew the binder, and get right to work listening and reading.

And this was what brought Beethoven and Bach and Berlioz and Grieg and Tchaikovsky and a host of others into my life. I learned of Beethoven's deafness, and what his symphonies sounded like (I think they packaged two of them). I learned that something had been dreadfully wrong with Tchaikovsky's marriage (though not precisely what) and how he had been rescued from despair by the kindly benefactress Mme. Von Meck, and I came to recognize the sound of the *Pathétique*. And incidentally, I came across the perfect theme music to accompany one of my most gripping literary experiences.

I wish I remembered exactly when my parents introduced me to J.R.R. Tolkien. I'm pretty certain it was sort of an afterthought after I'd exhausted C.S. Lewis' Narnia series. I had literally grown up with the Narnia books; by 1958, though, I'd received (and inhaled) my copy of the last one. Somewhere my parents heard about Tolkien, and how he was somewhat the same kind of thing.

And so, kind of as an experiment, I think, they got me the first Houghton Mifflin edition hardback *Hobbit*. That took. So they bought me the first volume of *The Lord of the Rings*, and then the second, and then, inevitably, the third. I still have these copies, though unfortunately the dust jackets are long gone. I read them over and over. I copied Tolkien runes, and actually tried to send people messages using them. And of course I was making a movie in my head, though I had no idea how it could possibly be done.

I have a memory of reading *The Lord of the Rings* in my bed early in the morning. There was a second-floor window close to the head of my bed, and there was a mulberry tree below it on which birds liked to perch and sing. In summer the windows would be open (no air conditioning). So naturally I'd be up early. It was a wonderful, quiet time. And there I would sit with various books.

I could riff on some of the other books, but my point is that I very specifically recall the thrill of reading Tolkien sitting there. And while I was reading that, I often had playing softly, so as not to wake my parents (on my grey two-tone Columbia record player) one particular record from *The Treasury of the World's Great Music* (or whatever it was really called). This LP combined on one side the symphonic version of Borodin's *Polovetsian Dances* and Dukas' *The Sorcerer's Apprentice*. Now with all respect to Howard Shore's estimable soundtrack for the Peter Jackson's near-definitive movies, once you've listened to these pieces, you will never think of Shore as being in the same class in capturing the thrill of those books.

Yes, I know that these pieces were written to capture something rather different. Borodin (together with his posthumous collaborators Mussorgsky and Glazunov), was seeking to convey the exoticism of the Central Asian Polovtsi people, who are not Russian like the audience, and not the good guys. Paul Dukas was setting an ancient cautionary tale in a dark but humorous scherzo. And probably I would never have associated these things with Tolkien if I'd seen them in their more accustomed settings, the grand opera for Borodin, and Disney's *Fantasia* for Dukas. I was at least on notice with the Dukas, as there was in my booklet a still of Mickey Mouse as the Sorcerer's Apprentice from the 1940 movie. But it made little impression. If you can listen to these pieces without that baggage, though, you can see what wonderful accompaniments they make to Tolkien's epic. You think about what's in those books and, as they say, there's an app for that.

There's music that fits with traveling to unfamiliar and desolate places, music that might call to mind hobbits jumping along the road, music that calls troops of horsemen like the Rohirrim to mind, music for battle scenes or flights by night, music conjuring up crowded tones, and music for desolate and sinister places.

Obviously the books are long and the pieces are short, less than 20 minutes total, which is why they fit nicely on a single side of an LP. And obviously I was listening to lots of other things over the several readings I gave those books. But there was never any question what record of mine gave the most scope to my musing how to make – and score – a movie based on them.

8

THE GROUND WAS SHAKING

TEMPTATION, BY NACIO HERBERT BROWN (1933),
ARRANGED BY JERRY BILIK (CA. 1957),

PERFORMED BY THE UNIVERSITY OF MICHIGAN
MARCHING BAND, ENCOUNTERED 1962-1967

NO PLAYLIST TRACK

IT'S AMAZING HOW, when you check, some things that seem to have been constantly repeated parts of your life turn out to have actually been infrequent and relatively few in number. They just made outsized impressions on your memory.

One sterling example of this for me was University of Michigan football games. Like everyone else growing up in Ann Arbor, I encountered football as a secular religion with which no church could ever compete. In observance whereof, the town pretty much stopped doing business on home game Saturdays. Most locals were at the game: the Stadium held about as many seats as the town held people. And in those days, unlike these, it was possible for youngsters to attend even without the aid of a rich parent. If the game didn't sell out, the holder of a high school ID could obtain an end zone seat for a dollar.

So my unexamined recollection was that I was going all the time. My mom's diary says otherwise. It reflects that I went a mere 18 times in junior high and high school. Now that's not negligible, but it's not constant. About one percent of the days in my high school years. And yet the memory is golden and large for me. It feels like a constant and frequent thing.

I think the discrepancy between what I feel and what I know is to be explained by a number of things, not least that even if I wasn't there at the game, I was still listening to it and living it along with everyone else in town. (Along, even, with my parents, who believed that all this sports stuff diverted universities from intellectual pursuits. Therefore they affected far less interest and far more scorn than they actually felt.)

The games I did go to were especially cathartic. You entered what they now call The Big House by climbing a hill, walking under stands that towered over you, and then the world would suddenly open up, as the field was well below the outside grade, and you were suspended partway up this huge bowl halfway between the earth and the sky. And that was the environment in which you'd start to experience the whole thing, including the cheerleaders (the local contingent then an all-male gymnastic corps, very natty in Michigan maize sweaters, in sometimes piquant contrast with their mostly all-female counterparts for the visitors), the crowd, awash in the colors of the University and its rivals, the booming amplified voice of the announcers. And you'd be there with friends, and/or sometimes a date, and the sharing of the experience would add a whole other dimension.

And, then, of course, there was the marching band, almost as much a religious idol as the team itself. It would warm up in the morning elsewhere around the campus and march into the Stadium in the run-up to the game. If you lived anywhere near the heart of town, as I did, you'd hear them echoing through the streets. And they'd fill the field after the game and play some more.

And that's the part I want to write about here: where I could exit the stands and swarm on out to the field myself. Understand that it can get pretty cold in the stands, no matter how enthusiastic you might be and however much time you might have spent on your feet. The sun might be sinking lower in the sky at that point; 3:30 p.m. on a late fall day can be distinctly tinged with dusk, particularly if it's overcast. The glorious disorientation you might have felt upon emerging into the Stadium three hours earlier will have worn off, and you have been focusing on a patch of grass for most of those hours, but needless to say you have been kept from coming near that beautifully tended and inviting-looking field by ushers and cops.

And then suddenly, the constraints begin to come off just as the tension of the game, for better or for worse, falls away. In the last few minutes, win or lose, the marching band begins to file back onto the sidelines. And as the game actually ends, the band occupies the field and starts to play. The police officers who had blocked fan access to the field stand aside, and we fans who want the flavor to last for a few more minutes are unleashed to go down there, onto that legendary patch of grass, and stand almost amidst the band. (I understand fans can't go down there these days at any point, but I'm speaking of a more generous era.)

Though it's common now, the Michigan Marching Band reportedly was the first such ensemble in the country to put on a post-game show, and the inspiration came from nothing more complicated than the desire to dampen the crush of game-goers headed for the parking lots and the highways. But what a gift to be privileged to stand right in the band's midst for it! It is one of those in-person musical experiences that are so intense that nothing else, certainly nothing recorded, can duplicate them.

And the main reason why is the Jerry Bilik arrangement of *Temptation*, which rests upon a thunderous but dexterous drum foundation that rapidly hands the timekeeping and embellishment back and forth among a variety of timpani. You can stand right there a couple of feet from the bass drummers, as they shake the earth, unpredictably contributing to an overall boom-ba-ba-ba-boom-ba-ba-ba-boom-ba-ba-ba-boom in time to the song, and it is a form of aural ecstasy. (Unfortunately there's no video on YouTube that really captures it, but there are some that at least suggest it.)

It was an unlikely song to end up so powerful. The moral of the story may be never to underestimate the power of a good arranger. Jerry Bilik, the nonpareil arranger here, completed a thirty-year process in which the song was redesigned from a crooner ballad to a power number.

Wikipedia says that *Temptation*, music by Nacio Herbert Brown, lyrics by Arthur Freed, was originally published in 1933. Freed is better-known as the king of the early MGM musicals. And indeed the song appeared first in an MGM musical, *Going Hollywood*, with Bing Crosby and Marion Davies, in that year. Crosby also recorded it that year with Len Hayton's orchestra, an exercise in pure crooning. Others who gave it that treatment were Perry Como, who tangoed it up in 1945, and Mario Lanza, who did the same in 1952. The tango element was played up even more in a version played in the movie *Singin' in the Rain* (1952), where it was called *Temptation (Tango)*. But the man who taught the song to swing was bandleader Artie Shaw around 1940. In the syncopated tom-toms that propel his version, you can hear the beat that must have set Michigan arranger Jerry Bilik's imagination wandering, probably around 1957, which is when it first seems to have been incorporated into the Michigan Marching Band's repertory.

Not that Bilik merely transcribed Shaw's version for the marching band, not at all. Shaw's version is still a dance number, although the dancing would have had to have been pretty energetic (GIs just going away to war when the Shaw version came out would have been motivated to toss their sweethearts around with abandon, no doubt). Bilik took this slightly antique-sounding piece of pre-war pop (published the year Bilik was born), swapped in a bolero rhythm for the existing tango rhythm, axed the croony bridge, threw in something that Khatchaturian would have used for a dervish dance, and turned the number into a bellow of athletic power, causing the earth to tremble and the ears to tingle with the heavy use of cymbals. In his hands, it's nobody's love song; it's something much more brilliant and dynamic, but also more primitive. It's a hymn to the football war god.

In consequence, whenever I think back to the whole Michigan football experience of my youth, the recall always starts with me standing on that field under a darkening, cold sky, being consoled for a team loss if there was one by the indomitable sound of those drums and tympani shaking the earth. Mischance is being defied. For a moment at least, Michigan, and I as one of its fans, are transcendent. Whatever the score, the universe is ours. Go Blue!

9

PREVIEWS OF LOVE

DO IT AGAIN, LYRICS BY B.G. DESYLVA, MUSIC BY GEORGE GERSHWIN,
PERFORMED BY JUDY GARLAND (1961), ENCOUNTERED CA. 1962

LAZY AFTERNOON, BY JOHN LATOUCHE AND JEROME MOROSS,
PERFORMED BY MARLENE DIETRICH (1954),
ENCOUNTERED CA. 1962

PLAYLIST TRACKS NOS. 15, 16

STRANGE HOW POTENT cheap music is, a Noel Coward character observes. This understates the matter. Cheap music doesn't just affect our emotions; it also informs our thinking. Songs tell us what to expect about the world, not just how to feel about it. In the cheap ones (at least as I use the term) that information is erroneous, incomplete, or just plain wrong. And since, for most adolescents, songs are a vital vector of information, relying too exclusively on those cheap ones (i.e. songs plagued by prejudices, received ideas, or just laziness) can result in some rather strange notions.

I should know.

Let me talk about a couple of these songs that I consulted as I was beginning to think about girls. I was then about thirteen. I was trying to conceptualize some way of matching up my feelings with some kind of plausible scenario about getting close to girls. Enter two popular chanteuses to serve up suggestions: Marlene Dietrich and Judy Garland.

31

Bit of background: Dietrich, a husky-voiced, German-accented woman of the world, in her 60s at this point, had been an immense favorite during the War, but I think by the early 1960s she was becoming a bit *vieux jeu* with the public at large. Still, people of my parents' generation, then nearing their fifties, retained great loyalty. Somehow I sensed these dynamics, which I took to mean that I was a little bit sophisticated sharing my mom and step-dad's interest. (I was still just a year or so too young to be susceptible to a countervailing embarrassment just because something I liked was out of date.)

Garland, on the other hand, was having a different career trajectory, going up and down all the time, but mainly and right then up. At age 38 she had just enjoyed the biggest night of her career, her legendary 1961 concert at Carnegie Hall. Everyone loved the double album that came out of that night; it charted for 73 weeks on the Billboard chart, including 13 at No. 1. My frenemy Paul, a boy who was fiercely competitive with everyone, got the album first, before anyone, and knew all the songs by heart. I mention this because Paul possessed a firmer sense than I did what was in and what was out amongst us young teens, and he was not at all the type to have publicly indulged in a taste that was unacceptable.

The bottom line was, I was open to listening to each of them.

At this point, I was just trying to imagine what it would be like to – well, there isn't a good word for it. Sex (of which I'd understood the mechanics already for a couple of years) was definitely not what I was trying to imagine. As a good Catholic schoolboy, I still assumed that that kind of thing wasn't on the program until I got married. I guess the best way to say it was I was trying to visualize romance.

Judy gave me one idea.

You really shouldn't have done it,
You hadn't any right.
I really shouldn't have let you kiss me.
And although it was wrong, I never was strong.
So as long as you've begun it,
And you know you shouldn't have done it,
Oh, do it again.
I may cry no, no, no, no, no, but do it again.
My lips just ache to have you take

The kiss that's waiting for you.
You know if you do you won't regret it.
Come and get it.

The way Judy sang *Do It Again* in that Carnegie Hall presentation told me a lot about female longing. It made conceivable, perhaps for the first time, that women might like kissing, even if they didn't admit it right off the bat. Overcoming their reluctance sounded like fun, so long as the reluctance was only – what? – not feigned, but provisional and temporary, like Judy's. I never visualized forcing a kiss from someone who really didn't want to. But that was the problem in a nutshell: how could you tell if they didn't want it before you tried? And there was a secondary problem: how were you going to deal with the embarrassment if you discovered they really didn't want to? (A dilemma that I believe continues to haunt nice young men through the generations.)

It's not just the words, of course. Judy makes her voice soft and naive and virginal. Had Ethel Merman sung the same thing, it might have rung a bell or two with adult listeners, but not with a 13-year old. Thank goodness, too, I had the old LP, and not the CD reissue, which includes about 1:20 of monologue after the applause dies down, all about how Judy might have a cold, having perhaps "picked up an old fungi in Atlanta." And all of the sweetness is gone from her now-New York-accented voice, a cultivated but recognizably Gothamite accent like my father's and my aunt's – way too grownup. What my younger adult son now calls a buzzkill. My early adolescent fantasies might not have been the same.

In those fantasies, somehow I was going to get over that obstacle of finding the girl who actually wanted to kiss back – how, I wasn't certain, but it was going to happen. Then what? That was where Marlene came in handy with *Lazy Afternoon*. She presented me a plausible fantasy about what the blissful communion of two lovers might be all about. I should hasten to add that it was about the only completely graspable thing on the album where I encountered it: *Marlene Dietrich at the Café de Paris* (1954). This vinyl platter was a mass of confusing signals that it was going to take me years to work my way through, but I sensed I didn't get the half of what was going on. One of the few songs I thought I really understood was *Lazy Afternoon*. It suggested what I and the girl might do once we discovered we really, really liked each other. We could walk out to the countryside together and sit very, very still, and let nothing happen, and it would be incredibly intimate:

It's a lazy afternoon
And the beetle bugs are zooming
And the tulip trees are blooming
And there's not another human
In view
But us two.
It's a lazy afternoon
And the farmer leaves his reaping
In the meadow cows are sleeping
And the speckled trouts stop leaping upstream
As we dream
A far pink cloud hangs over a hill
Unfolding like a rose
If you hold my hand and sit real still
You can hear the grass as it grows
It's a hazy afternoon
And I know a place that's quiet
Except for daisies running riot
And there's no one passing by it
To see.
Come spend this lazy afternoon with me.

The orchestration is simple, alive with shimmering strings that suggest a sultry afternoon. It's all very, for Dietrich, unambiguous. In recent years, the song has been recorded by everybody (AllMusic.com lists 500 recordings including Barbra Streisand, Vanessa Williams, and Wynton Marsalis), but Dietrich's was almost certainly the first, and there still weren't many by 1962. So this came at me as a breathtaking first.

It provided me with a plausible picture for my fantasies of what might happen after the *Do It Again* kisses. In the Ann Arbor of 1962, you could still walk from the center of town to real farms (much harder now). And with my parents, I would sometimes be driven to places that were just a little further out that were so unpopulated you could truly be alone. I'd slip away from the grownups, and go for a long hike through deserted fields and ponds, and think about what bliss it would be to have someone who loved me to share it all with. That sounded pretty good to me.

It was all true, if incomplete. Even in *Lazy Afternoon*, the implication is strong that the lovers on the blanket in the countryside get up to more than holding hands. But I couldn't quite visualize it yet. I had a lot more to learn.

10

"PATRICIA"

I GET A KICK OUT OF YOU, BY COLE PORTER, PERFORMED
BY EILEEN RODGERS (1962), ENCOUNTERED 1962

PLAYLIST TRACK NO. 17

IN THE LAST two weeks of August 1962, when I had recently turned 13, I hopped the New York Central Railroad's Wolverine to New York to visit with my father Emile. At this stage of his life he was teaching at the Columbia Graduate School of World Business. He had just published his most important book, had either received or was about to receive his full professorship, and was three years into his successful second marriage. He and my stepmother had recently bought a country getaway home in Tannersville, up in the Catskills. In short, I was visiting a man at the top of his game.

It was an exciting time for him, and a good time for me to drop in. Three things stand out about that visit for me.

One was that he took me on the Staten Island Ferry to pass the Statue of Liberty. It was a big gulp of the sheer glamor of the town, and I was duly impressed. Another was that a girl from my hometown of Ann Arbor visited. And a third was that my dad took me to see the off-Broadway revival of Cole Porter's *Anything Goes* at the Orpheum Theatre and bought me the album.

I was now a rising eighth grader. A girl I'll call Patricia and I comprised half of a four-kid circle a charismatic teacher of ours had formed, back in my fifth grade. This teacher, Sister Rose Irene, had decided that the four of us were getting too little out of the grade school library, and had sent us up to the high school library instead.

The four of us, two boys and two girls, would not just climb the stairs to mingle with our elders, but we began to hang out together as a clique at each other's houses. I particularly bonded with Patricia, a slim, tall, thoughtful girl. We talked on the phone a lot, and with her I could talk about almost anything. I visited her home sometimes even if there were only two of us, and not the foursome. And by the beginning of eighth grade I was beginning to have feelings for her.

I've described in the previous chapter where I was then in my thinking about girls. Perhaps I'd moved on just a little from that stage to the moment I am speaking of, now that I was turning Patricia over in my mind. Having her as a friend, someone with valuable things on her mind to share, and to appreciate the most important things about me – that was of far more moment than the thought that, for instance, we might be smooching some time.

And what was one of the most important things about me then? Why, the fact that, though I lived in Ann Arbor, I had something of a second life, with an illustrious dad and stepmom in Manhattan. So when I learned that Patricia and her mom would be visiting in New York at the same time as I, it was like manna from heaven. I could bring Patricia into my New York life! She could see (and hopefully admire) that side of me. I agitated with Patricia's mom and my dad for a meeting in Manhattan. And the parents complied.

My dad lived on the Upper West Side in a University-owned apartment, so Patricia and her mom came up there. We were a couple of blocks away from the Riverside Cathedral, the nondenominational Gothic structure that towers over Morningside Heights. So we all went sightseeing there. You'd think, considering how important it was, I'd remember more details of that visit. But that's memory for you. I don't remember much about it. I remember climbing the steeple with Patricia and her mom. I remember being very excited about the whole thing. And that's about it, at least as far as events go.

But as far as feelings go, there's definitely more. The excitement didn't go away. Patricia may only have been a girlfriend in my mind, but now she was in on my second life. We could talk about it, which was huge. It made me long to get back to our phone calls, when I got back home.

In the meantime, though, I was also an avid theatergoer, a taste my dad shared. And so down to the Village we went, to the Orpheum, to see a revival of Cole Porter's *Anything Goes*. Although you could hardly grow up in that era with parents marinated in their own generation of pop culture and not be exposed to Cole Porter, you could (and I did) do it without listening to the songs very hard, and certainly without registering his name. Porter wrote first and foremost for the stage, and when you heard his songs in context, a lot of things swam into focus and you would not forget the name any more. Percy Hammond of the *Herald Tribune* commented on the original 1935 show that Porter's songs were "ribald and sentimental." That nails it. Much of the best of Porter is ribald and sentimental all at once. That's a combination that chimes with the deepest vibrations in a young adolescent's developing soul, whether or not he recognizes the receptors for them in his mind.

Although there's nothing too grownup about the lyrics (except for a mention of cocaine), and high schools can and do put on productions of the show without offense, when you see the whole package as I saw it in 1962 (chorines dressed as angels but fluttering their diaphanous dresses like strippers, a revivalist anthem, *Blow, Gabriel, Blow*, that says farewell to carnality and worldliness with utter Broadway razzmatazz, and a gangster's girlfriend showing off her underwear doing high kicks) you know you're in the presence of ribaldry.

But by the same token when you hear expressions of longing like *I Get A Kick Out of You* and *All Through the Night*, you cannot be blind to the fact that the lyricist knew a thing or two about the emotional side of love as well. He knew about being in love when the object of your affections doesn't reciprocate – which is in fact the situation in *I Get A Kick Out of You*. Indeed, that was the one obvious thing I shared with Cole Porter, after eliminating, for instance, being grownup, or gay but stuck in a straight marriage, the way he was. And the contrast was more marked with Reno Sweeney, the character singing the song (Ethel Merman in the original, Eileen Rodgers in the revival). Unlike Reno, I was a) male, b) young, c) unfamiliar with drugs and alcohol, d) not accustomed to flying in airplanes, and e) never known to go "out on a quiet spree," whatever that exactly means. (In Porter's case it probably meant trolling the louche bars of the Left Bank for the relief of easy male companionship.) So there was a lot I couldn't identify with in the song. But the heart of it was all me. Like Reno and Cole, I understood that the secret obsession one might entertain for the object of one's affections would make every other amusement pale a little. I don't think that I would have described going to movies, playing board games, or hanging with my friends (my competing satisfactions) as "my idea of nothing to do," as Reno phrases it, but there was no question that the pinnacle of my emotions right then was reached when I was talking on the phone with Patricia. This song spoke powerfully to that – and the distinctions between me and the writer, and/or me and the singer, were just static, statistical error.

And so I listened a lot to that album. It was more than getting a fix of ribaldry and sentiment. It contributed to my musical ear too. The musicals whose records I'd grown up with to this point had all had full orchestras. *Anything Goes* featured a charming but distinctly pared-back ensemble, in which you can hear every instrument clearly, and every instrument counts (it has to). I was in love with the sound of that pit band. I must have listened to the overture a dozen times just to hear its sonorities. And when it came to *I Get a Kick*, somehow the trumpet's melancholy in that song made it for me more than Rodgers' voice.

That was the beginning and end of my Cole Porter experiences until the Rock Era, when Porter would come back in a different setting altogether. But that's a later story.

The tale of Patricia took a while to wind down too, but I can summarize. Matters reached their crisis the following year, the Saturday after Kennedy's assassination. I was walking along with her and, in my mourning and my longing, tried to put my arm around her. The reaction I got made it clear that this was not at all a direction she'd ever thought we might go. She more or less fled. And that ended up being more or less that.

I get a kick,/ Though it's plain to see/ You obviously don't adore me.

Amen.

11

THE GREATEST SONG(S)

WALK ON BY, BY BURT BACHARACH AND HAL DAVID,
PERFORMED BY DIONNE WARWICK (1964), ENCOUNTERED 1964

PLAYLIST TRACK No. 18

SIXTIES POP MUSIC smacked me in the face. And before it hit me, I never saw it coming. There were a couple of reasons for my surprise.

One was the force of my parents' tastes. Almost everything I'd liked up to about 1964 was a selection from what my parents had made available to me. And why not? What they provided was musically nourishing. There is such a thing as being too fulfilled to look around. But for teenagers, that never goes on forever.

There will come a moment when a teen will look around, and I'd just hit that moment. Up to that point, I hadn't ever asked myself whether my parents' tastes were in any sense old-fashioned. And I'm not sure that even then I put it in quite those terms. But on some level I had begun to sense was that my parents had "gone about as fer as they could go." The original cast albums from Broadway musicals my stepdad bought my mom might be the latest, but they were not advancing the art much beyond where Rodgers and Hammerstein had left it. Chanteuses that my parents liked, like Judy Garland and Marlene Dietrich, about whom I've already written, were still singing, but with rare exceptions not exactly breaking new ground.

And my parents' radio habits were similar. My folks listened to WJR in Detroit and the University of Michigan station, WUOM. WJR, to the limited extent it was about music at all, was kind of middle-of-the-road-ish, and WUOM was for classical music, educational fare, and Michigan football. There was nothing wrong with them, but again, they were just not breaking new musical ground.

That was okay with my folks: they had no use for new musical ground. Well, not just that they had no use for it; they were actively hostile. And so here we come to the second factor I had to overcome: parental disdain. Both my mom and my stepdad had entertained a visceral revulsion toward the ever-so-slightly-oppositional-defiant style of 1950s American youth icons (e.g. James Dean, Elvis Presley, or Marlon Brando). To them, this wasn't a minor matter of style, it was a fight for the very soul of our society. Such revulsion not only left out of the question any serious parental attempt to listen to or hear what the first generation of rockers were providing, but also extended to expressions of disgust in which I was expected to share.

And, out of sheer loyalty, that's what I did. For a while. My parochial school, which covered twelve grades, had but one cafeteria, and I remember sitting there as a grade schooler in the late 1950s and making scornful remarks over lunch about the high school girls in their signature bobby socks and saddle shoes (standard footwear for girls of that era who might be listening to Elvis and his ilk) – about them and their music – really for no other reason than that that was what my mom would have done. Nobody else ever joined in, but I never stopped to ask myself why that might be.

Becoming an adolescent, though, I started thinking more for myself. And that, in turn, would inevitably involve me in an embrace of a lot of things my mom hated. All the same, one generally does these things by steps. And I'm pretty sure that the first step of my initiation came through WJR, the very station my mom with all her musical prejudices found comfortable to listen to almost every day.

In 1964, however, WJR itself opened up a little bit, rehiring (from a spell in San Francisco) the slightly adventurous DJ and all-around radio personality J.P. McCarthy, who had both the Morning Music Hall and the Afternoon Music Hall programs. McCarthy was not orthodoxly opposed to new sounds. And a lot of new sounds were happening in 1964. April of that year saw Barbra Streisand charting with *People*, and Dionne Warwick charting with *Walk On By*, both of which I am pretty certain I first heard on McCarthy's

41

program. I remember Mother commenting with astonishment but not disgust at the then-new Streisand phenomenon. I don't remember her saying anything about Warwick.

If she had looked into Warwick, though, she'd have known that Warwick was the test pilot for many of the songs produced by Brill Building tunesmiths Burt Bacharach and Hal David, but also that Bacharach was just coming off a six-year occasional gig as the conductor for – Marlene Dietrich's orchestra! But Marlene wasn't doing Burt's kind of music.

I remember being blown away by both *People* and *Walk On By*, but being aware, immediately, that Streisand's and Warwick's hits came from entirely different musical countries. The former was my parents' music continued, maybe freshly repackaged. The latter, on the other hand, was – well, what was it? That is actually a surprisingly tough thing to say. Here's how the very artic-ulate Alec Cumming phrases it in his notes to the wonderful 3-CD Bacharach anthology The Look of Love (1998).

> *"Walk On By" has the ability to stop you dead in your tracks. Maybe it's the flügelhorn. Or those pounding doubled-piano breaks. Or maybe it's the echoed background singers, with their desperate little joke ("Don't. Stop. Don't. Stop.") Or the strings that at one instant swell up like a sea of tears, then next moment slink away.*

In less than three minutes, Bacharach takes you on what seems like a compressed tour of the whole territory of heartbreak, courtesy of his amazing mastery of the pop orchestra. He composes, he orchestrates, he conducts, and he creates a sound that is uniquely his, one I would come to know as the quintessential sound of 60s pop.

Part of the wonder is the rhythmic uniqueness of it. When you look at the sheet music, it seems to be in 4/4 throughout. But the introductory rhythm break ups the bars in a way you can only hear, not count. It feels as if there's a shift every half-bar, as if fragments of bars are being fused in weird places. It should slow the singer and the flügelhorn and the strings down to a halting crawl, but somehow it propels them to lyrical heights. Don't ask me how he does it. Half a century later, it still seems wondrous to me.

Which is not to say it's all about the composer and the orchestra. It's also about the lyricist and the singer. Especially the singer. In commenting about each of them, though, I'm even more at a loss for words than I was in talking about the music. What can one say about utter perfection? For once I am not even going to try.

In the years since then, I've heard lots and lots of songs. This one remains my very favorite.

And when I first heard it, early in 1964, as a high school freshman, I knew immediately I'd found something my parents knew nothing about and wouldn't care to, but that I desperately wanted more of.

Well!

And so, at age 14, I started to explore.

12

PEN PAL

RESTA SEMPRE ACCANTO A ME (TRUE LOVE NEVER RUNS SMOOTH),
BY BURT BACHARACH AND HAL DAVID, PERFORMED BY
GENE PITNEY (1964), ENCOUNTERED CA. 1964

QUE FAIS TU LA, PETULA?, BY PETULA CLARK AND PIERRE DELANOË,
PERFORMED BY PETULA CLARK (1965), ENCOUNTERED CA. 1965

PLAYLIST TRACKS NOS. 19, 20

ADOLESCENTS HAVE A particular talent for living in imaginary worlds. Mine was Europe, a particularly suave and sophisticated idea of Europe. I suspect that this fantasy was inevitable, given that for a brief time in my earliest years, I'd actually lived a Viennese version of it, as I've described in Chapter 2. But as I've also made clear, by the time I hit my teens, it had been years since I'd lived remotely like that, and I was probably much closer to privation at times than I was ever allowed to realize; certainly I was well out of the gilded phase of my life. Still, a part of me never stopped harkening back to the possibility of a miraculous return to it.

These dreams did have one solid tether, in the person of a friend named Fiona. Our mothers were old friends, and when her mother, a Canadian national who lived in Rome with a diplomat husband, came to visit our Ann Arbor abode, she brought Fiona with her. Over their two- or three-day visit, we children thoroughly hit it off, and initiated a correspondence that, in one way or another, has lasted all our lives. In retrospect, it was nearly inevitable, as we truly were kindred spirits. Each of us is a congenital writer, and a congenital memoirist to boot. The earliest letter I have from her dates from Christmas Eve 1959, and the earliest letter to her of which I kept a carbon copy is dated October 1963, when I was just starting high school. But the bulk of our correspondence was written and sent in our upper school years.

What did we write about? Certainly about school and our family lives and the things that interested us. But as one might expect, first and foremost, she wrote about boys and I wrote about girls. Condensed version: she kissed a lot of different guys, falling and unfalling for many of them, and I yearned, mostly from afar, for a lot of girls. There were some variations on that theme at my end, some of which I'll get to eventually, but the usual gist was as described. In any event, our letters amounted for some years to fever charts of our respective love lives. And if we were mostly talking past each other about mostly dissimilar experiences, what harm? Each of us was getting things articulated and figured out. (And considering how little either of us knew about life then, and how many basically incorrect received notions were being fed to us by the cultures we were growing up in, we had a great deal of figure out.)

Of course I had more than a slight crush on Fiona myself, but most of the time each of us was realistic enough to recognize that romantic connections between us were impossible, given the distance and the absence of opportunities to meet for years at a time.

But, even apart from romance, what a fabulous fantasy Fiona presented! For almost all my high school years, her family lived in part of a Roman *palazzo* and owned a *castello* in the countryside near Assisi. The *palazzo* was no merely honorary palazzo, either, but a universally-recognized full-scale one that you could find in the guidebooks. (Yes, I consulted guidebooks at the Ann Arbor Library, and found out, for instance, that her Roman home was near the Spanish Steps and had a facade by Bernini. And while I'd not heard of Bernini before, I recognized at once that this was a name to conjure with, and I was duly impressed.) She was educated in international schools, and the boys she wrote about had names like Armand and François and Eckhardt and Zaidun and Sten and Shuki and Jean-Noël. Their dates consisted of things like going to Fellini movies and parties and dances. It made me jealous; it made me feel like a hick, while to her it was as normal as breathing. And frequently I'd get upset at this disparity, which I'd try to justify as outcroppings of my natural blunt American personality, and she'd have to calm me down.

Reviewing the correspondence now, I can see, though, that there was a strain of competitiveness in it on my end. If she was having adventures, I wanted to have equivalent ones. The truth, though I couldn't articulate it well then, was that equivalent adventures really weren't possible in my more insular milieu. In my world, there were no group skiing trips, no dancing contests, no international community, little availability to or acceptability of alcohol for young teens, and no night spots at all where upper schoolers could hang out until the wee hours, all the sorts of things that formed a background to Fiona's young life. And – oh yes – I had that Catholic thing going on as well, full of rules that inhibited me in small but definite ways. As a result of all these deficits, there would just have been no way for me to match or top phrases like one Fiona tossed off casually about one of her boyfriends: "Since he has been gone, Rome has been boring."

How many of us have wished we could live a life in which Rome could be thought boring? Knowing Fiona, I'm certain she was not showing off when she said things like that, only reflecting the world she lived in. But it made me wish I had things like those to be casual about. Sure, I was probably inaccurately glamorizing the world of expats in Europe – with a generous assist from Hollywood, let me add. (Think *The Pink Panther*, *Charade*, *Roman Holiday*.) But the stream of letters from Fiona confirmed that something somewhat like that actually existed.

It surprises me, in retrospect, how enterprising I was, feeding that glamor-lust. Like most members of my generation, I'd ingested a generous helping of pop music fandom. But I extended my version of that generational taste to unusually international objects – well, unusually for a Midwestern American boy. For instance, it was easy, in that era, to be familiar with and appreciative of the hits of Gene Pitney (*Town Without Pity*, *(The Man Who Shot) Liberty Valance*, *Only Love Can Break a Heart*), but I don't think many of my contemporaries had developed a taste for those hits in Italian. I did: my good friend Stefan had been given an LP called *Gene Italiano*, and after he played it once for me, I begged him on various occasions to play it again. I think all of the songs on the album were straight Pitney performances in Italian translation, with the same orchestration as was used on the U.S. versions of the songs. But Pitney's voice, what his obituary in *The Guardian* accurately called a "quavering tenor," seemed to go perfectly with the dynamics of the Italian language and what I could call an Italian sensibility, and thus the songs just worked best in Italian. Case in point: *Resta Sempre Accanto a Me*, loosely translated from the Bachrach/David hit *True Love Never Runs Smooth*; with its crooning accordion and mandolin backdrop, it just sounds more Italian than American.

Perhaps I mentioned my interest in foreign pop to a friend behind the record counter at Discount Records, my favorite record store; I was prone to having such conversations. This was in the time frame where Iggy Pop (James Osterberg) worked there, though I have no recollection of what any of the staff looked like; conceivably Pop may have been the very guy who put me on to this. Anyway, someone alerted me to Petula Clark's foreign-language records. Again, this was the work of a singer every American kid would have known (e.g. *Downtown* or *Don't Sleep in the Subway*, among many hits). It turned out she recorded her hits in at least four languages, and most of them could be heard on imports from her French label, Disques Vogue. I bought three or four of those French Clark LPs, on special order.

It's easy for me to pinpoint the French Clark song that quickly meant the most to me, however: *Que Fais Tu La, Petula?* – literally "What are you doing there, Petula?" This wasn't a translation from an English-language original: it was a humorous French-language version of Clark's own story. As I'd quickly learned when I started looking into Clark's foreign recordings, in her youth, she'd gone off the reservation and married a Frenchman and moved to France. In the song, she recounts her British relatives' initial horror at her marriage and her expatriation – and then their gradual acceptance and their own moves to France. I have no idea how much of denouement is historical, but the fact of Clark's marriage and her own move abroad certainly is. At around the same time, Clark recorded a more soulful meditation on her story, *Two Rivers*, extolling and pledging a kind of sentimental allegiance to both the Thames and the Seine.

In my heart with every beat
Two rivers flow, two rivers meet
And love. And love.

These songs told me that one could actually move to places where they spoke other languages, beautiful languages, and that one could become part of a glittering transnational circle, without necessarily losing one's grounding in one's native land. It could happen. And if it could happen to Clark, then maybe it could even happen to me. Only time was going to tell.

So I suppose, in a way, consoled by the notion that I stood at least a chance of entering that world, I was able to face the requirements of my mundane American existence with greater equanimity. And at the same time, I had Fiona's letters that allowed me to interact in a way with a world I had once in my earliest youth been headed for, and still wished I could return to.

13

KIND OF A BIG DEAL

A HARD DAY'S NIGHT, BY JOHN LENNON AND PAUL MCCARTNEY,
APERFORMED BY THE BEATLES (1964), ENCOUNTERED 1964

NOT A SECOND TIME, BY JOHN LENNON AND PAUL MCCARTNEY,
PERFORMED BY THE BEATLES (1963), ENCOUNTERED CA. 1964

PLAYLIST TRACKS NOS. 21, 22

I BELIEVE I can remember the first time I heard about the Beatles, sometime during late winter 1964 (my freshman year), in the boys' locker-room of my high school, after a junior varsity basketball practice. I think someone was saying he was expecting to watch them on Ed Sullivan, which means we were probably two of three days before either Sunday, February 9 or Sunday, February 16, the dates of the Beatles' first two appearances on the show. I took it in, but didn't make any personal plans to watch. (There was no TV in my house until June of that year anyhow.) I understood the Beatles were kind of a big deal, but this was a month or so before my ears started opening up, as described in the previous chapter.

Had I even heard their music at this point? I think I must have, as I was already attending high school dances at least sporadically. Surely by early 1964, they were already playing the Beatles at the dances. (*I Want to Hold Your Hand* had charted on January 18 and *She Loves You* the following week.) But evidently I just wasn't listening yet. I'm quite certain that when my classmate spoke up about Ed Sullivan, I could not have called a single Beatles melody to mind.

No, my path to satori was a by-product of my growing interest in girls. It was no secret that the youngsters doing most of the screaming at Beatles concerts were female. If you wanted to have something to talk about with girls, knowing something about the Beatles might come in handy.

There was one Beatles fan in particular, I'll call her Becky, whose mom and my parents met at the beginning of that summer of '64. Her mom was part of my parents' academic crowd, and I think everybody thought Becky and I were suitable companions. Well, all the grownups did.

Her mom also had the reputation of being a scalp-hunter, out to sleep with academic stars and to flirt with smaller fry. I can't speak about whom the mom really slept with (or didn't); it could all have been unfounded gossip. But the flirtatiousness I had myself observed, aimed at my stepdad. In fact a little bit of it was extended in my direction (and a little bit was powerful stuff).

I know Becky had observed this too. And would you want to go out with a callow boy who had been conspicuously buzzed by your mom? I'm asking the question, not answering. All I'm certain of is that it was complicated.

She may have felt as confused as I did, given the pretty obvious enchantment her mom exerted over me. Sometimes Becky treated me like a confidant, and at others as if I were an annoyance. Because our families quickly became intimates, I was constantly visiting with her throughout the summer and fall of 1964. She certainly held me at arm's length, with off-putting remarks like: "Kisses shouldn't be handed out; like jewels, they're valuable because they're rare." On the one hand, this kind of comment kept me from trying to kiss her, and in retrospect I'm sure that was an intended effect. On the other hand, it spurred me to try finding shared topics to fascinate her with.

Which is where Beatlemania came in. The on-ramp for me was the Beatles' movie *A Hard Day's Night*. The soundtrack album came out in June, soon followed by the movie itself. When I was visiting with my father in New York that August, I persuaded him to take me to see it, largely motivated by the desire to have something to talk about with Becky. But not exclusively for that reason.

I was getting intrigued on my own. By now I was listening to the right radio stations back home, CKLW in Windsor and WKNR in Detroit, which certainly featured Beatles music prominently. And the stores in Times Square all seemed to be playing the songs. And so I must have heard it all on the radio before ever seeing the movie (seven songs from the movie/album having charted by that point in the summer).

When I heard just that first unforgettable George Harrison chord (possibly, say the experts, G eleventh suspended fourth), I knew I was in for an adventure. No great distinction for me to perceive that, of course: everyone in my generation had had that same moment of epiphany. What followed the chord in the movie, though (the madcap chases, the lower-class Liverpudlian attitudes, the sneering toffs, the hard-rocking love songs with the soft-core centers, the camaraderie of the four lads) was an initiation into a brand-new and exciting world and made me fall even harder. There was something, too, about the fourths and fifths the Beatles liked to harmonize with – different from the thirds my ear had been trained up till then to anticipate, that forever came to be associated in my mind with the bracing strangeness of the life on the screen in that movie.

Remember, too, I myself was from England, sort of. So I felt as if this should have been part of my birthright. But my dim memories of the place held nothing that looked or sounded anything at all like this. Like most impressionable youngsters of that day, I wanted to go to England, to be English, and part of that scene.

I bought a copy of the album for Becky as a birthday present – which, by good luck, was the only Fab Four album she didn't already have. But of course, to a teenager in 1964, Beatlemania was like a Roach Motel: you could check in, but not out. Of course I had to have the record myself. I bought my own copy three days after handing over the first one to Becky. And then I went and saw the movie again with my Ann Arbor friends six days after that.

I got to know the songs. I played my harmonica alone in my room along with them. I bought a songbook and played the songs on the piano (to the best of my limited ability and the dismay of my parents downstairs who were hoping for something more along the lines of Chopin). I became happily obsessed.

There was a lot more to the music than a chord, I was learning. Not that I was exactly thinking; I was just responding to the straight-ahead rock 'n' roll of the early Beatles. It drew me in with the just the right mix of challenge and coziness.

And I began to develop a dollop of sophistication. Top 40 Radio brought me this incredible mix of excitement (#1 hits from that year – apart from those of the Beatles, who had five of them – included vintage stuff from Peter and Gordon, Roy Orbison, the Beach Boys, the 4 Seasons, the Animals, the

Supremes, and the Shangri-Las). There were dances on Friday nights at the high school where you could hear these things cranked way up (and I got a young woman neighbor to show me how to dance properly). And I spent hours in the record store, looking at the posters and the album covers, and taking in what they were playing on the PA system.

Somewhere in that fall, I remember being at a dance, and actually telling a girl "This music is the sound of our generation." Why would I say something so obvious? Well, partly because it wasn't quite so obvious then. We had scotched the snake of the Mitch Miller sound, not killed it. (It's worthy of note that Dean Martin also had a #1 hit that year.) And we also hadn't converted our parents, to most of whom it was and remained nothing but noise. (It was surely just noise to my mom and stepdad, though, blessedly, my father Emile seemed to be hearing something.) But that remark was also a statement of allegiance. I was refusing to follow my parents' likes and dislikes any more.

In later years, my mom spoke reproachfully of having "lost" me. She was, of course, talking about a lot more than my music. But in a real sense it started with the music. Implicit in her thinking was that she had laid down a course for the two of us to walk together, and then I'd inexplicably wandered off it. My perspective was the opposite: I'd gone on a voyage of discovery that her own tastes had done a great deal to send me out on, and then she'd refused to accompany me where the path naturally led. And, as I'd said before, the Beatles (especially of this era) were actually a pretty cozy lot. Our moms should have loved them. But for some reason some of them, including mine, couldn't figure that out.

Of course I went on and bought all of the Beatles' records, mostly monaural. I still have them, sacred relics. Shortly after I secured the soundtrack LP of *A Hard Day's Night*, I bought their first Capitol album, *Meet The Beatles*. More actually than *A Hard Day's Night*, that album – the whole album – was the theme music of my late 1964. But if I have to choose just one number from the album, I'm going to take *Not A Second Time* as my Theme Song.

You can argue about whether it's the hardest-rocking song on the LP; in my opinion it is, because of George Martin's pounding piano, and because of the awfully jazzy minor keys (G minor and E minor) alternating between which John Lennon (sole writer and singer) carries on proceedings. Allegedly the melody comes down on an "Aeolian cadence," something Lennon had never heard of. No more had I, nor do I understand the technical lingo to this day. I just know that it was the song that ended the album, a powerful finish that amounted to a calling card.

And I, as it happens, was accepting visitors.

What then of Becky, who had helped precipitate these discoveries? Things there never got unweird. We did share a few occasions that could reasonably be labeled dates, but she resisted any efforts to get physically or emotionally close. And then came a climactic moment of weirdness. Two different strands of my life suddenly got snarled on each other, and I was left not knowing whom to believe. Becky told me that "Patricia," of whom I have written above in Chapter 10, was spreading word that I in turn had been spreading trashy calumnies about Becky and her sister. Apart from the shock of being accused of saying things it would never have occurred to me to say about anyone, the notion of Patricia and Becky having any contact was surprising (they attended different schools in different grades). I had no idea whether Patricia had actually said these things, or whether Becky was making up the story that Patricia had said these things, or whether some intermediary had started the rumor. And though I protested I was innocent of the accusations, Becky's stated way of dealing with it was not to go out with me anymore. She deigned to come to a party of mine, and we did see each other through our parents a while longer. Eventually, though, Becky's mom left town and never had any contact with her former circle again. And so there the story truly ended.

Or it did until 2017. At some point in the first half of the year, I became aware of a slight possibility my path might cross with Patricia's on a trip home later. And by now there was such a thing as the Internet, so I was able to locate Becky and simply ask her to set me straight. She was glad to talk to me, and I learned much from her about a lot of things. Regarding the strange upshot of our not-quite-anything teenaged relationship, she said she never had had any contact with Patricia. Piecing it jointly together, we concluded she had hit on this falsehood as a way of making me go away – a falsehood improvised in the midst of distracting family circumstances I had only dimly perceived which required all of her attention. Which was fine. I had not mourned long. But I had a fine legacy from the relationship, an introduction to the sound of my my my generation – someone sang a song with that as the title. And half a century later, a resumed friendship.

14

STEREOPHONIC

SAMBA DO AVIÃO, WRITTEN AND PERFORMED BY ANTONIO CARLOS JOBIM,
ARRANGED BY NELSON RIDDLE (1965), ENCOUNTERED 1965

PLAYLIST TRACK NO. 23

WHEN IT CAME to technology, my two sets of parents could not have been further apart.

Louise and Ernie, my mom and stepfather, resisted each advance in consumer electronics. Television, as I've already mentioned, was kept out of the house until 1964, and then only was allowed in because my stepfather's grandmother had died and left her set behind. My folks insisted on asking telephone operators to make their long-distance connections for them for as long as that was a viable option, and one of the first skills my mom lost later on when dementia set in was dialing the phone (I think because numbers then called for 10 digits as opposed to the six or seven that had prevailed earlier in her life). My folks never mastered the VCR I gave them nor the microwave. Though each wielded the typewriter a lot, there was never an electric typewriter in the house, let alone a PC (and each lived over a decade after PCs became commonplace, my mother more than two of them).

My father Emile, by contrast, loved gadgets, especially gadgets connected with music reproduction. In his mountain getaway cottage, there was a trestle table supporting nothing but hi-fi, or as we came to call it, stereo gear: turntables, tape recorders, amps, pre-amps, tuners, speakers, headphones, all patched together in unique ways. Whatever wasn't on top of the table was beneath it. This assemblage wasn't always a success from an audio reproduction standpoint, and was never ever very sightly, but my stepmother Etta did not mind, bless her. One of my real regrets about losing my father so early (1978) was that he didn't live to see the dawn of the really good gadgets. Of course he would have been about 90 year old when iPods arrived, 100 years old when Blu-Ray came in, 105 years old when BlueTooth became ubiquitous, etc. So, if he had lived that long, who knows if he would have kept his zest for mechanical novelty late enough into his old age to enjoy them?

But in the times I'm speaking of now, he was the guy who opened the wonderful world of sound-making gadgets to me. Somewhere around 1964, probably for my birthday, he provided me some entry-level but serious hi-fi gizmos: a turntable, a tuner, a combined preamp/amp, and a single speaker. I think that solitary speaker was all my dad could spring for at that time. So though it was definitely the most sophisticated rig in the house, it remained mono for a while. I knew that stereo was supposed to be way better, but I couldn't just go out and buy a quality speaker. If I wanted one, I had to save up for it. And I think I put money away for a year. I believe it was shortly after my 16th birthday in the summer of 1965 that I had the necessary sum gathered together. I went out to a store called Schochet's, put down my money on a companion speaker, and waited a week or so for delivery.

Eventually, I got the second speaker home, hooked it up with heavy-gauge transparent wire, flipped the switch on the amp from mono to stereo, and cued up my first stereo record. And that was *The Wonderful World of Antonio Carlos Jobim*. After discovering the Beatles and their cohort, I was all about exploring rock right then, so an album of bossa nova might have seemed like an odd choice. But I was always a musical omnivore, and bossa nova, not to mention Jobim, was all over everyone's radar screen after *The Girl From Ipanema* had become the Grammy Record of the Year in 1964. And I think I was also aware that the acoustic impact of an album like this was likely going to be greater than that of a collection of rock music. I probably didn't then recognize the name of the arranger and conductor, the great Nelson Riddle, but I believe I'd heard (probably read in Stereo Review, which I'd begun subscribing to) that the sound of the album was gorgeous.

So there I was, tone arm poised over the black vinyl with the gold Warner Bros. label in the middle, with "STEREO" written in an arc across the bottom in big red letters. The needle dropped, and I was transported. When I closed my eyes, I was in a different aural space, floating out there somewhere with the strings. It sounded as if Jobim was singing and strumming his guitar up close to you, with a chorus of growling trombones behind him in the middle distance, percussion to the left, piano to the right, with strings encamped all the way out to the luminous horizon.

Damn! This was stereo!

I just kept playing it. I'd keep coming back to those two speakers and the fact that I could close my eyes and lose myself in an imaginary space. I was so taken with the sound that the music almost didn't matter to me for a while. Of course eventually I stopped listening to the sound and started paying attention to the record. The effect was subtle, like the very sound of the bossa nova itself. Still that rich Nelson Riddle orchestral palette (the trade-mark, for instance, of some of the great Frank Sinatra albums of the late 50s and early 60s) elucidated part of the truth about bossa nova, which is that, while it may be quiet and subtle, it's often about passion and excitement. It's not just in the breathless frustrated eroticism of *The Girl From Ipanema* that appears in this album, a song which everyone knows is about the habitués of a seaside bar watching a passing 15-year old girl with hopeless and slightly inappropriate lust. On this very album you can also hear *Surfboard*, which somehow captures the thrill of waiting for and then riding a wave. And then there's *Samba Do Avião*, which is about riding a plane coming in for a landing at Rio de Janeiro's Galeão Airport, and looking down at the town as one goes. (Not coincidentally, I'm sure, Galeão is now called Antonio Carlos Jobim.) And maybe a word needs to be said about exactly why this is so exciting.

Avião is just Portuguese for airplane. But this was an era in which airplanes were conjuring up new feelings. Take a look at the TWA-branded cover of *Come Fly With Me*, Sinatra's 1957 smash album (well, recorded in 1957, released in 1958). Notice something odd to modern eyes about the aircraft? Look hard and you'll see, at least on the plane in the background, that they were prop-driven. Yet in the iconography of that cover, these old-timey planes are the magic carpets to carry the lucky listener to all the destinations Sinatra sings about: New York, Paris, Capri, Brazil, Hawaii, etc. 1957 was also the year the first commercial passenger jetliner, the Boeing 707 was first licensed for commercial flight. And people my age will recall that the 707, followed shortly by the DC-8, changed everything, glamorized everything, about air travel. By 1965, a song about taking off in an airplane (all right, this song is really about coming in for a landing, but I didn't know that then) would have had the listener thinking about being thrust unaccustomedly back against the cushions, about plunging recklessly upwards, about sexy stewardesses (sorry, "flight attendant" was a neologism years in the future), and about getting to interesting places ridiculously fast. Not to mention that the most glamorous folks in the world were called the Jet Set then. And this was all new.

Even if it weren't, it had the association of forbidden fruit for me. My Luddite mom and stepdad were deathly afraid of my flying. As a result, with but one exception (still in the prop craft era), all the comings and goings between my home in Ann Arbor and my home in New York were by car or rail. I had some wonderful rail and road experiences that way, but obviously the fact that my mom wouldn't let me made me all the eagerer to fly. And the song made it possible to do in my imagination, at least.

So that song carried those associations for me. I'd also seen *That Man from Rio*, with Jean-Paul Belmondo and Françoise Dorléac, twice, the previous year. So I knew what the statue of Cristo Redentor that the singer admires looked like, and about the staggering hills above Rio. I knew it was an exotic land well worth visiting. In short, I was a sitting duck for the way the song, even in a language I didn't grasp much of, evoked its subject.

So this was a part of my introduction to the stereophonic effect, to the sounds of bossa nova, and to the lust for travel. All have remained with me to this day.

15

ON A LOSING STREAK

(I CAN'T GET NO) SATISFACTION, BY KEITH RICHARDS AND MICK JAGGER, PERFORMED BY THE ROLLING STONES 1965, ENCOUNTERED 1965

PLAYLIST TRACK No. 24

ONE-TWOOOO, ONE-TWO-THREE! ONE-TWOOOOO, one-two-three! First you hear Keith Richards' fuzz guitar playing this rhythm, lancing upwards and drifting downwards in one of the most famous riffs in all of rock. And then Charlie Watts lays down almost the same rhythm on the drums, an abortive march ending each measure with the little cha-cha-cha that keeps the beat as jerky and unfulfilled as the lyrics proclaim the singer to be. Lyrics full of sexual frustration and disdain for commercialism – and what could more potently capture the psyche of a 16-year-old in the summer of 1965?

Certainly nothing I was listening to that summer.

I'm convinced the way most of us listen to most rock lyrics does not include taking them in as a whole at first. Partly because of the vexed acoustics they're embedded in. (For instance, when Mick sang "I can't get no girl reaction," I'll bet half the listeners heard what I heard: "I can't get no girlie action" – which is a little bit more risqué. And on the other hand, I'll bet lots of people heard "I'm trying to meet some girl" rather than the blunter "I'm trying to make some girl," which was what Mick actually sang.) Another reason is that little fragments of words and music mean so much they tend to distract you from the bigger picture. It took me a while to get past "I try and I try and I try and I try" sung as a rising cadence, because that spoke to me. I was trying very hard the summer of 1965, and not provoking much girl reaction. Or any other kind.

That was a summer in which it seemed as if everywhere, people were doing big things. The Great Society had been proclaimed. A Michigan grad was doing a space walk. We were told we were winning the Vietnam War – or would anyway, once we responded properly to that Gulf of Tonkin provocation. And here I was, not doing much.

One of the ways I wasn't doing much was musically. With rock at what many would consider to be its highest tide ever, we all wanted to "join in a rock-n-roll band," I as much as anyone else. But my instrument was unfortunately the harmonica. I'd sort of flamed out on the piano, owing in equal parts to a lack of talent on my part, my mother and stepdad's interest in making me play classical music, which just didn't cut it in 1965, and my father's inability to stake me to a Farfisa organ despite my begging him. I think if I'd been given that Farfisa I would have been able to fight my way into some kind of music group. I would never have had people in ecstasy over my fingerwork, but I might have been just good enough.

But instead I played the harmonica. And not just any kind of harmonica. A couple of years before, my father had given me, out of the blue, a Hohner Chromonica 64. It's a classic; the same instrument is sold to this day. It's extremely versatile, with a huge four-octave range, and you can play it in any key, which all sounds like a plus, but playing it in almost any key except C major and A minor takes a good deal of practice, and it is not as exquisitely tuned in any individual key as are key-specific diatonic instruments, aka blues harps. And it's really only for melodies; it's not built to play chords on. Also bending notes is quite hard. So you have to work at it to sound really good. The day would come when I would sound pretty good at this monster, but that day was not one of the days featured on the 1965 calendar.

So it wasn't going to be me up on that stage. I would have to content myself being one of the crowds who would hang around and listen while others played.

I'm called to mind of one sticky summer evening. I was on a corner on the east side of the campus. Some early version of a band called Aftermath (later known to Motor City fans as Rhinoceros, and then as The Charging Rhinoceros of Soul) was playing up on a temporary stage. Actually, I don't think they were even Aftermath yet, since that name was a rip-off of the Rolling Stones' album name, and the album titled *Aftermath* wasn't released until mid-1966.

But I remember them as Aftermath. They had guitars and, if memory serves, horns. And they were playing *Satisfaction*. And my frenemy Paul was playing with them.

I remember listening to those lyrics, and feeling they were written about me. Paul of course was playing an instrument they wanted. Well enough to get invited to participate. Had the girls looking at him. And the band was very good, by local standards, anyway. I could see that. Paul was getting some Satisfaction.

As for me, I had nothing to show yet. Only the folkies in my circle would let me play my harmonica with them. And high school hootenanny parties simply did not compare to wowing a bunch of university students right up there in public.

Oftentimes in all the years that have passed since then, when I hear that song, I think of that evening.

... 'cause you see I'm on a losing streak.
I can't get no, oh no no no.
a Hey hey hey, that's what I say.

16

AN EARLY SENTIMENTAL EDUCATION IN THREE LESSONS: "ELLA"

I GOT YOU BABE, BY SONNY BONO, PERFORMED BY SONNY & CHER (1965), ENCOUNTERED 1965

PLAYLIST TRACK NO. 25

IF YOU'RE BOTH a romantically-inclined person and a red-blooded one, your earliest amorous adventures are likely to be fueled by a strange combination of starry-eyed devotion and crass calculation about what liberties you can get away with. Both the hearts and the bodies of the objects of your attention are unknown territory, and you're eager to explore them both. Nor are you able to forget for long that you are in a status competition with all your peers, and that your progress in both aspects of the mating game is likely a part of that competition.

My journal entries certainly confirm I was confronting all these dynamics when, as a 16-to-17-year-old, I crossed paths with three friends I'll call Ella and Zsuska and Kate.

It started where a thousand songs tell us romance is likely to begin: a high school dance. (It may sound strange to some nowadays, but in that era, dances were a regular staple of high school life.) It was a Saturday night in early September 1965. I was just beginning my junior year of high school.

The most uncomfortable thing you did at a high school dance was stand around. I did that for an hour and half, while friends who unlike me had dates were dancing to the music of a rather unimpressive rock band. I chose to content myself chatting with an English teacher. But eventually the band relented, and someone started playing records.

Cue Sonny and Cher's *I Got You, Babe*, with the ostenato two-note oboe figure that positively begs you to dance. Cue Kate, a tall freshman, darting around the room with a friend. I had noted her the last few days, had registered the new arrival in the high school, had been struck by the thick red mane parted in an unusual direction, and by a quality I could not name then but would later recognize as an art student air. (And she was indeed an artist.) She looked unconventional, different, and very, very attractive.

And yet, cursing my ineptitude, I could not get up the courage to put myself next to her and talk, let alone ask her to dance with me. Then the band started to play once more.

This nudged fate into my corner, because the band had left a ukelele on the stage. Picking it up and plucking at it, I found I could more or less fake my way through a melody along with the group. I worked my way over to the window where Kate and her friend were standing, picking along. Kate's friend broke the ice, and asked me if I played. No, I said, but we started to talk. I mentioned the band, probably overpraised them just to be saying something, and the friend told me that Kate was stuck on one of the members of the band. And sure enough, in a moment Kate was consulting the friend about ways to get a chance to talk to the band member. And in another moment after that, Kate was off to flirt with the guy.

That left me talking to the one I call Ella here. She was attractive too, dark with a finely-chiseled face and (I have already acknowledged a crassness at work in me too) terrific breasts. Whereupon the chair of the Social Committee, sponsor of the dance, happened past and more or less ordered the two of us to hit the floor. And one thing then led to another. At one point, Ella let me hold her hand, and I let Ella order me to accompany her to her locker to pick up things for her ride home.

In due course there was a bowling date, and another dance with Ella. With Kate, I could have fallen hard. With Ella, I knew that whatever love was, I wasn't in it. Still, it seemed like a good idea to date her for the moment; unlike Kate, she was available. Soon we had been dating for four weeks, and obviously, whether one considered the heart or the hands, it was time for things to progress, or not. Events would show it probable Ella was considering the same principles as I, albeit reaching a different result.

We came to a football Saturday night, a social occasion we both attended. My journal bears witness to my obtuseness. I wrote in my journal that Ella and I had "prearranged to sit together," but didn't. And she wasn't looking in my direction. To be brutally precise, I recorded that she was looking "every way but in my direction." I have to conclude now that if there had been any better male prospects out there that evening, the night probably would have ended differently. But apparently there weren't, and meanwhile I was all determination. So when my companions mainly took off, and Ella was standing alone in the bleachers, I made my move. I went up, we sat together second half, and then, as it came time to walk away, bliss. I took her hand, and she pressed the back of mine against her thigh, where I could feel the complicated underwear girls wore then to hold up their stockings. We went on holding hands while we waited at the gate of the field for the bus that would take us back to the school. There was a dance then, presumably up in the gym this time, where she pressed her breasts against me, no longer holding back as she had that first night. Overwhelming stuff if you're a teenaged boy just starting out.

As it happened, she lived three blocks from the school. So I got to walk her home.

Forty years later, I retraced those steps on a similar night. I was struck by how dim the street lighting is, and I'm guessing it probably always was. Perfect for my purposes at the time. By now the physical closeness I was asserting and she was acceding to could only lead to one conclusion, even for a boy as inexperienced as I.

It actually took a little while, even then, even there, for me to get around to the kiss. We arrived at her house; I went in and met her mom, who had a gentleman caller of her own. And then we stepped back outside, and I, all afumble, nonetheless managed to land one, with her cat looking on.

And that was my First Kiss milestone. I could have died and my life would have been complete right then.

There was a fly in the ointment, though, as I confided to my journal a week later. You could sum it up in two words: What next? I didn't want to go steady with Ella; Kate was still the one on my mind. And Ella, it seems, did not have me on her mind either.

As witnessed by her behavior. For two weeks she "sprinted" – my contemporaneous word for it – in the other direction when she saw me coming in the halls. I did catch up with her the night of the next football game, and got her to sit with me. She had her half-sister with her. And rereading the details of the rest of the evening, it is painfully, painfully clear they were trying to get rid of me and I couldn't be gotten rid of. I followed them home, but, needless to say, received no repeat goodnight kiss on the porch.

No more Ella after that. By December, she had said NO firmly when I invited her to a party I was giving. (My comment: "I know she never wants us to speak again, and I'm agreeable.") Not too long after that, she turned up wearing maroon bell-bottoms at a dance with Tim, a guy from my old grade school, plus the half-sister.

So that was that with Ella. And Sonny Bono's song, playing that September night when I met Ella and Kate, was mocking me:

HIM: I got flowers in the spring
I got you to wear my ring

HER: And when I'm sad, you're a clown
And if I get scared, you're always around

HER: Don't let them say your hair's too long
'Cause I don't care, with you I can't go wrong

HIM: Then put your little hand in mine
There ain't no hill or mountain we can't climb. Babe

BOTH: I got you babe
I got you babe.

I was a long, long way from finding that kind of love. And I was still hoping that maybe I could find it with Kate. But in the meantime, a kiss was still a kiss.

17

AN EARLY SENTIMENTAL EDUCATION IN THREE LESSONS: "ZSUSKA"

I'VE GOT YOU UNDER MY SKIN, BY COLE PORTER, PERFORMED BY THE 4 SEASONS (1966), ENCOUNTERED 1966

PLAYLIST TRACK NO. 26

IT'S REASONABLE TO ask why I hadn't given up on Kate by this point. Partly it's because she hadn't clearly signaled how she felt about me. Kate did come to my party that Ella had refused to attend. We talked a lot, as well. We attended the monthly student matinees of a professional theater company resident at the University. Sitting next to her in the dark, I would hope that our arms would brush, and once is a while they would.

Come February I asked her to the Sophomore Prom. Kate said yes, to my delight. I gathered that her parents were sick of some guy in a band she had been dating, and were very pleased to hear that someone else was taking an interest. That nugget of information should have worried me, but I obstinately took it as a good sign.

On the evening of the Prom itself, I was a little ahead of time. I might have wanted to loiter in the vicinity to contrive a less premature appearance, but Kate's dog heralded my arrival, and hence there was Kate at the door, in a turquoise dress, wearing lipstick.

I met the parents; Dad, I wrote down in my journal as "a television paterfamilias." I believe he had a red cardigan sweater and even a pipe, and seemed to my untutored eye to be radiating calm and maturity. Mom seemed pleasant, too. What I wasn't seeing! In reality this was a household in agony, well down the path to dissolution. Within three years, Dad would be teaching in another state, living with a girlfriend. You'd think that as a child of divorce, I would have picked up on something, but no, not a clue. And Kate, whatever she might be going through, was giving nothing away.

The main thing I remember about the evening was Kate's thick red hair tumbling in front of her face so much when she danced, I couldn't see it clearly. That just made her prettier to me. And I do remember that at some point Ella and Tim made an entrance. Kate dragged me over to talk to them at the refreshment table. Ella obviously still didn't want to talk to me, though Tim and I got along fine. (I later learned that a mutual friend had given Tim a backgrounder on Ella and me, to ease any diplomatic awkwardness.)

And the dancing went well. When you're 16 and you dance a number of slow dances with a girl, she does get more comfortable after a while, gets into the little liberties you take. I'd been taught, like nice boys before and since, that girls know what they want, what their limits are, and you can operate only within those limits. In truth, however, I don't think it is really all that different for girls than it is for us: flirtation lays down a logic all of our bodies have a hard time not following. And dancing is a license to flirt. The closer the dancing, the less escapable the logic.

So, no escaping for Kate right then. My head was resting on the nape of her neck. (I did have to disengage a couple of times because her hair lacquer stung through the pores of my heavily-shaven face, and that lovely red hair would get in my mouth.) I wasn't forcing anything; she was as much a part of it as I. We were both hot and sweaty and enjoying the moment, and I simply loved it.

But that was that. I could not maintain any kind of mutual electricity, either at a post-dance pizza joint, on the walk home, or on the doorstep, where I received no goodnight kiss.

It could have been more definitive. She did not cut me off. I kept my spirits up on the strength of another invitation – this to an April party at the house of one of Kate's friends.

The party itself was the kind of party that artistic intellectual White kids threw in that particular era: music on the hi-fi, arguments about Vietnam, lots of making out, and a lone Black boy, whom we still would have spoken of as a Negro. I was probably the oldest one there, most of the guests being freshmen.

This was all happening down in the basement. As I reached the bottom of the stairs, there stood a short, terribly buxom girl with, as I recall, a black page haircut, wearing white slacks and a green pullover. I stuck out my hand; she introduced herself as, let us say, Zsuska, whom I didn't find terribly appealing, but whose company I enjoyed.

Dancing was the big item that evening. And Zsuska wanted to dance. Matters were complicated by the fact that she seemed already to have a date, lets call him Henry, a diffident young man, and Kate was talking with someone else named Jim. So I tried to disengage myself, and insert myself into the Kate/Jim dialogue.

This was what you call not going with the flow. Kate, it should have been plain, was going to spend the entire evening with Jim, whatever I said or did. If I'd had gaydar then (or even a concept of what it was), I'd also have known to a reasonable degree of certainty that Henry was gay, and would have been unsurprised that Zsuska was bent on me, not him. I have a distinct suspicion now that my fate may have been a matter of negotiation between Kate and Zsuska before I even got there.

Somehow I kept on finding myself talking with Henry and Zsuska, not Kate and Jim. And presently Zsuszka said "Henry, don't you think we should let other people get a chance to dance with us?" – looking straight at me. Henry had to say yes.

"I don't know anything about you," she told me in a little while, though I already knew this wasn't strictly true, since she'd admitted Kate had told her something about me. As we slowly danced, we found we had in common having both been younger children in other lands. Soon she asked me what I thought of her. I tried to field this diplomatically, but I said I thought she was rather an aggressive person. She replied that she had to be, because otherwise nobody asked her to dance. I responded with remarks about breaks being bound to come one's way. She responded by pressing her bosom hard against my chest.

I said, "Hey you really are being aggressive."

She pulled back. "Don't you want me to?"

"No, I don't mind at all," I said, and she happily pressed even harder against me.

All the same I was worried about Henry, and when the lights were turned up to search for another girl's lost earring, I extricated myself and started talking with someone else. Then the other girl called it a night, and soon I was cutting in on Henry and Zsuska again.

"How's it going?" I asked Zsuska.

"Lovely, thanks to you," she said, and looked into my eyes with a look that even then I called "naked desire" – in quotes. It may have been sincere on some level, but it was also a performance. James Bond might have had that kind of effect on women: in my wildest fantasies, I knew that I surely did not. Shortly after that, Zsuska was telling me that I was too old for Kate, and that she (at 16 like me) was too old for Henry. Soon, Zsuska was trying to get me to kiss her.

Not there, I told myself, not in front of everyone. But Henry and a boy left together, and it was Zsuska's mom who gave me a lift home. Of course there was a date arranged.

I have seldom been so humiliated by myself as that date made me. We went to the theater to see a war movie, and from the moment I saw Zsuska at the theater, I knew it was all wrong. She really was not attractive to me. And I had to be polite and flirt, and hold her hand. And all I wanted to do was get away. I suppose that by now I was sort of in the position Ella had earlier occupied with me. I desperately did not want to hurt or humiliate Zsuska, but I also wanted the date to end. And I recognized that my lack of interest in her was not based on anything profound: I just didn't care for her looks. I would have given a great deal not to have been so shallow. But that's what I was, and I knew it.

There was only one other thought contributing to my insensitive treatment of Zsuska: she wasn't Kate.

As for Kate, she, I guess, continued to date that other guy, Jim, until the school year ended. That summer, she was somewhere else. I knew she was out of town, and yet somehow, I kept finding reasons to visit her home. Not knocking, not asking if anyone else was there. Just walking by.

I was a bit like Viola's notion of what she would do, were she in love with Olivia:

[I would m]ake me a willow cabin at your gate,
And call upon my soul within the house;
Write loyal cantons of contemned love,
And sing them loud even in the dead of night;
Halloo your name to the reverberate hills,
And make the babbling gossip of the air
Cry out "Olivia!"

I wasn't exactly making cabins at Kate's gate, and my hallooing was strictly internal. But the emotion was the same. And to get to her gate, I usually managed to take the way from the school past Ella's house down to Kate's.

That fall, the fall of 1966, the 4 Seasons came out with a song that expressed exactly how I felt, their cover of Cole Porter's immortal *I've Got You Under My Skin*.

Don't you know, little fool, you never can win
Use your mentality, wake up to reality
But each time I do, just the thought of you
Makes me stop before I begin
'Cause I've got you under my skin.

Not that I knew anything at that age about the 4 Seasons' version being a cover. Unbeknownst to me, the song had been recorded hundreds of times, from its premiere in the movie *Born To Dance* (1936) right up to the 1960s. But it had never, so far as I was or am aware, been sung or recorded like this.

Producer Bob Crewe had spotted something in the song that no other version I know of to that date had picked up on: one little musical phrase that he took out of context, changed slightly, and turned into the centerpiece of the production. This was the phrase sung to the words "go so well," in the line: "I said to myself this affair never will go so well." As written, it's F, F#, F#. (Well, actually transposed one half-note down for this version, one presumes to give singer Frankie Valli's falsetto a little more headroom.) Crewe took this phrase, and instead of starting with Porter's sophisticated and bluesy accidental, took the launching note for the phrase one half step down, thus: E, F#, F#. It sounded squarer, more sincere. And now Crewe had the essential building block for his recasting of the song. He paired the revised cadence up with bells and with the words "never win," and played it and had the Seasons sing it over and over. He gets some gorgeous chords that way, and manages to make the song less about obsessed hope and more about obsessed despair. ("Never win, never win.")

It might have been better if I'd taken Crewe's point to heart while I was listening to the song. But I still thought maybe I had a chance.

18

AN EARLY SENTIMENTAL EDUCATION IN THREE LESSONS: "KATE"

KIND OF A DRAG, BY JIMMY HOLVAY, PERFORMED BY
THE BUCKINGHAMS (1966), ENCOUNTERED 1966

PLAYLIST TRACK NO. 27

I LEARNED UPON getting back to high school in the fall, and finding Kate in my German class, that she was not tied up with Jim now. On a Saturday at the beginning of October, Kate let me take her to a University football game. She let me put my arm around her in the cold, and hold her hand, and she did not demur when I told her she was the only girl in the school worth troubling with.

But. But we talked about "making out," which I commented to my journal had been the real thing I thought had come between us the previous year. I paraphrased her stance as "She doesn't like to do it except when the situation calls for it." Whatever that phrase meant, it couldn't be good news for anyone hoping to do that with her. And she faulted the late unlamented Jim for spending all his time doing that with her replacement. She blamed his proclivities that way for her dropping him. So I thought maybe I could provide some kind of contrast.

I was smitten in a way I had never experienced before. Too beautiful for words, I called her. I admired her strength in class. I admired her vulnerability discussing her parents' impending divorce, a fact now shared with me.

She certainly kept me off balance. We went to the theater a couple of times. But then there were other times when she would not come out with me. Then she would tell me, for instance, that she would blow off her Saturday night Quaker group to go out with me, whatever I wanted.

And so we approach the crescendo. And here my journal fails me. It was too painful to write down coherently, and at the same time utterly clichéd. In brief, a competitor named Michael appeared at her Quaker teens' circle, and he played in a brass rock band. I should have known I held no cards to match those. But still I kept on, and still she accepted some of my invitations for a while. So for a time I regarded myself as in a contest I could perhaps win (the 4 Seasons' repeated refrain notwithstanding).

This much the journal confirms: There came a moment when I kissed her and told her I loved her, and that was kind of the end. I have a picture in my mind – a picture of whose accuracy I am not sure – of the location and some of the circumstances. I think this happened near my house, when we were walking from there. I cannot construct a plausible explanation of why it would happen so far from her house or so near to mine. I seem to picture her face filling with dismay after my kiss and my avowal, and her refusing to let me hold her hand the rest of the way to wherever we were going.

This I did not write down, but am absolutely clear on it: I lost several hours. I've never misplaced time like that before or since. After that moment when I had put my heart on the line and finally knew I had lost, I went back to my room, and lay on the bed for several hours, my mind a complete blank. I was not even conscious of being unconscious. The time just passed without my being in any sense aware of anything. Swoons were very popular in the 19th Century, I read. I think this may have qualified as a swoon. I came to with my mother calling me for dinner. My heart was officially broken.

And eventually, sort of – I got over her. In December 1966, the Buckinghams' *Kind of a Drag* started climbing the charts ("Kind of a drag/When your baby don't love you" – over upward cascading brass choruses) – and that became my theme music for a while. Well, until *Sgt. Pepper* pushed it and everything else into oblivion right around the time of my graduation that June.

Nor, interestingly, was it quite the end of the story. Just after graduation, Ella came back into my life for a few dates. They were fun, if frustrating. She let me take her canoeing, and allowed me to me nibble on her ear as July 4th fireworks went off, though I saw her holding hands with another boy a couple of days later.

Kate managed not to deal with sex with me, but she had to do it with someone, and in fact it was reportedly Mike from the brass band. She confided to me worriedly that summer that she was concerned that the liberties she was allowing him might result in her pregnancy. At my school, as I've said, that wasn't a far-fetched fear statistically speaking, but Kate was spared that.

You might think that at some point I would finally have washed my hands of the friendship underlying the yearnings. But that didn't happen either. Kate and I have stayed in touch, off and on, over the years.

The Buckinghams promise that "Girl, I still love you,/ I'll always love you,/ Anyway." That's the way it feels at the time, but of course we all move on. When I see Kate now, I am glad to see her. It is a very pleasant time, but I do not hope for sparks to fly, and they do not. Effectively, our relationship now is a descendant of our friendship, not of what I tried to make of it. My on-again, off-again romancing for a couple of years half a century back is not even referred to, and is simply not a factor, not even as a trying experience that somehow bonded us. If you live long enough, you can get over pretty much everything.

Ella never married, I hear from Kate. She lives happily on the West Coast. I think what Ella thought she was doing with me was summed up by a female colleague of mine who spoke appreciatively once of all the boys she had kissed. At first blush I thought she meant all the boys she had had sex with. But then I reflected that this woman is quite unembarrassed about herself (I learned in more clinical detail than I cared for all about a pregnancy of hers), and far freer with the expletives than I have ever been. If she had meant fucked, she would have said fucked. No, she meant kissed. She was telling me that there was a stage in her life when she had luxuriated in flirting with boys and sharing kisses with them. I believe that this was what I was to Ella: one of the boys she had kissed. Something fun that she correctly surmised would wind up, quickly enough, in her rear-view mirror. And I now know that there was nothing wrong with that, though it was a little harder to accept at the time.

Zsuska is not even mentioned between Kate and me now, though I'm aware they're still friends.

Though I do not long for Ella or Kate, I long for the feelings I had then. I long for the intensity that a few strains of music could stir up in emotions, when love was as yet unachieved, when sex (a somewhat distinct thing) was terrain I was exploring at my own leisurely pace, when, in one's expectations (doomed though one might have sensed they would prove to be), embraces and endearments could lead to lifelong magic, magic in whose presence the music in one's head would never stop.

19

ROUNDING THE BASEPATH

CALIFORNIA GIRLS, BY BRIAN WILSON AND MIKE LOVE,
PERFORMED BY THE BEACH BOYS (1965), ENCOUNTERED 1966

PLAYLIST TRACK NO. 28

THE PARTS OF the summer of 1966 when I wasn't writing loyal canons of contemned love for the absent Kate were largely devoted to my filling in holes in my education and curriculum. I count the Driver's Ed I took at Ann Arbor High in June as education, the Golf I took at Eastern Michigan University in July to satisfy a Phys Ed requirement as curriculum. The proof: I get behind the wheel almost every day; the last time I picked up a golf club was the last day of the class.

Almost immediately after the class ended, I again spent a week visiting my father in New York. I was also sporting my first beard. I liked the way it made me look older than my 17 years. And in 1966 a beard was also a political statement. Plus it made my mom nervous, always a plus.

She'd have been even more nervous if she'd known that my father had taken me to see *Dear John* up in the mountains, at the art movie house in Woodstock. It's a movie no one has heard of these days. It was quite a statement in its time, though. I quote myself in my journal — a nascent film critic:

...a Swedish movie drenched in sex. In fact it was the most sexually explicit movie I've ever seen.... It was the story of two people lonely

beyond belief who desperately try to find refuge in making love to each other. And then they discover that they really made love.... It stirred me deeply. It was truly a religious experience ...

That last phrase in particular might have alarmed my mom about what was going on in my head. I was beginning to reevaluate this whole sex sermon my church was preaching to me. If the mysteries of sex were sacred, then delving into them could hardly be wrong, whatever the official line.

And I have no doubt that my Quaker (and born Jewish) dad knew exactly what he was doing when he took me to that movie. After all, he read movie reviews in the *New York Times*. And his bookcases betrayed a taste for the offerings of the Olympia Press, purveyor of high-class erotica in that era. So there was no mistake there. I'm sure he wanted to get in a few licks for a more bacchanalian point of view than I was being taught courtesy of my ultramontane mom. My journal also contains some positive comments about Playboy at this point. So what was going on in my head wasn't hard to figure out.

And the day after I got back from my sojourn with my father, my mother, my stepdad and I were on the road, out to circumnavigate Lake Michigan. It stands out in my memory as the only strictly touristic trip the three of us ever took as a family. Every other voyage with them as a family centered on some kind of family visit and/or professional travels for my stepdad; there might well be side trips or treats, but the main object on those occasions had been more practical. This one time was about seeing interesting places and a few friends along the way. Period.

So there I was: bearded and curious. And on the road.

Our second stop was on a Saturday night in Whitehall, north of Muskegon, at a place called Murray's Inn. It sat at the end of a peninsula separating a coastal lagoon from Lake Michigan proper. To my parents, it was a kind of disappointing evening, I think. There was no liquor license, and I guess they must have gone to bed early. At any rate, I wasn't with them. I'd been tipped off by a bellboy that the kids, many on staff, all gathered together in the snack bar downstairs at the end of the shift. And sure enough the party started up. We played cards, Crazy Eights.

Sitting across from me was Betsy, my age, blonde, from a Chicago suburb. "I like Johns," she said when I introduced myself. (I did not go by Jack then.) Shortly thereafter she said, "I like your beard." Not too long after that, she was suggesting we go for a walk on the beach, which I said I'd love to do.

I wasn't too thick to recognize that this was a girl with an agenda, but, owing to the lack of experience I've already written about, I was unable to rush into making a first move. Of course she'd already made the first move, conversationally. But the ball, I knew, was in my court, and I was not bold about advancing it.

So we just walked and talked, with the light from a lighthouse brushing over us every twenty seconds. And the conversation was, as I recorded in my journal, "rather dull." Meanwhile the wind was blowing colder, and she was wearing shorts. We decided to go for a longer walk, but she had to check in with her parents (and I'm guessing she wanted to change into something warmer). We held hands on the way back to the hotel, but that was the end. The parents were upset that she'd gone out without checking in with them in the first place, and she was grounded for the evening.

We arranged to meet the next day, Sunday, and as I recorded, this was "the most unendurable and long night." I knew what was going to happen the next day – and I also knew there was a tight schedule. Mass was at 10:00, checkout at 2:00. Not very romantic to be thinking this way, you might comment, and I couldn't disagree. Kate had been mostly about romance; this was about something else.

Come the morning, my folks and I breakfasted at 8;30, and, leaving the dining room, met Betsy. (My parents were "not impressed," per my journal.) I told her I'd call as soon after 11:00 as possible, and with that, I followed Mother to a Mass service.

The service was at someone's private estate, high above the Michigan waters. I was wrestling with the right and wrong of what I was about to do. I decided, let us further say, that I could go pretty far into the sacred mysteries, if not "all the way." My conclusion: "I received Communion with a prayer for guidance."

Then back to the hotel, where I was told we'd be checking out at 1:45. I went by Betsy's room, picked her up, met her dad, who told Betsy I seemed like "a good boy." Her dad, she told me, always thought the boys she went out with were good boys. A remark full of implications.

The sequel was surprisingly long-drawn-out, considering our tight schedule. We went down to the end of the boardwalk and out onto the beach. I took a dip in the freezing water. My parents walked by, and either were or pretended to be oblivious. We returned to the sand near the boardwalk. My folks came back, exchanged pleasantries, left. We were all alone.

And then, finally, we got around to it. I went into the particulars in lip-smacking I detail in my journal, but that won't happen here. Call it a solid mutually satisfying second-base experience. We exchanged a ritual remark about not making out just to make out, that we felt something. But I cannot believe it could have been any truer on her side than on mine.

And two days later, it happened again, with a Kristine, in Traverse City. This time with the added fillips of being mean to another boy who had a real crush on her, and trying to charm the girl's father right after having had my way with her – or at least as much of a way as either of us was ready for. Call that one a solid third-base experience. And of course no sooner had I tagged third than it was time to pile into the car and make another getaway.

As I confided to the journal, though, I really wasn't comfortable. After all, what I'd done with Betsy and Kristine didn't have much to do with the apotheosis of sex, the sex-blending-into-love stuff I'd seen depicted in *Dear John* and which I'd used at that Mass above the waters to justify what I was about to do. And I tried to talk myself into feeling good about weaseling Kristine's old man and humiliating that other boy, but when I got down to it, it humiliated me to have behaved that way.

This Casanova stuff was certainly momentous, but in the psychotherapeutic language we all use today, I needed to process it.

We pulled into Charlevoix on Tuesday, with me sitting in the back seat, processing like mad. We got out and walked along the waterfront. I remember looking into a boathouse where three young guys were working on a boat. And I could plainly hear the LP of the *Goldfinger* soundtrack playing. (It had come out the preceding year, and I had that LP myself. I knew every note, and recognized it instantly.) James Bond, hero of that movie, was a master of the love-'em-and-leave-'em, the very stunt I'd just pulled twice. If I couldn't feel a little good about that, what was anything worth?, I asked myself.

We drove on to Petoskey, lunched, and then proceeded northwards to where the road climbed upward to where we could see far out over Lake Michigan. We pulled over the car so we could enjoy the scene.

And that's when I had my *California Girls* moment.

I whipped out my camera, the DeJur reflex my father had given me, with the huge-field 120 film, and just tried to encompass the scene in front of me. I still have the photo: the afternoon sun glinting off ten thousand billows.

After that, my parents let me walk down to the beach by myself. There was some kind of wooden stairway. And the wind was gently blowing in my

face, and for a moment I felt utterly at peace. And as I did so, *California Girls* came powerfully into my head.

It didn't happen because I was asking myself what was the perfect song to come into my head right then; it came unbidden. But it doesn't take much reflection to see why that particular song did come into my head. Let me count the ways.

First, there was something evocative of spacious horizons in that music that exactly fitted the scene before me at that moment.

Then too the melodic tension through all the key changes in the "Wish they all could be California,/ Wish they all could be California" is resolved in a way that sounds as if it's coming down in a strange and beautiful place, in a new key. (Actually it's not; it's the same Bb chord we started with, but Brian Wilson and Mike Love have spun us around so we don't hear it the same way.) You feel as if you've just arrived somewhere new, musically. Which I had just done in a different way.

There's the carnival feel in the organ chords, evocative of a locale devoted to pleasure – a locale on a left coast, looking westward toward sunsets. Exactly the kind of places I'd been visiting for the last three days.

And then there's the lyric, limning the charms of the girls of all sorts of places, topped off, however, by a somewhat ambiguous wish that they could be something else. No question that I had a someone else in mind too.

I've already commented in Chapter 6 that *Calcutta*, at least in its English lyrics, tells much the same tale: of a guy wandering around the world sampling everyone's charms but committing to none. If you're going to go down that road, however, the Beach Boys' approach is the way to go; the singer admires women the world over, but for aught the lyrics disclose, he may never have laid a finger on any of them. Possibly he's an admirer, a connoisseur, not a promiscuous lecher.

As for me at that moment, I didn't know – and don't know now – what I was, or what I should have been called. Partly I was intoxicated by the vistas opening up before me; certainly I was thrilled that if I wanted, I had some of the basic skills and equipment to be a ladies' man. But was I really going to wander out into those vistas just yet? Would I wander into the water, like that swimmer who's a speck at the bottom of my seascape photo?

Or would I, instead, clamber down to the bottom of those stairs, stand for a moment in admiration on the beach, and then clamber back up again, to continue riding around with my parents? And would I, in less than two weeks, surrender the beard upon demand of the principal and headmaster? Even before I reached the bottom of those stairs, I knew the general answer to those questions: My time wasn't yet.

But it certainly was time for that glorious song. I've indicated before that *Walk On By* remains my all-time favorite song; this is my all-time runner-up.

20

AN UNEXPECTED OPEN DOOR

ESSENCE OF SAPPHIRE, COMPOSED AND PERFORMED
BY DOROTHY ASHBY (1965), ENCOUNTERED 1966

PLAYLIST TRACK NO. 30

IF YOU'RE LIKE most middle-class American kids, your life is formally divided into predictable stages, sectioned off by academic years. As I was growing up, you knew that, after six years of grade school, you'd be moving on to junior high, and that after two years of that, you'd be moving on again to high school. And then came a really big divide, between high school and what lay beyond: college, in the case of pretty much everyone in my school. It was all essentially arbitrary, but emotionally meaningful, especially in its moments of transition, like graduations.

My senior year was filled with that kind of emotion. I was about to move up, but also out. I knew I'd be leaving Ann Arbor. I knew it was unlikely I would ever live there continuously after that. That final year, therefore, was not only consciously devoted to completing the high school life with a bang, but also, only a little less consciously, to completing my mastery of my hometown.

After the wanderings of my earliest years, I had been surprisingly grateful to wash ashore in Ann Arbor. But now that had been almost thirteen years earlier. I understood that this town of less than 100,000 population, no matter how much I loved it, was a small corner of the world. I was determined to try my luck in bigger, more central places.

Yet, as much walking and cycling around town as I'd done, I knew that I had not quite exhausted it yet. And before I gave up my citizenship papers, I wanted to know it more completely. So maybe without ever saying to myself that that was what I was doing, I set out to explore harder.

I could devote a lot of space here to the wonders of the town I uncovered in that last couple of years: the swimming pool nuclear reactor with the glowing blue heart I and friends twice wangled tours of, the other pool in which they tested ship hulls, the pathology museum with the pickled diseased body parts, the fields I walked and cycled out into further than ever before, canoeing under bridges, walking along rail lines. But the one discovery of which I write in this chapter will have to stand for all.

Unknown places are cool, but the ones I love best are places that are not fully known because they're too large and/or complicated and/or inaccessible. For instance, I thrilled to the parts of C.S. Lewis' *The Magician's Nephew* describing a dark passageway connecting the garrets of a set of rowhouses, in which the characters never quite locate themselves correctly. Or the 1965 Gregory Peck thriller *Mirage*, with a staircase that is sometimes there and sometimes not. The Michigan Union was like that in real life. It had been a constant for me from the moment I'd set foot in Ann Arbor, but I'd never really mastered its crenellations.

I'd started going there with my stepdad to get haircuts in the basement barbershop. Later, when my father came to town to visit, he'd often stay in the hotel operation run there, and I'd see a completely different set of features: a swimming pool where you wore no swimsuit, a bowling alley (which you could only get to by means of some kind of trick with the stairs that I had never reliably mastered), dining rooms. In the year I'm speaking of now, I'd begun to frequent the pool hall at the top of the tower, often with my friend Keith, where I learned almost everything I know about the game. Through all these visits, I came to recognize that the only the parts of the building I really understood were at the front, near the main entrance where John Kennedy had first publicly announced the idea of the Peace Corps. This may have been partly owing to the subtraction of various features. For instance, there's no bowling alley or swimming pool today; they may have been removed at around this time. Or my not being able to find them may just have resulted from my not sufficiently grasping the topography.

One day, however, I was there on my own. I heard music from a room, one of the public rooms on the main floor with glassed doors and windows.

In the spirit of inviting myself in wherever I felt like, I opened the door and walked in. There was a three-piece jazz combo playing; I'd heard jazz before, as discussed above, but nothing like this. The leader was an African-American harpist, with drums and either a bass or piano, I don't remember which now for sure. (I think bass.) I had never heard a jazz harp before, and I was entranced. It was so powerful, so elegant.

The Beatles had recently come out with their second movie, *Help!*, which I knew had earlier been tentatively titled *Eight Arms to Hold You*. That was kind of the impression I got of Dorothy Ashby's harp – that she had some abnormal number of fingers and strings to syncopate with. It was a preternatural experience. Which, come to think of it, is exactly the kind of thing orchestrators rely on harps to convey anyhow.

I knew immediately I had stumbled into something special. I can remember nothing about the audience, none of the songs she played. I just knew that I was hearing something wonderful and unusual. I was willing to bet that none of my friends, none of my parents, none of my parents' friends, had ever heard a jazz harp being played. I remember being struck by the elegant appearance of Ms. Ashby as well, though I cannot now picture how she was dressed. I do remember sitting there to the end. My wanderings around town trying to find something new were over for the day.

I know as well that I shortly afterwards went and bought her album. It was probably a bit of a rarity even then, but less so in that neck of the woods, because, as I later learned, Ms. Ashby was a Detroit radio personality – and not only a radio personality, but active with a theater troupe seeking to bring Black theater to that town. And so of course I listened to it over and over.

I tried sharing it with friends, but it wasn't easy. None of my contemporaries still living in Ann Arbor were into jazz at all. So it was sort of a private thing.

When I hear it now, after all these years (recently reissued), two things strike me. First, it's as good and as fresh today as it was back in 1966. Dorothy Ashby herself is gone, having died unreasonably young, but if she had never done anything else in her busy life except cut this LP, she would have had nothing to apologize to her Maker for. Second, *The Fantastic Jazz Harp of Dorothy Ashby* reminds me of my time for exploring and finding new things, even in a town I knew pretty well. I wanted to locate things, not just places, that no one else knew were there. And this was one.

I've selected *Essence of Sapphire* from among the ten cuts of the album, although really the whole album qualified as a Theme Song in my life. I chose this track because it is the most stripped-down one in the album in terms of personnel: just Ashby herself, Richard Davis on bass, and Grady Tate on drums, quite possibly the very combo I saw playing that day at the Union. It conveys the essence of Ashby at that moment.

It conveys something about me at that moment, too. Ashby was nearly unaccompanied, and so in a sense was I. As busy as I was in my last year of high school, and involved with my academic and church communities, I was also spending a lot of time on my own, as I readied myself for a divorce from my whole environment. And that had to be a solo venture.

Finding music to nurture me, music that no one around me had had a hand in exposing me to, was a useful way to prove to myself that I was not only ready, but willing and able.

21

A BRIEF GLIMPSE

MAIN TITLE TO BLOW-UP, WRITTEN AND PERFORMED BY
HERBIE HANCOCK (1966), ENCOUNTERED 1967

PLAYLIST TRACK No. 31

MY MOTHER'S DIARY reflects that I first saw *Blow-Up* on Saturday, February 25, 1967 with my friend Keith, and again with my best buddies Stefan and Walter the following Saturday. It was far from unheard-of for me to see a movie more than once, but this one really seized my imagination – and my ear. I'm betting I dragged Stefan and Walter.

On the imaginative front, as I recorded in my journal, I responded to Michelangelo Antonioni's movie because it was Continental in sensibility, there was gorgeous photography, I liked the surrealism, and, oh yes, there was this bit about the "sexual candor," as I labeled it. As I've already mentioned, I'd seen some on-screen nudity the preceding year with *Dear John*, and now there was this: Vanessa Redgrave topless, and David Hemmings romping on purple paper with Jane Birkin and Gillian Hills, plus Sarah Miles making love. But if this movie was largely about sex, it sure wasn't about intimacy. Call it the anti-*Dear John* in that department.

In what seemed like a panoramic view of the Swinging London of that era, it seemed that intimacy, accountability, reality itself, had all gone missing. The conversations were truncated and stripped of context, people only had sex with people they didn't like, and the meaning of everything seemed to be constantly shifting. I don't want to play faux naïf; I'd been seeing other films with that hard, disenchanted European perspective. But this one seemed to nail it down.

I was personally quite the optimist, and didn't subscribe to the film's outlook myself, but I was braced by the exposure to it.

More important was the music. I walked home whistling the main title theme. I'd recently become a member of one of the record clubs that were popular then – I think the Columbia Record Club. This became one of my selections. I must have listened to that yellow-covered LP dozens of times. I still have it today.

The big draw, of course, was the main title and the rest of the source music and score by Herbie Hancock. Unbeknownst to me, Hancock was providing me a brief (far too brief) glimpse of the main current of jazz at that moment: modal jazz. If you listen to that main title, at least as rendered on the LP, you'll hear that about half of that brief minute-and-a-half is taken up with powerful rhythm guitar and then blasting trumpets doing complicated things that resonate with the G-major 7th and G-minor 7th chords Herbie Hancock is laying down on the piano. This willingness to work away at single chords for extended musical passages, along with not worrying much about orienting entire pieces toward single keys, is a hallmark of modal jazz.

While Hancock and his sidemen serve up a wide variety of jazz in a brief compass on the album, the main title and its companion closing title, are harder-edged than the rest, and clearly Black. I don't think a White-led group could have given us that sound in 1966, when the score was recorded. (Of the seven musicians that I think I can hear on that cut, only one was White.) Though racial generalizations are always dangerous, it's safe to say that Black and White jazz musicians of that era were largely involved with separate projects. Bop and modal jazz were deliberately off-putting to an ear trained to expect Western melody, and they made great technical demands on the players. Many of the players and composers were self-consciously pursuing a kind of racial authenticity. This was, after all, the beginning of the era of Black Power as slogan and ideal. And a sort of hard, somewhat inaccessible, and technically dazzling musicianship was the stylistic weapon of choice in jazz.

Later on, I also asked myself why, surely understanding all this, Antonioni put Hancock's music in *Blow-Up*. How is that music properly the theme for this movie? Reflect, there is no London jazz club pictured that I could discern (even though Ronnie Scott's, for instance, already enjoyed worldwide fame), no jazz musicians (indeed, the only musicians pictured are the proto-punkish rockers, the Yardbirds). In fact, there are hardly any African or African American faces to be seen (two Black nuns in the early going stand out, but nuns don't bring jazz to mind). If this was supposed to be the theme music of this story, what was the commonality? I've never come to a convincing answer. Some of Hancock's score makes it into the story as source music, which tells us that Thomas, the antihero, is a Hancock fan. And it appears the Hancock score that made it into the movie was actually recorded in New York, not London.

The best I can come up with is that the world of *Blow-Up* was hip and modern, and so was the sound of Herbie Hancock, and perhaps Antonioni thought as well he could create the same kind of splash with a Black jazz score as Louis Malle had done in 1958 with Miles Davis' contribution to *Elevator to the Gallows*, which snagged a Grammy nomination.

Whatever prompted Antonioni to invite Hancock into the movie, I was blown away by what Hancock did there. Because I didn't know what I was hearing, I didn't know how to look for more of it then. I had no one to teach me about it, and the rock was blaring so loudly in my ear (it was 1967, after all) that it's no wonder I laid down that thread and didn't pick it up properly again for some years.

But the loose end stayed out there and visible. Notice had been served that something remarkable was happening in the vast world of jazz, something I would need to get to know, someday.

Most of the songs I chronicle in this book stand out as reminders of something else. But my moment with the *Blow-Up* music was important for itself.

22

MY PEPPER MOMENT

SGT. PEPPER'S LONELY HEARTS CLUB BAND, BY
JOHN LENNON AND PAUL MCCARTNEY, PERFORMED
BY THE BEATLES (1967), ENCOUNTERED 1967

PLAYLIST TRACK NO. 32

GRADUATION. COMMENCEMENT. MOVING on. All hopeful, terrifying words. You hope and expect that wherever you're headed is more exciting than the world you're leaving behind, and yet you're terrified that you'll wish later on that you could go back. You're being expelled as though from a womb. The next stage, you know, is likely to put you and your parents in different places, in different households.

It has to happen. You and your parents have to disentangle. They need to have their lives be more about them, just as you need to have your life be more about you. On both sides, the "us" of your family identity needs dialing back.

Formally, the date of my own graduation/expulsion was Friday, June 9, 1967. Actually, the process had begun back on Sunday, May 14, when my stepdad had come down with violent abdominal pains. Over the next couple of weeks, much of them spent in the hospital, he was diagnosed with diverticulitis, a disease of the bowel. He would have to undergo a major resection of the bowel three days before my graduation. His life was therefore going to be more about him at this point, however I felt about it. I might be taking finals, going to honors assemblies and proms and such, experiencing the highs and lows of this inflection point; he wasn't going to be there in my cheering section.

And I wasn't going to be available much to support him, either. I was furiously busy, as absorbed in this final spasm of high school life and my other amusements as he doubtless was with his own uncooperative digestive system.

This proved to be a moment of transition for him as well. Up till that point, one would have described him as in decent health for someone with his generation's standard bad habits: smoking, drinking, overeating. He'd had a health crisis with scarlet fever a couple of decades earlier, but he'd done pretty well since then. And he would have stretches of reasonable fitness afterwards. But serious bad stuff kept menacing him from this point onward. This diverticulitis attack was the moment when the Reaper started sizing him up – and never looked away for long after that. My stepdad kept saying that he thought he'd live to an old age, but be sick the whole time. The prediction was based on grim experiences that began here.

It's hard to recall how bad it actually was, having him and by extension my mom subtracted from my affairs at that moment. The one place I do remember really missing him was at the graduation itself – and having the feeling that my mom was just going through the motions of being there. Our parish priest had driven her to the graduation direct from the hospital. There was no one to take family pictures; I only have official ones, including this from the yearbook photographer. (I'm the figure on the extreme left of the top row.)

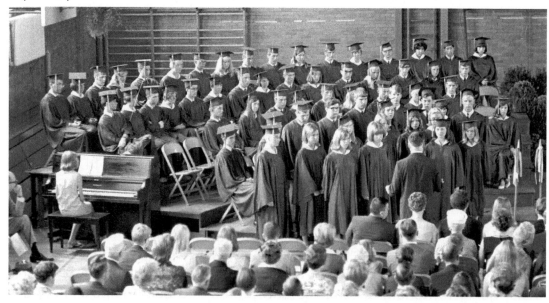

That was one of the reasons the ceremony itself felt rather empty to me. Another was knowing that we were leaving almost nothing behind us; it had been announced that there would only be one more graduating class after ours before our school shut down forever. When you're leaving a school, you want there to be something to return to from time to time, so you can draw sustenance from and measure yourself against some kind of ongoing tradition. Even if you can't return, you want what you had still to be going on for someone, in some form, or some way. At your graduation, you're supposed to be the one doing the abandoning, not the one suffering it.

So whatever people might like graduations to feel like, mine wasn't much for me. The after-party, though, was another matter.

There had been a series of class parties over the extended goodbye we were all saying to each other. The very last one was that afternoon, at our classmate Dave's house. This was the last time we would all be together before we'd have to call it a reunion. Dave was not a special friend of mine. We hailed from different class castes. I was one of the smart kids; he was one of the jocks, about the fastest runner I witnessed in my brief stint as manager of the track team. But I was glad to be there, if only because it was a great place to have a party.

There was a large pool in the back yard, and he'd set up (or maybe the family just had) a real live soda fountain to help us beat the June heat. I still remember that fountain with longing.

To explain this, I first have to explain Vernors Ginger Ale, to the extent anyone can explain it. Though I can now buy a product by that name where I live in Maryland, the true Vernors was a Detroit thing, an intense, pungent ginger-and-vanilla experience, heightened by the deliberate overcarbonation of the beverage. And if you happened to put that overcarbonated treat in a soda fountain beside a pool on a hot summer afternoon, it made for cold indescribable wonderfulness. You more inhaled it than drank it, especially if you knew to spritz in only shallow drafts. The foam gave you all the flavor and little else. I believe there were other flavors in the fountain, but I only had eyes for Vernors.

So there I was, drowning my sorrows (such as they were) in Vernors, and then someone turned on the record player. That was my first opportunity to hear *Sgt. Pepper's Lonely Hearts Club Band*. The album had been out a week. I might have heard something of it on the radio, but there were no singles from it in release. The album came out only as an album, the only right way for it to be heard. So I'm pretty certain that up to this point I'd only heard of it, not heard the thing itself.

Most critics call this the single greatest album of the rock era. I agree about that, but sheer abstract greatness was not the quality that made the first hearing unique for those of us sitting around that pool. What struck me, and don't think I was alone, was how strange the album sounded. It starts with an orchestra tuning up in a concert hall against a background of crowd noises, not a very typical way for any production in the world of rock to have started. As the vinyl rotated, we heard a whole lot of other stuff we'd seldom or never heard before: merry-go-round pipe organ sounds, sitars, an orchestra doing chromatic upwards slides, foxes and hounds, string chamber ensembles. We heard lyrics about things no one else was lyricizing about: a young woman leaving home, getting old, meter maids, and whatever *Lucy in the Sky With Diamonds* might be about. Picking up the album cover (and I remember I did that) was to encounter things we'd never seen before: a group shot that included the Beatles dressed up in Victorian band-leader uniforms and waxworks of the Fab Four, Marlene Dietrich, a bust of Oscar Wilde, Laurel and Hardy, you name it. The interior opened up to reveal a closeup of our heroes as the band-leaders against a harsh gold-yellow background. The back had them awash in scarlet with all of their lyrics (not a common thing in those days.)

Did everyone instantly drop everything and listen? No, it was a pool party. Did anyone ignore it entirely? I can't speak for everyone there, but I seem to recall a lot of dumbfounded comments. Those who were paying any kind of attention knew that they'd have to pay a lot more attention, later on, that we'd all have to listen to it several times to get out of it a reasonable helping of what the album had to offer. But hey, we had the time.

That was the beauty of the moment for us. We had the time. No more teachers, no more books. No more living at home. No more anything familiar. In our first official post-high school moments we were being offered something original, something we had not encountered before. It was bright and shiny and challenging and exciting.

I remember little else about that party. I do remember hearing that record, though, and feeling great. We were leaving home, bye-bye.

23

SUMMERTIME BETWIXT AND BETWEEN

DIDN'T WANT TO HAVE TO DO IT, BY JOHN SEBASTIAN, PERFORMED BY THE LOVIN' SPOONFUL (1966), ENCOUNTERED 1967

NO FAIR AT ALL, BY JIM YESTER, PERFORMED BY THE ASSOCIATION (1967), ENCOUNTERED 1967

PLAYLIST TRACKS NOS. 33, 34

So, I WAS leaving home. Only not just yet. College started in September. There was all that time between graduation in June and matriculation in September to get through first. It was, by my own choice, a rather solitary time for me, both busy and languid.

All three of us in the household withdrew into ourselves, under the twin shadows of my stepdad's convalescence and the foreknowledge of the coming separation that college would bring. My stepdad was in the hospital for most of two months, and seriously convalescent for another month.

My mother, worn out with nursing him, changing dressings, etc., hardly wrote an entry in her diary, which was highly uncharacteristic of her. And I nearly stopped journaling myself. I also stopped writing to Fiona, my confidante/pen pal from Rome, now studying in Montreal. I was too focused on other things. But as a side effect, all of a sudden there isn't much of a documentary record for a while, and I have to rely on my somewhat unreliable memories.

And what do those memories tell me? They pretty much confirm what one little scrap of evidence tells me, a letter I wrote to my step-grandmother exactly a month after my graduation. "My summer is perfect. I'm not working: couldn't find any. So I keep my own hours – noon to 3 a.m. I work on writing a book between 11 and 3. Nobody calls up and there's nothing else to do, and so there are no interruptions. I go to every single movie I want to. I share a fairly regular date with this other guy, and have enough friends to pass the time. I do chores around the house, read ... occasionally play tennis or billiards or canoe. I imagine this is the last chance I'll get in my life for this kind of existence."

So I was keeping to myself, and writing.

My writing project: the Great American High School Novel – based, of course, on my own recent past, despite the fact that, judging from what I produced, I really had nothing to say about high school. I lacked any theme.

I also was working from the wrong models. There was *Middlemarch* and *War and Peace* and *Tai Pan* (which had just come out the previous year) and *Kristin Lavransdatter*. And *Advise and Consent* (though as literature it doesn't measure up to any of these other models, not even *Tai Pan*, a potboiler if there ever was one). Popular or obscure, they were epics, one and all.

I should have understood that you can write about high school, or you can write epics, but you cannot do both at once. High school is for sensitive novels about the shaping of the artist, about first love, about sports, and, now that we have Young Adult fiction, about kids confronting various big life problems and social issues. But it's closeup work, not big picture material.

And even if I'd employed a reasonable focus, I had no idea about what tone to adopt, and no idea how to shape a story.

The result, of course, was that the 200 or so pages I completed that summer are about as unreadable as anything I've ever written. I don't think I ever supposed they were all that good, but I kept thinking I could fix it all later, that I could take this shapeless, toneless, theme-less mass and make something of it.

And, as near as I can tell in retrospect, there was a kind of unarticulated (even to myself) design there. The real plan was to write a story in which I got the girl. I've already recounted what had really happened. Whatever else I might have accomplished in high school, I would still have had to acknowledge that I didn't get the girl. As Don McLean so riotously put it: "All the victories I've led / Still haven't brought you to my bed." But I think my inchoate hope was that by making sense of it all through a fictional reinterpretation, I could still get the real-life girl to love me. She would read the story and see how foolish she'd been. And she'd come to that realization by reading a story in which a character like her sees how foolish she's been. Glancing at this huge unfinished typescript (I can't really bring myself to read it), I think I can see how that reinterpretation was expected to work. The character who stood in for me would achieve a kind of moral grandeur through dealing compassionately with other characters' difficulties and avoiding their shortcomings, persuading one or two girls (I think I hadn't worked out the number) to fall in love with him. Maybe, if there were two, he would break the heart of one of them because he had grown too lofty for her.

That might have been doable, in a jejune kind of way, if I'd had any idea how to plot a story, but I didn't. I wanted to afford the interactions of a bunch of high schoolers the kind of treatment Tolstoy gave to Russia's Napoleonic wars or Allen Drury gave to the machinations by which the U.S. Congress came to vote on a presidential appointment. I grasped from these sources that everything that happens is a consequence of a vast number of other events, and that providing a truly contextual understanding of anything requires the recreation of an entire web of human interactions. What eluded me, apparently, was that no one wants a truly contextual understanding of young love or the social interactions of a high school class.

Undeterred, I was listening to music that constituted theme songs to my one or two ultimate story lines. (This time the term is actually employed more conventionally; I was dreaming of having a movie made of the book, and was thinking along the lines of actually having these numbers played in it.)

The Lovin' Spoonful's *Didn't Want to Have to Do It* was the music for the story line having to do with the girl who didn't quite measure up. The singer has had to disappoint a woman who "keeps on a-tryin'/ And I knew that you'd end up a-cryin'." Actually, this was pretty much what had happened to me, not to the girls in my life, and I'm sure that's the real reason it resonated so much with me. It is an extraordinarily beautiful song, with heavy, heavy vibrato on John Sebastian's guitar (or is it autoharp?), while in the lyrics, Sebastian is continually if reluctantly drawn to the two words "the end."

Meanwhile The Association's *No Fair At All* was the song for the happier love story. Jim Yester's lyric is a scales-falling-from-the-eyes tale:

I've never seen the sight of you before
'Till now.

I've never knew that you could feel this way
'Till now.
After all this time we've spent together
Just doesn't seem fair
At all.

"No fair at all" gets sung at the end by several voices, in something like a round, while a recorder weaves in and out. It's devastatingly beautiful. That the scales-from-the-eyes experience conjured up by the song, of course, is what I wanted to happen to the girl in my life. I wanted to be seen in all my magnificence. And since in real life I was a little deficient in the magnificence department, and she seemed quite content to keep the scales on her eyes, fiction was the only route to that experience.

I know that The Association never gained much respect, as their music was too pretty, and too closely orchestrated. With around six male voices it could call on, and some slick arrangers, it could be called ear candy. (Although I challenge anyone to say that about their anti-war song *Requiem for the Masses*.) I've never liked putdowns like "ear candy." If it's moving, say I, it's good. So I wear my heart on my sleeve unapologetically for the Association.

Still, I'll grant you that it was no summer for profundity. As exemplified by the book I was trying to write, I lacked enough depth, perception, or experience to do anything except wait for the seasoning that college and the life beyond were about to bring.

24

AN EMPTY ROOM, GREEN TROLLEYS, AND BRUBECK

DIALOGUES FOR JAZZ COMBO AND ORCHESTRA:
III - ADAGIO-BALLAD, BY HOWARD BRUBECK,
PERFORMED BY THE NEW YORK PHILHARMONIC
WITH THE DAVE BRUBECK QUARTET CONDUCTED BY
LEONARD BERNSTEIN (1961), ENCOUNTERED 1967

PLAYLIST TRACK No. 35

IN A NEARLY empty room, after perhaps weeks of silence, music can be heard.

A group of cellos speaks first, meandering through a series of desolate chords without a clear direction, while above them a lonely oboe hesitantly picks out a melody as if trying to find a footing in the insecure and seemingly trackless chordal morass. Then, after two minutes, the chaos resolves, and a saxophone picks up where the oboe left off, and confidently navigates the chord pattern, swinging effortlessly where the oboe stumbled. A piano then picks up the stride, and marches with the entire orchestra to a bluesy, melancholy conclusion.

This was the music I played on the stereo in my college dorm room the night of Saturday, September 2nd, 1967, my very first, very solitary night there. At the time, I couldn't have told you why I'd chosen it, but that was the music I chose.

I'd had no way of picturing this moment in advance. As was more typical then than now, I had never before set foot on the campus of the University of Pennsylvania in Philadelphia, where I would study for the next four years. I'd had no aids to visualize it, no websites to visit, very little in the way of counseling to advise me, and my mother and stepfather were, for a pair of academics, singularly clueless about where I should go to college, or why.

In preparation for my trip from my Michigan home, I'd acquired a big green footlocker, and packed a lot of my stuff, including some records and stereo gear, into it. My stepdad and I had entrusted the trunk to the care of the Railway Express Agency, for it to be delivered to the Agency's Philadelphia office.

And then he and my mom and I drove, reaching Philadelphia at about 5 in the afternoon on Friday, September 1st. Typically for my family, though, by the time we reached Philly we'd stopped at least one night with my folks' friends, and when we got to Philadelphia, there were a total of five grownups gathered to see me installed. I loved them all, but I would have preferred to have been on my own. I wanted to start life in my new world. At once. Alone.

But no, my parents would not be rushed. Instead, they congregated with the others at the Sheraton in Center City. Then we had to go to one of the two rival Bookbinder's restaurants for dinner. Finally, after dinner, my parents consented to take me over to the campus; a campus cop let us in. We found my dorm room in an ivy-covered quad.

I was enchanted. My window would have been too high off the ground for a Sebastian Flyte to come and vomit into my room, a la *Brideshead Revisited*. Still, I could expect something like a ground-level vantage-point on whatever might happen out there on the quad.

The following day, we retrieved the Railway Express trunk and moved my things into the dorm. I got to make my bed, and pulled my precious stereo components out, but I don't think I had time to wire them up. The six of us went out to dinner at the other Bookbinder's. And then, gloriously, I slipped away ...

I could have walked it, and I'm sure for that matter my parents would have staked me to a cab. But I really wanted to do it the way a Philadelphian would, by the underground trolley. I'd researched it, and worked out that there were four lines that ran through a station a block from the hotel, and that they would deposit me right on campus outside the dorms. (Just avoid the Number 10, I was warned.) So, as soon as I'd made my leave, I went down into the portal of the 19th Street Station.

I was excited and nervous. I remember being struck immediately by what I would come to recognize as the peculiar smell of that tube, something reminiscent of steam and heated electrical copper. I grew nervous, though, when the train I boarded waited for a switch to reset right ahead of us. Had I done something wrong? Could I be on the 10 line after all? So I bolted at the first stop after the switch.

It was what I would later know as the Sansom Street stop. There's nothing sinister about the neighborhood now, but it was a little sketchy in 1967. Still, I felt that I was in about the right place, and struck out in what I figured had to be the right direction. And damn, I was right! I found the dorm and got inside without trouble.

So I settled in, all by myself. Finally I could hook up my stereo components, and sit in the semidarkness.

The first work I played was something I'd been turned on to a year earlier by a high school classmate, *Dialogues for Jazz Combo and Orchestra*, the four-movement concert piece composed by Dave Brubeck's brother Howard, which gave the orchestra set things to do and periodically opened up windows for the Dave Brubeck Quartet to jam in. There's no doubt, though, that that night it was the third movement, the Adagio, the one I've described above, that mattered.

The next day was one more day of family reunion and tourism. But I cut out when I could, got back and met and spent the night with my new roommate, with whom I hit it off well (a friend to this very day). So that was exciting.

That would be a nice note on which to end this chapter, but there's still a little more to tell.

The following day, after all, was the one I'd really been anticipating and dreading. For sheer guillotine-like intensity and definitiveness of severance, nothing in our society short of divorces and funerals begins to compare to the moment when parents leave kids off at college for the first time. I have now been through both sides of the experience, and I know. Talk about necessary; talk about wrenching!

There was a brief reprieve for the Dean's reception in front of the Annenberg School. Then came the moment of goodbye. I'd been eager to be on my own before; now I had this terrible hollow feeling. I don't remember the hugs and what was said, but I do remember, after my parents had left, being unable to talk to anyone. I just needed to get out.

The campus block that includes what were then known as the Men's Dorms is perhaps a mile around. I went out walking, head down, crying softly.

Suddenly, someone honked at me. I looked up, and there were my folks, one more time. "Hey," my stepdad yelled, "can you tell us the way to Penn?" and then they sped off.

I burst into tears. I may have misted up and even sobbed to myself before, but now I was bawling. My childhood, at this very moment, was completely gone, all used up. A door had slammed behind me.

I finished the long walk around the block, pulling myself together as I went. I made it back to my room, and sat down and wrote letters to my two closest friends, advising that I had "a king-sized case of the blues."

Still, I promptly went out and began my campus life. They had something called Tradition Night that evening. I described it to my parents as "an orgy of chauvinism backed by the Glee Club." I also wrote:

> "One of the funniest things that happened last night was when this doddering old alumnus, representing the big alumni organization, stepped up to the microphone and said, 'Welcome aboard.' My first response ... was 'Who in the hell is he?' It was obvious that anybody of his mental caliber couldn't possibly make it into Penn today."

I nearly choke when I read these words half a century on. The misapplied negative is the least of it. I probably am now no younger than that "doddering old alumnus," and odds are I couldn't make it past a 21st-Century admissions committee myself. Still, I take that letter as overall a good thing. Surely the return of the insufferable arrogance of youth meant that some kind of equilibrium was being restored.

I was launched, thanks to a million and one things, including that unfairly-maligned alumnus, a small victory over the green underground trolley cars, and Brubeck's *Dialogues*.

And I have come in recent times to understand the reason why I focused on that Adagio that night. The draw for me was that shift at the midpoint from those hesitant, wandering chords to the confident stride of the clarinet. That was what I was hoping this final exercise of my adolescence, the adventure of college, would be: a working-out of all the formlessness I could feel in my life, and a move to definition and purpose.

Time would tell whether I would or could achieve it. But that, at least, was what I would be working on.

25

MINDWORMS, MUSICAL AND OTHERWISE

BLUE JAY WAY, BY GEORGE HARRISON, PERFORMED BY
THE BEATLES (1967), ENCOUNTERED 1967

PLAYLIST TRACK No. 36

WHILE MY COLLEGE freshman experience was full of good things, there were difficult, frustrating, and sometimes downright horrifying ones as well.

Within a few weeks of my arrival, a young man who had just matriculated with me, and whose face was on the page facing mine in the freshman directory, was strangled by a campus tobacconist whose shop stood just a block away from the dorm where I slept. Although I was not quite unfamiliar with violent death occurring in my immediate vicinity, it had never before happened to a peer of mine.

More mundanely, my courses proved harder than I could have guessed (I pulled a first-semester GPA of only 2.8), and I wrote a friend, and meant it, that "everybody here's smarter than I." My study habits clearly needed upgrading, but I was slow figuring out how.

The city itself was challenging, too. I wanted to explore, but Philadelphia yielded itself up slowly. There was lots of dirt, neighborhoods where it wasn't necessarily safe to go, unpredictable train schedules, distances that were a little uncomfortable to walk (and this was before backpacks, wheeled briefcases, or any technology for miniaturizing the information you needed to have available for your studies). The air was full of soot that would mess up your record grooves (and you'd best believe I noticed something like that.) Frequently there were nasty smells from the nearby oil refineries. People were harder than in my hometown. The barber at the student union practically cursed me out when I (not then knowing better) didn't tip him. I got into a fight with the petty tyrant who checked to assure we were wearing ties for dinner at Freshman Commons, as required.

So, as exciting as it all was, there was a queasy underside to it that kept me off balance. It reached its apogee the day I bought *Magical Mystery Tour*, the Beatles' follow-up to *Sgt. Pepper*. I was more than ready for whatever the Beatles were about to dish up, even though the first few people I'd heard talking about it were disappointed. I bought my copy on Saturday, December 9th. I was finished with all my courses then, and studying for finals. (Complaining jokingly to my parents the previous day that "I should be out wenching ..., but I'm going to be reading Kierkegaard.") *Magical Mystery Tour* was a present to myself for getting through the semester and an encouragement to myself to study hard.

I think on my first couple of listens, I found a lot to like about the album, but there was one totally creepy song, George Harrison's *Blue Jay Way*. My Beatles *vade mecum*, Ian MacDonald's *Revolution in the Head*, objectively describes the song:

> *Written in the fog-bound Hollywood Hills of Los Angeles on 1st August 1967, the blurred harmonic oscillation between C major and C diminished which is almost the entire musical matter of BLUE JAY WAY all too successfully conveys its author's jet-lagged dislocation while waiting for publicist Derek Taylor to arrive. A four-minute pedal-drone laden with [Artificial Double Tracking] phasing, and backwards tapes, it numbingly fails to transcend the weary boredom that inspired it.*

I just found the song scary. It seemed like a descent into some kind of languorous madness. (To be fair, probably not what Harrison intended.) Not only was the song unattractive, but it wormed its way into my head and I couldn't get it out. It's not just the songs you like that do that to you. By the third play-through I deliberately lifted up the tone arm and skipped that song.

Predictably, I was far from the only person celebrating that day. The fraternities and sororities were doing their end-of-semester thing. A block from me, at the Delta Tau Delta house, a party was in progress. Around 1:30 on the

Sunday morning, someone mishandled a cigarette near some combustible Christmas decorations. The ground floor was promptly engulfed in flames, which then quickly spread up the one stairway to the second floor. People on the second floor were trapped. Many jumped from the window, some were pushed from the window by frantic partygoers behind them, and some injured themselves in the fall. Three died, two frat brothers and a high school girl. (Heavens only know what she was doing there at that hour.)

The word was all around campus, of course, when I awoke that Sunday morning. I was dumbfounded. That frat was at the east end of the fraternity row, on the main campus block. I passed it every day. And now people had died there! I was scared. I was horrified. I tried but failed to get images of people on fire out of my head.

When I first walked on campus after that, I stole a glance at the charred entrance with the tape around it. Then I looked away. And for the next several days, I wouldn't look that way. I knew that what had happened was a sample of the random disasters that come along from time to time. The next time might not be a frat party, but something else I hadn't even thought of. There but for the grace of God, I was feeling.

It's obvious, then, why *Blue Jay Way* serves as touchstone for that moment. I didn't want either to look at the one thing or to listen to the other. But I had to keep encountering them. And I couldn't get either one out of my head.

I had not been the only person celebrating, and now I was not the only person avoiding. The following summer I received the yearbook. On the Delta Tau Delta page, it's as if the event had never occurred. "This was a good year for Delta," the page informs us, "as brothers remained active in every major aspect of University life." Football heroes are mentioned, and service clubs. Toward the end, remarkably, this: "Social activities were climaxed in the fall with the annual Christmas formal and the spring semester was full of promise as we gained another outstanding pledge class." That's it? That's all that's worth mentioning about Christmas season at the frat? Nothing about the three lives snuffed out and the desperate people being pushed out the window, and the charred entrance, and the trauma for the entire campus?

I kept hearing George Harrison's refrain in my head, *Please don't be long/ Please don't you be very long*, like a plea to the missing, as if George were invoking them to delay no further their return from the dead. But George was too spaced-out for his voice to reach them, and so they wandered off further into the land of shades.

26

CASHING IN ON CACHET

I'M INTO SOMETHING GOOD, BY CAROLE KING AND GERRY GOFFIN,
PERFORMED BY HERMAN'S HERMITS (1964), ENCOUNTERED 1968

PLAYLIST TRACK NO. 37

I RECEIVED A very early tutorial in social hierarchy and sexual privilege among college students in the late 1960s. My early efforts at on-campus romance didn't come to much, but Philadelphia was quite the college town, so there were lots of places where young women from other schools were to be encountered. My first or second Sunday at Penn, our dorm counselor took us to visit a couple of such places.

Including the counselor, there were nine guys jammed into his little green 1957 Rambler station wagon. After a brief tour of historic downtown Philly and breakfast, we went off to see Bryn Mawr College, but the place hadn't opened yet, so we dropped in on its nearby neighbor, Harcum College, a two-year institution, then a women's school.

It was move-in day there. We rolled up next to an authority figure talking with some parents, and asked him, probably a shade too boisterously, if we knew the way to Pennswood Dorm. This dorm was where a friend of someone in the car was supposedly going to be living. The authority figure didn't like the look of us and warned us to stay away from the campus that day, or he'd have us arrested. "We only want gentlemen visiting this campus."

We drove away, laughing as soon as it was safe to (our dorm counselor included), and found Pennswood Dorm on our own. Things didn't immediately improve there. We walked in the front door, all nine of us, probably coming on as a bunch of storm troopers. I actually saw a parent's jaw drop as we passed. The young lady we were seeking turned out to be elsewhere, at a meeting with the dean, but her friends were very friendly, and very helpful. Soon, though, we came up against a den mother type, accompanied by a campus cop. And the cop was not simpatico.

"Hey, are you guys the ones in the blue Studebaker?"

We weren't about to get pedantic over nameplates or paint colors, but we did intend to stand our ground if we could. The one who knew the girl protested that we had an invitation.

"What did the man tell yah?" the cop interrupted.

"I was trying to say, sir," began our friend again.

"What did the man tell yah? He told yah to stay out, didn't he?" And he poked one of the guys with his stick to emphasize the point.

Clearly, it was not time to stand our ground after all. We let him herd us in the direction of the door. But as we neared the door, someone got through to him that we were Penn men. The change in his demeanor was instantaneous; no more toughness.

And just in time, as we were met at the door by the authority figure. "Gentlemen," he said, "I'm the head of the Harcum physical plant, and I told you to stay out. We could throw you guys in jail."

The cop protested. "Oh, they're all right, Mr. Wilson. They just didn't know." Here he actually threw his arm around me. "They're just guys out to have a good time." He addressed me: "I know. I was a boy, too, once. I wasn't born like this, you know." Referring to his girth.

Mr. Wilson wasn't placated. "Now I want you gentlemen to get out of here right now, and we won't press charges."

The cop intervened. "But they're just Penn boys."

Wilson didn't bat an eyelash, but he did change his tack. "Well, you can come back tomorrow, but we don't allow boys on the campus when the girls are moving in. If you act like gentlemen, you're welcome here. If not, don't bother coming back."

So we learned that being a Penn guy gave us preferential access to women. In a town filled with colleges and universities, many of them dedicated to the education of women, this was welcome information. And later experience only confirmed it. In that town, apart from Princeton University, safely sequestered over an hour away, Penn, my school, had the most – the only word that comes to mind is what Frank Zappa called "groupie status." Not a perfect analogy, but it will do.

During my freshman year, I took full advantage of this advantage. In practice this meant that I went to mixer dances at schools all over and met young women there, or they came to mixers at Penn. And then I'd date them, but always briefly or superficially. Lots of us were dating lots of people. I had a couple of real heart-flutters, but they weren't returned.

In the midst of all this I met Cindy, who had long black hair. We encountered each other at one of the dances, somewhere on our campus. This would have been around the end of the first semester, or the very beginning of the second. Cindy went to Rosemont, a Catholic school, then single-sex, though since that time, like Harcum, it has gone co-ed. Cindy seized onto me right after our first dance together.

I wish I could remember her more clearly, but the fact that I can't exactly underlines the problem. The tone of what I do remember about her is all class markers, from her smoking to her accent. Think of the bridge-and-tunnel strivers in *Saturday Night Fever* and you'll have the picture of what I saw.

And I fear it was class that she saw as well. I was a Penn man, with all that that entailed. Everywhere I'd ever been, everything I'd ever done, had equipped me for this, and for the life I and my compeers were training ourselves to pursue next. It was who our parents were, it was where we were going to school, it was in our aspirations and our accents. And I don't think for a minute she was blind to that. If I'd looked exactly the same but gone to a different school, I doubt I would have held nearly the allure. After all, women of my own social class at my own school were finding me perfectly resistible so far.

And now we get to the Theme Song. We parted, I'm pretty sure, somewhere in downtown Philadelphia, most likely the Suburban Station, and I know we had made a promise to get together at a date both certain and soon. I believe it had been raining, and I had my umbrella (furled), as I was walking across a wet square. That's when *I'm Into Something Good*, a song from three years earlier, came unbidden to my mind. And why not? The lyrics fit my situation pretty closely.

She's the kind of girl who's not too shy: Check!

She danced close to me like I hoped she would: Check!

We only danced for a minute or two/ But then she stuck close to me the whole night through: Check!

I walked her home and she held my hand / I knew it couldn't be just a one-night stand / So I asked to see her next week and she told me I could: Also check!

There had been something about the way she kissed goodnight that had made it clear to me I could probably go anywhere on the proverbial basepath with her. I started singing the song to myself. I went through it several times, clicking the point of the umbrella in rhythm on the Philadelphia sidewalks as I made my way back.

I was all set to cash in on my cachet.

The prospect became more explicit on my next date with her. Again, I wish my memories were clearer. But putting together little clues in my memory, I believe we started the evening at my dorm room, where there was some making out, then dinner and a movie downtown.

Only two things vividly stand out in my mind about that date. One was that when I first caught sight of her, the long black hair was gone. What I'd seen the previous occasion had been a fall, not her real hair. With it shorter, she wasn't nearly as attractive to me; I was silently taken aback. In retrospect, I believe she was posing me some kind of test: was I sufficiently attracted to her without the help from the fall that she could trust her body and her heart to me? And beneath that test, a bigger one: was I okay with the class difference?

My other recollection is a picture of the two of us, at the end of the date, necking hot and heavy in some underground corner of the catacombs under Center City, not far from the Suburban Station, before I took her to her train. I seemed to be passing her test. But I was failing the bigger test of my own character. *Droit de seigneur* corrupts the lord as much as it degrades the serf.

But in the end I acquitted myself somewhat better. Somewhat. After agonizing over it for a few days, I sent Cindy a letter telling as much of the truth as I could bear to tell. We weren't right for each other, I wrote. And that much was true. I didn't spell out the reasons for the mismatch, and the hints I gave were deliberately wrong. But the rest of what I wrote was true. I said it was obvious we were going to be having sex if we went on, and while I wasn't sure where I stood on the official Catholic line on this, I knew sex was serious, and if it wasn't kept for marriage, at least it should be kept for something committed. Strange, now, to note that I was speaking my mind about sex, but not about class. My Catholic upbringing had given me a vocabulary and a straightforwardness for the one but not the other.

What I was leaving out, probably not fully articulated to myself, was that I was recoiling. Not from anything wrong with Cindy, but from the class mismatch she and I were on the verge of embarking upon. Better, of course, to know myself and my snobbery than not. But better still not to have been that snob, to have been able to make my choices free of such attitudes. Cindy, bless her, wrote back, saying that it was a great compliment to her that I would look at the relationship so squarely. She acknowledged that the impending sex would have put her in conflict. (We Catholic kids had that burden.) And she ended by addressing, somewhat more squarely than I had dared to, the class issue. She was sorry she had "disappointed" me in that regard, she said.

She could have spared herself that apology. None of us has anything to apologize for about where they come from, Cindy least of all. In a strange way, then, I guess the promise of that song was fulfilled. I was in for something good when I met Cindy. It was brief, it was abortive, but it was good, especially in how it ended. And it left me confronting, if not remotely solving, my own classism. If one's early affairs are about learning, this was at least a partial lesson, and hence something good.

27

THEATER DAYS

*IN AND OUT, WRITTEN AND PERFORMED BY BRIAN AUGER
& THE TRINITY (1968), ENCOUNTERED 1968*

*GATES OF EDEN, WRITTEN AND PERFORMED BY
BOB DYLAN (1965), ENCOUNTERED 1968*

PLAYLIST TRACKS NOS. 38, 39

I WAS THEATER-SMITTEN before I ever got to college. Coming to Penn, then, I simply assumed that I'd get involved with the student theater company, the Pennsylvania Players, and I did. My resulting involvement with them ended up being tougher, shorter, and more interesting than I would have predicted. In the end, I took part in three shows.

The first was a big original musical about GIs and nurses during the Korean War. The tale, of a concert pianist who gets his arm blown off in combat, but then discovers meaning in life taking care of a little girl with leukemia, was a little too upbeat and square for a show being produced during Vietnam. I served as assistant stage manager. My experiences were frequently sort of *Rosencrantz and Guildenstern*-y, with me stuck occupying a corner of a scene that other people were barging into and out of paying little heed to me.

I did suss out some truths that should not have but did come as off-putting surprises. I learned that the theater is full of temperamental and cliquish people, for instance. I learned that kids with aristocratic pedigrees from

Philadelphia's Main Line and similar spots further up the Eastern Seaboard had a sense of entitlement, not to mention quaint names. I learned that some theater people were highly flirtatious, and that in an organization drawn from four college classes, a lot of the romantic histories and/or rivalries among the older members were important, extensive and not readily learned by newcomers.

Despite these shocks, I managed to do all right with that show, and suddenly started "feeling the love," in the modern phrase. In recognition of my success, I was now placed in line to direct a show somewhere further up the line. My next step, in the spring, was being given a stage manager position on one one-acter in an evening of short plays that had won an undergraduate playwriting competition. Unlike the very limited assistant stage manager role on the big musical, this was effectively an assistant directorship, and looked on as readying me to direct.

I surely don't want to exaggerate how much of a step up this was for me. Looking back, I can see this was the bottom rung of the Penn Players' farm system. The play we were given, called *Blues Man*, by a senior we'll call Meyer, was described by him in a handwritten note on the script as: "… the story of the necessary self-destruction of an emasculated white liberalism and the subsequent emancipation of the Negro Psyche." It depicted the fracturing of a friendship and working relationship of a pair of jazz players, as the Black one rejects the well-meaning but ultimately blind and patronizing support of the White one. As the (White) author pointed out to me when I got in touch with him a decade ago, this was sort of an attempt to follow in the footsteps of the Black playwright then known as Leroi Jones (later Amiri Baraka). For juvenilia, the play's not that bad. But with the limited resources of talent Penn Players devoted to it, we made a hash of it.

Beyond the fact that we wrote the play a new ending and destroyed the playwright's vision, we had terrible casting. For the angry Black man we had a whimsical and utterly unmenacing guy I'll call Charles. For the White guy we had a foreign grad student with a significant accent I'll call Dieter. Now, the White liberalism being dissed in the play was specifically American White liberalism. Foreign jazz enthusiasts, of that era especially, were just different from American ones; they liked and were reacting against different things. Dieter could effortlessly have come across as some kind of clueless foreigner, rendered insensible to the values of truth, justice and the American Way by too much food with garlic, powerful tobacco and reflexive Marxism. But he couldn't be a convincing U.S. honky trying to sidestep White guilt. Also, he looked far more conventionally masculine than Charles. Acted that way, too. I remember him at parties, absolutely relentless in the pursuit of women, which Charles never was, despite his once quoting me the saw about "once you go Black, you never come back." In Meyer's and Leroi Jones' imaginations, this would have been wrong; the Black guy should be the studly one, not the – to use Meyer's word – "emasculated" White liberal.

So, okay, we couldn't do typecasting. Worse yet, we couldn't do music, and that was on me. For our play, the choice of cue music for some reason was mine. Now you'd think that I'd have been sophisticated enough to realize that in a play about two blues-oriented American jazzmen, one of whom is Black and plays the sax – the White guy tickles the ivories – we would lead in and out with small-group jazz that might remind one a little bit of saxophonists like Coltrane or Parker or Rollins or pianists like Bill Evans. But the sad truth was that I knew nothing about those guys in 1968. Rock was shouting pretty loudly in my ear right then. My knowledge of jazz was spotty.

I ended up picking out from my meager selection of jazz albums *Open*, by the Brian Auger Trinity, a bunch of Brits who had obviously heard rock once or twice. The rock intonations were probably what I liked about it – well, that and the cover photo of spacey but sexy Julie Driscoll, who, however, only sang on one side of the record, which had its own subtitle, *Jools*. The cue-in music from the album was a number called *In and Out*. So, yes, technically I got the small group aspect right: as the name implies, the Trinity were Brian Auger and two other musicians, a bassist and drummer. But the keyboard Auger was playing on this number was an organ, a Hammond B-3, notwithstanding that neither character played the organ. Trinity's performance could best have been described as a jaunty Hammond tour-de-force. It was swinging more than soulful, funky without the spirituality of the Coltrane types. Kind of a strut with a sporadically walking bass line. Call it Carnaby Street Jazz.

Whatever I was thinking, and I swear I don't know, the result of my little musical contribution to the theatrical end product was to strip out any musical context for a racial argument largely couched in musical terms. It is not one of my proudest memories.

And whatever I was thinking then, whenever I play that number or that album these days I think of my experience helping put on a little play in a strange and somewhat hostile environment – a sort of microcosm of how I felt about freshman year at a strange school in a strange city.

It's not the only song that makes me think of the experience. You also have to take *Gates of Eden* into account. It was, as I have said, a three-play evening. The first play, called *Necropolis*, has vanished from my memory (and the author hasn't answered my e-mails asking to be reminded). But the music that accompanied it is still with me: Bob Dylan's haunting, mystical, not-to-be-understood slice of what? Gnosticism? Apocalyptics? It was at about this point in the second semester of my freshman year that I was came to the realization that an English major would be a far safer course of study for me than a lot of other things. I was starting to think and listen like one. And my ear, increasingly sensitized by what I was getting in my courses, recognized both music and poetry amid the ramblings.

No mistake; the song did ramble. I defy anyone to make cold sense out of lines like:

The lamppost stands with folded arms, its iron claws attached
To curbs 'neath holes where babies wail though it shadows metal badge.

So one mistake would be to take every word as if it were seriously meant to denote or depict something. Another would be to take the whole as if there weren't anything meaningful going on. There are two clear poles of meaning in the song. It starts and ends with wonderment at the elusive meaning of war, and it contrasts the bafflement and confusion the speaker experiences with the certainty of Eden. We know a few things about Eden; among them:

No sound ever comes from the Gates of Eden.

You will not hear a laugh
All except inside the Gates of Eden [which seems to contradict the previous point]

There are no kings inside the Gates of Eden.

And there are no sins inside the Gates of Eden.

... what's real and what is not. It doesn't matter inside the Gates of Eden.

And there are no trials inside the Gates of Eden.

And there are no truths outside the Gates of Eden.

Is the land beyond the Gates of Eden real in the universe of the song? Unclear. And is the peacefulness of Eden anything more than that of the grave? Ditto. There is something uncompromising and bleak about this music, though, which made Eden seem forbidding, even with all these basically positive attributes Dylan posited. Easy enough to sense. But I craved that bleakness for some reason.

Of course, like everyone in my generation, I'd been somewhat familiar with Dylan for at least three years. But I'd known him as a protest singer *(Blowin' in the Wind)*, who also wrote grouchy love songs *(Don't Think Twice, It's All Right)*, and grouchy songs in general *(Like a Rolling Stone)*. The phase he was entering now, half Lewis Carroll nonsense versifier, half mad prophet, appealed to me much more. It was around this time, as I recall, I spent a good part of a skiing trip at my dad's Catskills cottage, with the two of us playing Dylan's double-album *Blonde On Blonde* speechless with laughter. How can you not laugh at lyrics like:

The fiddler, he now steps to the road.
He writes "Everything's been returned that was owed"
On the back of the fish truck that loads
While my conscience explodes.

This is so preposterous, so inconsequential, so syntactically wrong, the mind just goes into overload. And Dylan was churning this stuff out by the bushel at this phase. But amidst the cheerful syntactical chaos, you could sense someone whose least utterance was powerful, whether for laughter, bleakness, or anger. Dylan was important.

So *Necropolis* was, in the final analysis, my real introduction to one of the great artists.

I'll discuss the third play and the ending of my Penn Players involvement in a later chapter.

28

SHARING

COMIN' HOME BABY, BY BEN TUCKER, PERFORMED
BY HERBIE MANN (1966), ENCOUNTERED 1967

THE HILL (O MORRO), BY ANTONIO CARLOS JOBIM
AND VINICIUS DE MORAES, PERFORMED BY
TAMBA 4 (1968), ENCOUNTERED 1968

PLAYLIST TRACKS NOS. 40, 41

ONE OF THE great things about the coming-together of college classes is simply
this: The records get shared. I know I'm dating myself by saying it that way.
A contemporary collegian would perhaps say that the streaming gets shared.
Tomorrow another phrasing will probably be necessary. Choose your own words
for it, then, but my point has probably been valid, *mutatis mutandis*, since colle-
gians first started teaching each other ditties on the lute and the recorder.

No undergrads, particularly in the mere 18 years they have to ready themselves for college, get to experience or learn to treasure all that the vast trove
of music has to offer. As the ancients put it, *Ars longa, vita brevis*. But pool
a bunch of brief 18-year stretches of musical experience and you've got something collectively much older, and definitely ready to pool. Put the collective in
one space and the pooling begins.

All over my dorm I was hearing new things, or hearing old things in a new
way. Take my roommate Billy. He was the one who first made me aware of

Burt Bacharach as an auteur and performer in his own right. I first heard the enchanting waltz melody of *Wives and Lovers* on Billy's copy of Bacharach's *Hit Maker* LP (1965). (Since it was a purely instrumental rendition, I'm not sure when I became aware of the alarmingly sexist lyrics – but I think it was later.) Billy also focused me on the Mamas and the Papas, who had simply been part of the Top 40 wallpaper to me before that. A bright and earnest young man from down the hall made me listen to the Byrds beyond their big hits. And I would hang in the record stores, especially a place called Jerry's, on Walnut Street, and just note what the sophisticated kids were buying: Jimi Hendrix, Jethro Tull, Cream, Dylan, Big Brother, the *A Man and a Woman* soundtrack.

One of the most dramatic discoveries for me was courtesy of a guy named Steve a dorm block or two over. Steve played the flute really, really well. I heard the sound of his instrument coming from his window, then traced it to the dorm room it came from, and, if memory serves, invited myself in. I not only heard him play, but listened while he put on one of his records, Herbie Mann's incendiary performance of *Comin' Home, Baby* at the 1965 Newport Jazz Festival. This would have been close to my introduction to jazz flute. And here, with Herbie Mann's record, I was suddenly happening upon the Mother Lode.

Though Steve was not destined to be a great friend, he was palpably marked to be a musician of some consequence, and if he was excited about *Comin' Home, Baby*, it was an endorsement of my own instant rapture. This was the nearly 11-minute capstone of Mann's July 3, 1965 set at the Newport Jazz Festival, with the composer, Ben Tucker, on bass. First Mann solos, zooming around like a mosquito, making this simple blues pattern sparkle with all kinds of colors, with just Tucker giving rhythm and the hint of a chord pattern for about three minutes, followed by a couple of minutes of solos from the sidemen, followed by more of Mann. The crowd goes wild, and Mann leaves the stage. Per the George T. Simon liner notes: "Herbie had already left the stage, with no idea of returning, when producer George Wein grabbed him and yelled, 'Get up there again! Hit 'em again!'" I'm not sure that this story isn't a bit of hokum (what star leaves the stage after a set that kills without planning to provide an encore?), but it captures the intensity of the moment.

People shared with me, I shared with them. I can remember proselytizing for my own discovery, the Tamba 4, whose album *We and the Sea* was, so far as I can recall, something I just picked up in the campus bookstore. Probably what attracted me was the cover, a gorgeous thing in what I subsequently discovered was the trade dress of the CTI "imprint" within A&M Records: big photos wrapping around from front to back covers, leaving room for only one commensurately-sized photo of the performer(s) on the back. I'm not sure what this particular cover photo, a sailboat captured from above, adrift on a golden sea, had to do with the music, but of course when I got the shrink wrap off and could listen to the record itself, it stood on its own merits.

And merits it had. The big number is Jobim and deMoraes' *The Hill (O Morro)*, in the original Portuguese (I am told) an evocation of Rio's hillside favela slums (though you barely get a hint of that in the standard English translation). I don't think there was any intention on Tamba 4's part to use the jazz setting of this song to convey any particular message. Instead, it is to blend some distinctly highbrow, north-of-the-border piano styling with Jobim's plaintive southern hemisphere melody. The liner notes mention Ravel, Debussy, and Gershwin; I think those are very apt comparisons. Luiz Eça, the keyboard man, builds an astonishing set of classically-inflected variations on Jobim's line. The most astonishing moment of all comes at about 4:45 into this nearly 8-minute song, when Eça, slowly ditching the accompaniment of the other three musicians, sneaks his way up to a pianissimo E three octaves above middle C, and then slides down with a sudden vertiginous drop, as if going down a roller coaster, with a driving beat in the left hand and a silky tour up and down and up and down the treble clef with the right. You think a little bit of Art Tatum, it's so ornate, but as with Tatum at his best, the show-offiness is all in support of real thematic variations.

I had never heard anything like this at all. I knew (though I wouldn't have used this vocabulary for it at the time) that it was at once sophisticated and of the vernacular. And it was a bit of my own unique taste that I brought to the great record sampling. I remember guys standing in the door of my dorm room chatting while I was playing these songs. Sometimes they would pay attention, sometimes not. But my dorm room had a certain flavor, of which this was a part (along with a picture of David Hemmings in Blow-Up and a poster some friend at the Daily Pennsylvanian copied for me in the photo lab: a hippie-ish young man holding a burning piece of paper (evidently meant to be a draft card), with the legend at the bottom: FUCK THE DRAFT). I was adding my little bits to the cultural stew, and taking my little bits out.

An exciting time.

29

SCHOOL'S OUT

NIGHT IN THE CITY, WRITTEN AND PERFORMED BY
JONI MITCHELL (1968), ENCOUNTERED 1968

PLAYLIST TRACK NO. 42

IT WAS ABOUT halfway through 1968. And just like that, my exciting first year of college was over. True, there's always relief in getting to the end of a semester. But I wasn't eager for it to end.

I wish I could write more fully about my classes, the one topic from that year I haven't touched on in these pages. But my memory is selective, and my studies have largely been selected out. And in any case, there's no music that specifically triggers memories of my studies, not that year. I think it's safe to say, though, that I knew, coming out of that year, that I was going to be an English major. And there was no doubt that, in my mind at least, I'd worked as hard as I'd played. This equivalence would not have satisfied my demanding mom, but it suited me.

I believe I finished up about Friday, May 10. My parents couldn't come and pick me up until the following Friday. They had their own classes to teach during the intervening week (and indeed for a week or two thereafter), and they wanted to be in Baltimore that following Friday for the 25th reunion of the Johns Hopkins University Class of 1943, of which my stepdad was a member. So obviously I had to stay East somehow for a week. I had one additional reason of my own, a philosophy paper I still needed to finish, which, thankfully, my professor had let me hand in late.

The Penn dorms had closed, however. That meant I had to find someone to put me up, or perhaps, better said, to put up with me. I have no recollection of asking or being invited, but somehow I ended up staying with the family of Steve, a classmate who lived in Northeast Philadelphia, son of a dentist. At that time it was a love of poetry that drew us together. We had talked about rooming together sophomore year, but for whatever reason, that didn't happen.

I wrote a friend about that week at Steve's house: "Their place and food are lovely, not to mention [the family] ... His mother urges food on me – 'Force yourself!' she says. My beard put her off at first, but she's figured out I don't mean anything by it." (This in an era when beards signaled political dissent, and the dentist dad was of the generation forged in the patriotism of World War II – as a soldier he had been part of the liberation of the first concentration camp discovered. I actually got rid of the beard while staying at their home.)

Most of my stuff was packed away in the trunk for Railway Express, but I know there was one album that wasn't: Joni Mitchell's *Song to a Seagull*. Well, at least that was the name at one time; sometimes it just gets called *Joni Mitchell*. Whatever it was called, it was stunning. Of course there's nothing original to be said about Joni Mitchell these days, but her ethereal voice, unique chords, and confessional lyrics were like nothing most of us had heard then. I can picture sitting in Steve's parents' front room and playing it when I probably should have been finishing that Philosophy paper. I must have played it enough so that two weeks later, writing Steve, the first thing I did was mention the album in a way I would only have done if I had known him to be as familiar with the order of the tracks as I was.

My guess is that sensitive young women of that era responded more to the songs on the album about how tough it was to be female and sensitive in New York or about the liberating influence of the seaside. My favorite, though, was the most masculine song on the record, *Night in the City*. In the comments with which Joni had prefaced her performance of the song the previous year (captured on a YouTube video), she intimated that it was inspired by impatience with a roommate who was taking too long to get ready for a night on the town. But the real subject of the song is simply how exciting the big city is at night.

Night in the city looks pretty to me
Night in the city looks fine

Music comes spilling out into the street
Colors go flashing in time

And what really made the song for me was Steve Stills's slightly funky bass, which made that one song sound much more like rock and less like folk than anything else on the album. Cities rocked, and the bass line confirmed it.

Well, my whole freshman year had confirmed it too. I might have been a bit homesick for Ann Arbor, but downtown Philly, on one's own, was an intoxicating place to me. And now I was leaving it for awhile.

Come that Friday, I trained down to Baltimore, my first real visit to the town where, though I didn't know it then, I'd end up spending the biggest portion of my life. My parents had flown into Philadelphia and were supposed to have caught a shuttle flight to Baltimore, but their flight was canceled, and they too had to take the train down, a later one. In consequence of this delay, I checked into their Baltimore hotel room some hours before they did. Talk about none of us knowing what we were getting into …

The Baltimore my parents thought they were visiting had just been given the *coup de grace*, though the dying would take years. After the Martin Luther King assassination on April 4, the town had been plunged into eight days of riots, which any Baltimorean can tell you changed everything. The town was in for years of sliding downwards, losing corporate headquarters offices, heavy industry, White citizens, pro sports teams, and civic pride. When my folks had been there in the 1940s, it had been a genteel, economically powerful Southern town (which was great if you happened to be White and genteel like them). It was never going to be like that again.

By the time I turned up on the town's doorstep on May 17, law and racial order had been restored, and I don't think I saw any of the destroyed neighborhoods – though I later discovered there were plenty of those. But another source of civic chaos had just erupted which would stand in for it. This was Preakness weekend. And we were staying at what was then called the Sheraton Belvedere, a faded dowager of a Beaux Arts hotel that was being respected by the party-hearty race-goers in about the same way that the virtue of Blanche Dubois was respected by Stanley Kowalski. There was constant yelling and running in the halls, raucous laughter everywhere – and a couple I'll call Drew and Lacy.

I think Drew was a college pal of my stepdad's. In my recollection he was a southern-fried lout, and his wife made some nasty insinuating remarks about my status as stepson, not son – and insinuated accurately, but as if this did me some discredit, that I was partly of Jewish heritage. I think there were also some arch comments about Mother being somewhat older than my stepdad. I don't know what my stepdad was doing being friends with such lowlifes. But they seemed to fit right in with the overall picture at the hotel that weekend.

I saw some of Hopkins too, but I really don't remember it. What really sticks in the mind was getting off the bus on North Charles Street at Hopkins, just outside the campus. It was hot and dusty, and the street seemed too wide (I hadn't yet learned to allow for the subtraction of the trolleys which had imposed breadth upon so many urban thoroughfares and then disappeared from the scene.) I remember thinking that this was a much less entertaining place than the stretch of Spruce Street running by my dorm at Penn. As dull as this bit of Baltimore was, life got even duller on the streets of Ann Arbor, to which I soon returned.

There was no doubt that I wanted to be back in that exciting city night that Joni had sung about:

> Moon's up, night's up.
> Taking the town by surprise.
> Stairway, stairway,
> Down to the crowds in the street.
> They go their way
> Looking for faces to greet ...

Well, I'd be getting back soon.

30

SLOW-DANCING ON THE SAND

THIS GUY'S IN LOVE WITH YOU, BY HAL DAVID AND
BURT BACHARACH, PERFORMED BY HERB ALPERT
AND THE TIJUANA BRASS (1968), ENCOUNTERED 1968

PLAYLIST TRACK No. 43

I HAD STARTED this chapter intending to call it "A Perfect Day." But then I went back and looked at the evidence of my journals. I realized that, glorious as the day was, perfect was not the word for it.

Call her Carolyn. I have her photo: shoulder-length brownish-blonde hair, freckles, proper long-sleeved blouse buttoned up to the neck, short skirt, seated and facing the camera with a slightly challenging grin.

Friday, April 26, 1968, at the outset of Penn's version of the college spring festival, in those days, known as Skimmer. In the idealized version of this idyll, we'd wear skimmer hats and sit with our dates watching rowing

119

races on the Schuylkill. I did not have a date, however. Fortunately the institution next door, Drexel Institute of Technology, had a mixer. And that was where I met Carolyn, good-looking, friendly, smart, a coed at Chestnut Hill College, a Catholic women's school. I invited her to do the riverbank thing with me the next day, followed by other Skimmer excitements.

She agreed to come in for the evening, which I'd planned to spend at my roommate's new fraternity. Come the evening, she turned up, we rode some carnival rides on the field outside the women's dorm, and then we went back to my dorm room to wait until it was time for the frat party.

So we started kissing, but it didn't go on long. The next thing I knew we were arguing about kissing. We were arguing about roaming hands. But the argument was being waged while we were lying side-by-side on the narrow single lower bunk of a bunk bed, from which neither of us was actually getting up. I was very politely calling her narrow-minded and she was very politely getting indignant, and then we were kissing some more, and then we were arguing some more. Oddly, this combination was raising both the lust level and the respect level.

We didn't bother with the frat party. It was somehow incredibly romantic, just lying there arguing about what I wanted to do and she didn't. The photo came during a break in the grappling.

Finally, we had to end the evening with a mad rush to catch the 11:30 Suburban to Chestnut Hill at the 30th Street Station. She fell down once in our haste, and even that was romantic.

We couldn't get together again until Saturday, May 11, my last night in the dorms before my freshman year tenancy expired. I must have done most of my packing already, because I had time to take her to a matinee of *Gone With the Wind*, in revival in one of the big old movie houses downtown. I hated the movie, but loved the rest of the evening: dinner at a favorite pizza joint, then watching as she finished packing my trunk, at which she was surprisingly efficient. We also carried my boxed-up speakers over to Railway Express in the rain. My description of the evening to my now-former roommate ended this way: "After we got back, she showed me some judo, and then some more necking and back to her sister's dorm."

You would not have expected that all this non-sex and judo and packing would have made us boyfriend and girlfriend, and it didn't, but it left us intrigued with each other. We wrote back and forth for the next few weeks, including a bit of jointly working through the Robert Kennedy assassination, which befell that June. And she invited me to visit her in her home town of Avon, New Jersey. I made a stab at taking her up on her visit offer – with the notion that I might drop by during a then-scheduled stay with my father in New York. Between our schedules, there turned out to be a one-day mutual window of opportunity: Monday, July 22.

And that was the perfect-ish day.

On this stay with my dad, I was fortunate to have my old grade-school friend Walter with me. Carolyn had secured a date for him too. So at around 11 we boarded a bus at the Port Authority Terminal, bound for Asbury Park, a few blocks from her town.

I was supposed to phone ahead before we left, but the line was busy when I tried to place a call from the Terminal, so we were fretting all the way down that Carolyn might have thought we'd stood her up. Worse still, the bus was over an hour late, as we seemed to be going round Robin Hood's Barn making additional stops that didn't appear on our schedule. But when at last we alit in Asbury Park, I found a phone, called Carolyn, and she said she'd be there in a few minutes. I walked back to Walter, shared the good news, and we both sort of collapsed. There was hardly a cloud in the sky.

Then we heard a honk, and there was Carolyn's freckled face beaming at us from behind steel-rimmed sunglasses out a car window. She whisked us out of the touristy downtown and took us somewhere residential, where Walter's date lived. And at the front door was Jan, a girl-next-door with something mischievous in her eye. Jan went to yet another Catholic women's college somewhere in New York, which she described as a place where they didn't do anything but drink legal beer and make out. That sounded good.

Better news yet: the girls had planned for us to spend most of the day at the beach, which meant, in the first place, that we got to spend most of the day at the beach, and secondly that we guys weren't going to have to spend much money, a not inconsiderable thing. Jan gave us one for the road (though I abstained). We sat around chatting about the movie of *Rosemary's Baby*, just out, which only Walter had seen, but everyone wanted to.

Then we all piled back in the car and drove to Avon (pronounced Ah-von). Carolyn lived with her mom in a bungalow with a sort of stolid Irish interior: big solid chairs, family photos, a Blessed Virgin statuette. We put something on the record player (*Days of Future Passed*, I think it was), and I helped Carolyn get lunch together. Alone together in the kitchen, Carolyn embraced me suddenly and told me she was glad I'd come. We took lunch out to the awning-covered front porch and sat and ate in the breeze. I don't remember what we ate, but shortly afterwards we all went upstairs and changed into beach stuff. When the girls emerged from their room, Jan was wearing something in two pieces, yellow and sexy, and Carolyn was in something brown and demure.

"So," as I wrote, "off to the beautiful beach." Walter and I then made our only cash outlay for the entire day, bar our bus fares: $1.75 each for badges that entitled us to use the beach that day. Then we were actually on the sand. I took off my shoes and buried my toes. It felt great. Walter and Jan ran on ahead, threw down their stuff and dashed into the water. They were as good-looking as models in a suntan lotion commercial. Carolyn and I couldn't compete on that kind of looks, but I felt no envy.

Shortly, the two of us joined Walter and Jan in the water. We dove in the waves, and did water fights with the girls mounted on the boys' shoulders. Then we lolled in the sand, letting the sun and the wind dry us. That may all seem quite standard-issue to some, but not to me. I had never before played in the surf with a date.

Eventually Carolyn and I went off on our own, down as far as the beach went, and wandered out onto a fishing jetty protecting the outlet of the Shark River that flowed under a drawbridge just behind us. We talked seriously.

In her letters to me she'd mentioned having awakened recently to certain what she called permanent aspects of her character. I wanted to know what she meant. Not surprisingly, it had to do with another guy she was seeing (this one from West Point) who had taken her out on this same jetty in the moonlight, and I guess had beguiled her with notions of sharing an urbane life; she said she had realized then that she was at heart a country girl. I'm sure it will not surprise you to learn I couldn't focus very well on the country girl aspect of the discussion; I was stuck being envious of Mr. West Point, whoever he was.

It grew to be time for a break. Carolyn, who'd commandeered the family car for our excursion, had to take her mom home from work and then, shortly thereafter, pick the rest of us up and bring us back to her house. Back there, we met her mom, a dentist's receptionist. She had a polite but disapproving look. I sensed I was being sized up; well, I could size up back. To my instincts I was looking at the source and pattern of the boundaries of what Carolyn would allow in our embraces. As a parent nowadays, of course, I have more sympathy. But I wasn't thrilled right then.

It was time for boys to be boys and girls to be girls. We boys showered in an enclosure in the back yard; Carolyn had a laugh by popping open a window directly above and proffering Walter a towel when he was in the nude, which annoyed him. I don't think she actually glanced at him, but the joke was had. Walter, as it happened, had just been musing about Jan's swimsuit: "I could see her nipples and everything." So arguably Carolyn's joke was a case of turnabout being fair play.

The girls came down and packed dinner, and Walter and I carried it out to the car. Carolyn tried to sneak some beer into the cooler past her mom, but failed.

We drove back to the beach again, setting up camp near the base of the jetty. A little later, I had some words with Carolyn about her mom. I criticized what my journal dubbed "the parochialism of her mind." I cringe when I read these words; I was a teenager who had never earned a penny looking down my nose at a woman putting two daughters through college without a dad. I feel a little better when I read the next thing I wrote: "Carolyn was quite right being upset with me. I was just shooting off my mouth."

In retrospect, there was more to it than that. I think my unspoken class prejudices which had surfaced with Cindy a few months before (Chapter 26) were surfacing again.

We had a repast of chicken washed down with soda, since Carolyn's mom had interdicted the beer. We turned on Jan's transistor radio and listened to WABC out of New York, then a big Top 40 station, and danced in the sand. I remember the feeling of utter peacefulness holding Carolyn in my arms, as we moved to the sound of Herb Alpert singing *This Guy's In Love With You*. We played leapfrog. And then we sat down and entwined toes in the sand. When the game stopped, Carolyn's toes and mine remained entwined, and then we held hands. For a while the only sound was the radio. We heard Alpert's song again. (Radio station playlists were short in those days.)

And then the sun sank behind us. The holding hands turned to kissing, and the blood was pounding in my temples. Walter and Jan realized it was a cue to absent themselves. When they were gone, I asked if we should go steady. I wasn't exactly requesting it; I was trying to make sense of where we were. Indeed, the next thing I said was that I didn't think we should. I thought we were too different. In my blundering, vainglorious way, I said something about me being an intellectual – with the other end of the comparison implied. I wasn't trying to be offensive. And this time I didn't offend. Her eyebrows had shot up when I said what I said, but her response was that she was surprised that I felt that way, and that she had come here to tell me the same thing.

Then I surprised her again, as I said that I'd known that that would be her attitude. And I guess if I hadn't known it in advance, I would not have spoken out, so I think I was telling the truth.

The two of us sort of danced around the reasons why we didn't want to go steady. Eventually, I more or less summed it up: "I could never see being married to you." She agreed, saying she'd thought about it, and all she could see was such a marriage falling apart.

Of course that mutual revelation begged a question we naturally both turned to: what were we doing buzzing each other with all the kissing and the slow dancing? She said that it might just be sex. I said, thinking back to my recent experience with Cindy, that if I just wanted sex, I could have had that. This pleased her, and led to some more kissing.

But we were still looking at the question of where we went from there. And it soon became clear that though neither of us had moved on the not going steady understanding, we wanted to keep up a special connection at the same time.

While we'd been wrangling, the lights had come on along the boardwalk, and clouds had rolled over the stars, and we were in the dark. Through my sweaty glasses, everything was suffused with a soft glow, making everything appear lit like a love scene in a sophisticated movie. Somehow the visual cues also made me happy, as if I were in a love scene, instead of – whatever I was in.

Walter and Jan rejoined us at this point, walking along the boardwalk, hand-in-hand. One of them sang out "Where have you two been?"

"We ain't gone nowheres!" I replied cheerfully. So we started picking up and carrying things back to the car. Carolyn and I went ahead, and as we neared the boardwalk, she reproved me: "You said we hadn't gone anywhere; I think we've come a long way."

Things happened quickly then: back to the house, clean up, pack up, say goodnight to Carolyn's mom, and then Carolyn and Jan took us sightseeing and showed us the bright lights of Asbury Park, what everyone would come to know in a few years as Bruce Springsteen territory. We ended up in a park opposite the bus station; our bus was already there. Carolyn and I crossed a little bridge over a pond , and we looked out at Asbury Park's twinkling lights. We allowed that we were anxious for college to begin again.

"It's going to be good, having something real to go back to this fall," she said dreamily.

"And what we have, if nothing else, is real," I said.

And then it was time to board the bus. I'd given Carolyn some money to hold for me, and she brought it out, saying in a loud voice so the other passengers could hear: "Here you are, Mr. Gohn, here's your change, and if you're ever in the area again, give us a call!" The girls broke into hysterics. Then, after a few moments they were gone.

Well, almost. We parked ourselves on the street side of the bus, and it was very quiet. Suddenly they drove past us, shouting out the window again: "If you ever come this way, give us a call!" I smiled and waved goodbye.

Then sleep. A little waking. Lights. Faces. More sleep. And then the Port Authority Terminal, and the walk back to the 7th Avenue IRT. The next morning we were on a homeward-bound plane by 10:30, and by 1:00 we were back in Michigan.

When I remember the day that we slow-danced in the sand, that song I remember that the radio played *This Guy's In Love With You* probably five times in all. True, contrary to the title and the lyrics, neither of us had declared love for the other. Still, against some odds, we found the time to get together, we had the double date, we played in the surf, we had two meals and necking and lots of dancing on the beach.

Close enough for a day.

31

MUSIC IN THE DARK

CAPRICORN: THE UNCAPRICIOUS CLIMBER, BY CYRUS FARYAR AND
PAUL BEAVER, PERFORMED BY THE ZODIAC (1967), ENCOUNTERED 1968

SO MANY STARS, BY ALAN AND MARILYN BERGMAN
AND SERGIO MENDES, PERFORMED BY SERGIO MENDES
AND BRASIL '66, SUNG BY LANI HALL (1968), ENCOUNTERED 1968

PLAYLIST TRACKS NOS. 44, 45

SOMETIMES DARKNESS MAKES music more intense, especially music about things you can only see in the dark. This one is about that experience.

It is at this point in my story I met the woman I would marry – and later divorce. This book is not her story, and I do not intend to invade her privacy to tell my own tale. I cannot give her a pseudonym as I have done with some of the other people I've been talking about in these pages; the world knows of our connection, and we have children and grandchildren in common. Hence I shall call her only S., and tell those parts of my story that involve her in such a way as to leave most aspects of her history and personality respectfully to one side. All you need to know to start with is that we met as fellow-students at the University of Pennsylvania.

I'll skip, then, all the preliminaries of our relationship, and deposit you along with us on the not terribly clean rug in the front room of an apartment on Walnut Street, in a building that no longer exists. There are four of us either lying on the rug or sitting on the grungy couches: me, S., and my roommates Jim and Elliot. It is my sophomore year. We call the apartment house Graudensville in honor of our heavily-accented landlord, Mr. Graudens. Let me say this gently; Mr. Graudens does not run a first-class establishment; this is a student tenement. The furniture and the rugs come with the apartment, and they look as if they have come with the apartment for a good long time. There are three guys living here in an apartment designed for two.

In my memory, it is daytime but the curtains are drawn (nothing to look at but a space between rowhouses anyhow). The lights are low or out. Music is playing.

In years to come I shall look up my roomies' whereabouts on the Web, and find that Jim has become a lawyer in Youngstown, and Elliot a musician and political activist in suburban Philadelphia. You might think that as a future lawyer with a giant music obsession, I'd really hit it off with each of these guys. But not so. We haven't bunked down together out of any great interest in each other; we've simply been cast out of the men's dorms by the University's lottery, and hence found ourselves required to find flatmates quickly. But being stuck together means it is to our mutual advantage to try to find things to do and enjoy together. Clearly music is our best bet.

Elliot, the future musician, has the best equipment, as one might expect. I myself am the proud owner of an Ampex reel-to-reel tape deck (I think another present from my father, who, as recorded in an earlier chapter, had given me my core hi-fi components a few years before). Elliot has either a better Ampex or a TEAC, which is coming to be known as the gold standard of reel-to-reel decks at this point. We hook the two up in series and feel like the kings of audio, swapping content with cheerful abandon.

Someday, the significance of two tape decks will not be so obvious. But today, in 1968, everyone knows that it is the only way to get taped music for free without actually shoplifting. Elliot has a lot of cool stuff on tape, some of which naturally ends up dubbed onto mine. Elliot also has some pretty cool records.

We're listening to someone else's record at this moment: *Cosmic Sounds*, by The Zodiac. It is a reflection of this cultural moment that the cover sleeve could also be read to enclose an album called *The Zodiac* by Cosmic Sounds. And there's no reality-based context to settle the matter. This is an album all about the Zodiac, and there is no real-life group or act called Cosmic Sounds. So it's just as plausible either way.

On the front of the cover is a trippy distorted zodiac, so we know this is true psychedelia. On the back is written in hot pink "Must be played in the dark." Perhaps there will be revelations in the dark that light would interfere with? In any case, following the instructions and the ethos of the era, we close the curtains and douse the lights.

"Psychedelic," initially a technical term for a class of recreational drugs, has come to mean as many things as "hip-hop" will later do. It is a drug style, but also an art style, a music style, a set of social and political views, and two or three fashions in clothing. It says something about the breadth of the label that of the four of us sprawling attentively in the dark, none of us is on drugs. No, not even pot. Yet this is a psychedelic moment for us anyhow.

The record is unique, and perfect of its sort. I quote the Richie Unterberger reissue liner notes, reproduced in the informative Wikipedia article on the album:

> Divided into 12 separate tracks, one for each astrological sign, it appeared just as both psychedelic rock and astrology itself were coming into vogue in the youthful counterculture. In some respects it was similar to other instrumental psychsploitation albums of the time, with a spacey yet tight groove that could have fit into the soundtrack of 1966 Sunset Strip documentaries, played in large measure by seasoned Los Angeles session musicians. In other respects, it was futuristic, embellished by some of the first Moog synthesizer ever heard on a commercial recording, an assortment of exotic percussive instruments, and sitar. The arrangements were further decorated by haunting harpsichord and organ, along with standard mid-1960s Los Angeles rock guitar licks. For those who took the astrology as seriously as the music, there was the dramatic reading of narrator Cyrus Faryar, musing upon aspects of each astrological sign in a rich, deep voice without a hint of irony.

Here, by way of example, is a part of Faryar's lowdown on Capricorn: *The Uncapricious Climber*:

> Eight notes scale an octave. Master the scale and you master the score. Uncapricious Capricorn captures each note, holding it tight until it surrenders. The mystery of music can meld into black and white, then dissolve into grey. Capricorn, convinced, can make grey glisten like white onyx.

I don't think any of us, in the language of those album cover notes, "[takes] astrology as seriously as the music." But the tour of the varied personalities associated with the astrological signs is entertaining, the music is definitely trippy, and there is something cool about lying around as if we were drugged, even if we aren't.

This is the way that good middle-class kids of that era make their peace with the ethos of free love and drugs fueling what's coming to be called the Counterculture. We're all Ivy Leaguers, for heaven's sake! Three future lawyers and a musician/politician! And yet we're all as sober as judges (give or take a few swigs of Mateus, a questionable Portuguese rosé that everyone is drinking at this point), giving a respectful listen to what was meant to be a drug experience-like trip based on a mythos none of us have the least belief in!

It's the fashion of the times.

How firmly we have one foot planted in the world of Woodstock (set to happen in about ten months) and the other in that of our parents can be gleaned from another star-focused song on a different record we listen to in the dark. This LP is a contribution from me: *Look Around*, by Sergio Mendes and Brasil '66. Despite the candy-colored scheme of the album cover, by the standards of the time, this is square music. (Delightfully so.)

Mendes is unique in the Brazilian Invasion, having immigrated to New York in 1964, and having started a quartet (a quintet on records) called Brasil '65, which was really a jazz outfit with a strong Brazilian accent, then replaced it with a pop sextet he called Brasil '66, in which half the personnel are U.S.-born. By compromising his Brazilian-ness this way, he can never be exactly cool, but he certainly is popular. Partly it's the great A&M Records covers, which look almost good enough to eat, partly it's the equally glossy production inside.

Look Around, his third Brasil '66 album and by far his most pop one to that time, excels in both departments, and goes to Number 5 on the charts. But the songs are the main thing, including the two big hits from the album, the remake of Bacharach and David's *The Look of Love* from the *Casino Royale* sendup movie and the title song, *Look Around*. These are finely-crafted pop-delivery devices, and we all appreciate them.

But the song that gets to me the most is *So Many Stars*, a lovely collaboration of Mendes with lyricists Marilyn and Alan Bergman, who are probably twenty years older than the people who had put together The Zodiac, and first broke big writing for Dean Martin and Frank Sinatra about a decade before.

And however swinging Sinatra will appear later on in posthumous reconsideration, to members of my generation right now he is suspiciously, well, old. So this piece is right on the edge of what we would all be comfortable listening to – together, anyway.

So Many Stars speaks to me, though. Reflect: I have my first real girlfriend, after having dated a lot – admittedly, I've wanted a real girlfriend for the longest time – but I am comfortable dating, while I've had no experience with being anyone's steady. So the effect of lyrics like these (especially as served up on a bed of lush strings orchestrated by Dave Grusin) may be imagined:

> *The dawn is filled with dreams*
> *So many dreams.*
> *Which one is mine?*
> *One must be right for me.*
> *Which dream of all the dreams,*
> *When there's a dream for every star,*
> *And there are oh so many stars,*
> *So many stars?*
> *The wind is filled with songs,*
> *So many songs.*
> *Which one is mine?*
> *One must be right for me.*
> *Which song of all the songs,*
> *When there's a song for every star,*
> *And there are oh so many stars, so many stars?*

I am certainly elated at having found someone as interesting as S., who has done me the great compliment of reacting to me the same way. But at the same time, I'm aware that I'm foreclosing other possibilities in a world full of them. And of course I have the recent history with Carolyn, just to exemplify what I'm surrendering. This song speaks wistfully to those very misgivings.

In later retrospect, where everything is crystal clear, I will say that I should have paid more attention to those misgivings, that a person feeling that way was not ready to settle down, even to the extent that going steady was settling down, especially at such a young age, and even more especially if the person was afflicted with Catholic scruples. But what I am telling myself at that stage is that life was full of tradeoffs, and that I'd be experiencing some kind of emotional confusion no matter what "star" I happened to be choosing. In other words, I'm feeding myself the wrong kind of adult wisdom.

I should be listening closer to the music in the dark.

32

OF LOVE AND CAFFEINE

MAIDEN VOYAGE, BY HERBIE HANCOCK, PERFORMED BY
RAMSEY LEWIS(1968), ENCOUNTERED 1968

PLAYLIST TRACK No. 46

IN LATE SEPTEMBER 1968, I was writing home to my mom and stepdad about the breadth of the things I was studying at the university. In Philosophy, Russell, Ayer, and Wittgenstein. In Psychology, all about ganglia, and stimuli and responses (I wasn't wild about the way this approach made us all resemble machines). In one English course, *Beowulf*, Gawaine and Mallory in translation. In another, Chaucer's *Canterbury Tales* in the original, which I acknowledged to them was "one of the greatest books in the world."

This was the relatively safe discussion to have with my parents. I knew that at least the literary part of my news would please my folks, as English literature was still my stepdad's field, and had once been my mom's.

There were two other discussions I could have had with them that weren't so safe. One I did have, one I didn't, or not then.

The one I had, though with some difficulty, was about my new girlfriend. Naturally, there was some reticence about that, and in any event words were lacking. For all that poets and pornographers and everyone in between have tried their best to describe it, there is something about the sweetness of a first serious love affair that exceeds and eludes description. It was all-absorbing, though; that was concrete enough to state intelligibly. More prosaically, and more to the point here, my girlfriend S. and I were "seeing each other almost just about every day," as I wrote my friend Walter.

Tough as it might have been to put words to it, no doubt my parents were ready for that. I was of the age where that sort of absorbing attachment was to be expected. What I didn't feel I could write about at all was something that should have been and maybe was obvious, which was the way that my budding love live combined with my theater commitment and my studies to overwhelm me. And as September turned into October, the theater part became the most overwhelming part of all.

I have already written in Chapter 27 that I had been given a one-acter to direct. I was learning, as had generations of student thespians before me, that as you get closer to that first performance, the available study time approaches the vanishing point. For the duration, I wasn't studying, I was directing. My little production came off the weekend of October 17. My postmortem to my friend Walter: "The play went over, at least in a small way. It suffers from almost total incomprehensibility, which mars its audience appeal."

But then I added these grim and true words: "[T]he play ... took all my time, and I'm now two weeks behind in everything, with bleak prospects for the grades if I don't shape up fast." I was clearly in overload. I had so much to process (throw in the disastrous Nixon election along with everything else) that by the end I had failed to communicate with my mom and stepdad for about three weeks, which provoked the predictable unhappiness.

So where do you go to catch up and sort out, if it's the fall of 1968, and you're a student at Penn, and you live in an overcrowded apartment with inadequate study space and your girlfriend is living in a dorm from which men are rigorously excluded overnight? But of course: the underground study hall in the Men's Dorms!

Talk about your basic study hall! This was a glorified corridor walled with cinder block and illuminated day and night with fluorescent bulbs. In my memory, carrels were lined up three or four abreast down the length of the room, like airline seating for the intellectually dogged. There was a more sociable study hall at the library, known informally as the Rosengarten Mixer, and not without cause. But that was for study as a social event, and in any case it kept library hours and was useless for that serious late-night cramming. There was also a far more plushly-furnished study hall in one of the picturesque dorm turrets nearby, but that, as I promptly discovered the wrong way, was for stretching out on something soft and falling asleep when by rights you should be staying up and cramming some more.

Because, yes, endurance was the name of the game. And this anonymous study area, basic though it was, had one amenity critical to endurance: a coffee vending machine from the Macke Vending Company parked near the entrance. Incredibly basic: Coffee black or with heavy or light cream, with or without sugar, plus hot chocolate. No cappuccino. (If you'd mentioned cappuccino to me in 1968, I'd have stared blankly.) An incredibly basic machine with the Macke Vending label. Yet it was the *fons et origo* of great things. How to sing its praises?

I'd been around coffee all my life, but for whatever reason I'd never had much interest in it before. I'm not one much for drugs. Lifetime tobacco score: one cigarette, one cigar. Moderate drinker. Marijuana experimentation only a few times and long, long ago. But coffee was my addiction waiting to happen, and here's where it did.

In a sense, it parallels the love affair with drugs every other addict describes. Ecstasy those first few times, diminishing returns of bliss thereafter, lifelong servitude nevertheless.

But this was my first, mad moment of infatuation. I'd wander down to that stark subterranean corridor, park my books on a carrel, and stride back the way I came in lordly fashion, back to the Macke machine. I'd put in a quarter (I think that was the going rate), and out would come – well, I have a feeling that today I'd find it bland and unsatisfying at best, undrinkable at worst. But to me then, it was a bolt of lightning that would infuse me with a raised pulse, a sense of ecstasy, and the certain knowledge that I would be equal to the rigors of the night ahead. (All right, to be fair, sometimes I had a chaser of No-Doz.)

And this, I think, is the point to explain my choice of Ramsey Lewis' version of *Maiden Voyage* as the Theme Song for this memory. I heard it courtesy of my girlfriend. My earlier observation in Chapter 28 that in college records get shared, of course applied, nay, applied to the nth degree, with boyfriends and girlfriends. In the course of getting to know everything about each other, my new love and I ransacked each other's LPs. And a gem of hers I found at around this stage was her copy of Ramsey Lewis's album *Maiden Voyage*. The title song, a gentle reworking of Herbie Hancock's 1965 masterpiece, was my ear's full opening to the evocativeness of modal jazz.

Lewis has taken his basic trio, and embedded it in heavy string and chorus arrangements, with Minnie Riperton (uncredited) keening in the background. This combination gives the feeling of new, unexplored horizons, a feeling that the song itself was cunningly written to evoke. Why cunningly? Well, when you listen to it, you're apt to wonder how Hancock/Lewis can wander through so many keys. Every key change sounds as if it's taking you somewhere new. Actually, though the composition is modal and so not wedded to any key, it sticks to only four chords. It spins you around and lands you right back in the key you started with, while making you feel you've gone somewhere else. But you, the listener, are not going to know that, unless you have keener ears than mine, or are blessed with perfect pitch, or have cheated by looking at the sheet music. The secret, I think, is in the complexity of the chords; you can go anywhere with them and it still feels like hazarding unknown seas rather than plying a trade route.

Well, seriously, can you think of better music for studying while high on caffeine? You want to feel that you have transcended time and space, and that your reading and your writing is taking you somewhere new and exciting. I can assure you that Ramsey Lewis' expansive sound was very much in my head on those long, long nights, and helped me get through them, as did thoughts of my new lover, the bringer of good things who had blessed me with this celestial melody. And, of course, I was also helped by desperation about my grades.

So the marathons began. On 16 November I reported to my friend Walter that "I pulled four all-nighters in the last two weeks … I'm pulling a D in French at the moment. The amount of reading I have to digest is enormous… I just wish I had thirty-six hours a day." On 5 December I wrote Walter: "The play did such damage to my studies that it has literally taken until the very end of classes to catch up." On 20 December, I reported to my father: "I am now in the last and longest (36 hours) of my enforced waking periods of the semester… [I] studied nine and a half hours straight [today]." That's an awful lot of Macke coffee and Ramsey Lewis. And mind you, I was not trailing clouds of glory through this whole ordeal. To the contrary, I recall nights of sheer physical torment trying to stay awake and mentally absorbent as strange and challenging new information fought to enter my head. Being at my carrel all night also did not mean that I might not pass out with my head in my hands, only to wake between ten minutes and an hour later with pins and needles in my arms, or a crick in my neck, or some other little indignity.

But it worked. I failed nothing, escaped with only one D, and pivoted to a regimen of studies that in time led to a *cum laude* overall plus honors in my major.

There were two other effects, each of which was undoubtedly foundational to my subsequent success with the GPA. One had to do with Penn Players. My break with them was quietly dramatic. On December 9, in the midst of this torrent of studies, I walked into the Penn Players offices, after a class had been canceled and I had a little bit of time on my hands. Someone congratulated me. I asked why, and was told that I had just been admitted to the Club. As I wrote my parents the next day, "I was a little astonished, inasmuch as I was not in the formal heeling program, and had not done the things you have to do to get into the Club, like selling tickets and painting sets... So apparently they've changed the rules – I don't know." Weighing whether to accept, I considered whether I wanted to commit to the stipulated minimum 30 hours a semester, and whether it was worth it just to have a say about those who would have a say in choosing the Artistic Director (the very same professor who was giving me the D, as it happened, an injustice for which I never forgave him till or after the day he died). But I knew ousting him wasn't likely. For that reason, and others, my conclusion, with regard to this unexpected and unsought honor: "I have bigger fish to fry." This was not meant to insult the organization; it was merely an assessment of where my priorities now lay.

The other effect of all this study was profound. Force-feeding does fatten the goose, after all. I was beginning to think of myself as a man who'd read Chaucer and Spenser and Milton and Corneille and Sartre. It was hundreds of pages, to be sure. But, as I wrote my parents (for now I could share the whole situation with them), "Most of the stuff has been of some genuine value. In fact I discovered that, for the first time in my life, I was fighting to cope with a tide of reading that was ... really significant and relevant to me."

The aha! moment came when I was consulting C.S. Lewis' most important critical work, *The Allegory of Love*. In September, that book would have been utterly incomprehensible to me; by December, I had the tools to read and understand it. As I wrote my parents, "For the first time in my life, I've really felt a little learned, as opposed to just well informed." Thanks in good measure to Herbie Hancock and Ramsey Lewis and Minnie Riperton and Macke Vending, the die was cast. I was going to be an intellectual, and not just an aesthete.

33

LOVESICK ON THE SHOP FLOOR

*SWEET CAROLINE, WRITTEN AND PERFORMED BY
NEIL DIAMOND (1969), ENCOUNTERED 1969*

*CRYSTAL BLUE PERSUASION, WRITTEN BY EDDIE GRAY,
TOMMY JAMES, AND MIKE VALE, PERFORMED BY TOMMY JAMES
AND THE SHONDELLS (1969), ENCOUNTERED 1969*

*WHAT DOES IT TAKE (TO WIN YOUR LOVE FOR ME)?, BY JOHNNY BRISTOL,
HARVEY FUQUA AND VERNON BULLOCK, PERFORMED BY
JR. WALKER & THE ALL STARS (1969), ENCOUNTERED 1969*

PLAYLIST TRACKS NOS. 47, 48, 49

THE FIRST CAR may frequently be more important in a young man's life than the first sex. I received my first car sometime in the first two weeks of May 1969. It was a well-used blue Chevrolet Nova, and it ranked up there with sex, no question.

That importance was immediately demonstrated the very day we took delivery, because I got into a fight with my father over it, one of the only two big fights I ever recall with my father. He, I, and my girlfriend had been slated to drive up together that evening to the family cottage in the Catskills, for one farewell weekend before I would take the car on to my summer back in Michigan. And, since I wasn't really familiar from my learner's permit experience with negotiating New York City traffic or the mountains at night, my dad insisted on being the one to drive the car up to the cottage. I was equally insistent that I do the driving. Voices got raised. I stormed out, till my girlfriend (who'd walked out with me) prevailed on me to call him from a phone booth. And of course he talked me back in, and I think we ended up starting for the mountains that night, just as planned, and with him at the wheel. My independence in my car would just have to wait another couple of days.

As I have indicated, my father and I almost never fought. He was the parent I always got along with. The huge blow-ups were for my mom. And this fight too should have been with my mom, as the Nova represented a victory over her protectiveness. She had been so fearful I'd kill myself behind the wheel that she had actively sabotaged my efforts to win a driver's license even after I took driver's ed, and made it so that I did not have a license when I went to college. As I quickly found out, it's damned hard to obtain a license as a nonresident college student in a strange state – and you don't even have a car to practice or take the road test in. Hence, though I cannot call to mind exactly how I finally pulled it off, I remember some of the hard times I went through to land that damn piece of plastic, including flunking the New York driver's test at least once in Albany, which I could only have taken courtesy of the very dad I was having the fight with, the one who had parlayed his New York City residence into a phony claim of New York citizenship for me so that I could be licensed there.

But it wasn't about the slightly deferred independence alone, that fight. It also happened because I was emotionally overwhelmed at that point, not only by the gift of the car, by also by the prospect of leaving my girlfriend behind, and by the thought of spending another summer in Michigan. I loved Michigan, then and always. But going back right then was going to be tough.

For one thing, I'd be interrupting the studies I was starting to love with a new intensity. And I'd have to leave the dyad my girlfriend and I had become, knowing (as we'd agreed) that we were each free to date others, and feeling quite ambivalent about it. And there was going back to living with my parents after the freedom of college. Worse yet, I knew that it was likely going to be a period of great depression for my parents; my mom had lost her college teaching job, and she accurately foresaw that there would never be another job for her again that was as meaningful. She no longer possessed the adaptability of youth, and I was expecting her to obsess over her unrecoverable loss, and that would be no fun to be around.

I was hoping the car could give me some distance from that.

If I couldn't be a college student at study, I reasoned, maybe I could be a college student at play; maybe I could live like the Beach Boys on the album covers, make like the college kids I read about partying on spring break. Cars were good for getting to beaches and parties and places where young people congregated. If I was going on dates with unknown women, a car would be immensely helpful, especially five hundred miles away from the public transportation grid of Philly I had so come to rely on. And if I had to be with my parents, at least I could use the car to get away by going to work, because the car finally necessitated that I get a job, in order to pay for insurance.

Well, that was the theory, anyway. Things turned out a little differently.

When my mom finally contemplated her defeat in the form of the blue Nova sitting in the driveway, her joy at my return took the sting out of it for her. I have a recollection of a frantic hug and her blurting out "You're home, you're home," and being taken aback because I wasn't so glad to be home, or, candidly, to see her, but having no words for what I felt, and knowing I would have had no right to say the words if I'd had them. And all she recorded in her diary was "[Jack] returns – in his car." The dash said it all if you knew her.

That was on a Wednesday. The following Monday I was at the gate of the Grove Street plant of the Ford Motor Company in Ypsilanti, the next town over from Ann Arbor. Ford's need for assembly line workers was immediate. I took a physical in the morning, and received an offer. I went home and wrote the girlfriend:

This is the hang-up: Ford will probably want me to work the second shift, which is 4:30 pm to 12:30 am. But it would phht! my recreational and social plans, let along virtually cut me off from my family. So for once my parents were rational and indicated that the idea didn't send them into paroxysms of joy. Job-hunting isn't as difficult as I feared. For one thing all the auto plants are hiring right now, because people are going off for summer vacation, and the auto makers expect the business to hold up well all summer.

It all sounds so like science fiction now, with manufacturing jobs as scarce as hen's teeth. Yet in those times it was true.

It turned out, though, that Ford decided it wanted me to work a shift that started at 7:00 a.m., not 4:30 p.m. as feared, so I took the job the next day.

That Friday, I wrote S., my girlfriend:

My wild summer plans have come to nought so far: my job eats up all my time. Tomorrow, for example, is a Saturday: Ford Motor Company, however, needs 165,000 shock absorbers pronto, 1/16th of which, approximately, pass through my hands. So tomorrow I work from 5:00 a.m. to 1:30 p.m. Time-and-a-half the whole time, so it comes to forty dollars for one day. Not bad for a day's work. But it's hard,... very hard.

I described having seen a performance of *She Stoops to Conquer* one evening, but feeling out-of-place amongst the cultured audience.

My hands ... are getting covered with dirt that is too deep to get out with mere soap. I am beginning to feel like an hourly laborer... [Last night] I ... found myself telling myself once or twice "You're an auto worker from over at the Ypsi Ford Plant." Not a student... An auto worker at General Parts.

And this, mind you, was after only four days on the job. I described it this way:

[It's] so simple it took me about ten minutes to learn it: Take a washer, slap it down on the block, reach down to the conveyor belt simultaneously and pick up a shock absorber (weighs anywhere from ten to twenty-five lbs.), slap the absorber on the block, pick up mallet and pound the washer onto the shock screw, put the shock back on the belt, facing the other way, and start again. I am one of four people doing this job. I've got to know one of [the others] a little bit. He has been doing this same wretched job for seven years, and he still doesn't have enough seniority to work one of the four hydraulic machines up the line. What kind of a future is that? Yet most of the thousands of automaton-men who work in the same room with me are spending their lives doing something quite similar. And most of them are quite happy to be doing it.

I topped off the letter by describing my night on the town after this day "down the works." I went to a coffee house and saw no less a personage than the legendary Sun Ra, but I wasn't ready for his kind of jazz, which at the time I dismissed as "pure noise." Then I went to another coffee house, where a folkie soloist was playing guitar and singing, and saw a couple of guys from my old high school trying to pick up a pair of lost-looking teeny-boppers and failing. So much for high times!

Then, during my second week, my job got harder.

Today I was elevated to operation of a steam-powered dingus known, I think, as a bushing ram. Never mind the specifics: it is hell on earth. I have to perform an incredible number of operations with sticky and uncooperative equipment at the rate of about five times a minute or more. Furthermore, if I don't complete them, I can screw up ... a quarter of the shock operations in the plant. Three times today I inadvertently shut the whole line down! And it looks as if I'm going to be doing this awful job for ten hours both tomorrow and Thursday!... You should have seen me swearing and cursing, while I was fighting that monster. Nobody seemed to do anything except criticize, except at one point at which I was getting a bit faint ... and this guy I didn't even like much came up and relieved me for a bit.... Whatever else he does, he's my friend now. I always thought it looked pretty vulgar, all those workers chewing gum. I found out why today: your mouth gets incredibly dry.

Clearly, this match of job and employee was doomed. The qualities that made for a successful auto worker had passed me by. Worse, I had yet to acquire basic skills even for holding down a job; my mom came home one day in the third week and found that I had not reported to work as scheduled, nor had I called in sick. The truth was, I was exhausted, and did not know how to deal with it.

I had gone to the shop steward and complained about the overtime, saying I had agreed to work on regular shifts, not the overtime. To my outrage, I had met no sympathy. I asked my Congressman if the employer could force me to work more than 40 hours a week, and was crestfallen when I found out it could. I may have had a fair amount of book-learning by that point, but I didn't understand the basics of assembly-line industrial relations, like the fact that allowing each worker to pick and choose hours would precipitate chaos, and the fact that almost everyone on that line welcomed the extra hours and the extra pay. If I was going to be a revolutionary, I would have to do it without followers. When I realized this, absenteeism and sullen silence had proved my only recourse, and my only response.

I have written elsewhere some disparaging things about Ford and the old Detroit auto industry; I take back nothing, but would be less than honest if I failed to add that I brought plenty of my own failings to that brief relationship. If I had come to that workplace a more mature and less snobbish person, I still don't know if my body or my mind would have stood up to the challenges of the job for much longer than they did, but at least I would have handled myself better.

As it was, my mom and stepdad had an out to offer me, and I took it most gratefully. After years of trying to find a way to move to a better house, they finally closed the deal on a much nicer home in the Burns Park neighborhood of Ann Arbor. This move was obviously going to be a huge project, and they actually did need me to stay home and help them do it. There was no make-work about it. I guess they must have picked up the cost of the car insurance at some point.

I believe I worked another three weeks, and I listened to my parents and did give the proper notice before quitting. I was now freer, if not absolutely free, to try having something like the kind of summer I'd hoped for.

Right out of the gate, I was able to host S., my girlfriend, over the July 4 weekend. I had been conjuring up images of her and feasting on the frequent letters she sent as a way of coping with the rigors of the shop floor. Longing was not as good as having, but it gave me some kind of motivation. The song that had kept going through my head while I thought of her was Neil Diamond's *Sweet Caroline*, which came out toward the end of June. "Sweet Caroline" sort of scanned along with S.'s name (if you tossed in her middle name). It kept me going. When Sweet S. actually came, it was a wonderful visit.

Then too, I was able to be of substantial help to my parents in a grown-up way. I was pretty certain (not to mention determined) that this would be my last summer at home. With a car, and, frankly, more mechanical skills than either of them possessed, I would give them something real to earn their respect and my exit visa. My memory is full of things like hauling boxes of books, digging post holes and pouring concrete for clotheslines, buying a lawnmower and cutting grass, helping assemble and stock bookshelves. My new wheels enabled me to go to the hardware store, and run out for carryout on those nights before the kitchen was assembled. Once there was a kitchen, I did some cooking. In short, I functioned as mostly an adult.

But that was it in terms of accomplishments. I wrote my freshman-year roommate that "I've been making shockingly bad use of my time, getting no writing done and very little reading read." But even that admission was only in terms of my formal business of being a student. In terms of the largely inchoate, unspoken agenda I have hinted at, I truly made little progress.

The only way to describe that agenda is to remember what the world promised young people my age at that moment. There was an exciting, authentic, fulfilled way to live, so the media told us. We could hang out at the beach and party all summer long, as the Beach Boys promised. We could dress up fabulously, so we heard from Carnaby Street. We could bring peace to the world and stop the War. We could have constant sex and touch the infinite: just ask Jim Morrison. I wanted to be part of all of that.

I may have managed a little bit of the beach thing. I got away to nearby Silver Lake with friends for an afternoon or two. I vividly remember *Crystal Blue Persuasion* playing on someone's transistor radio, which to my mind is the absolutely perfect beach song. Yes, when you look at the lyrics and examine the history, you find it's a song about God's beneficence from a Christian viewpoint, but beaches and the relaxation one experiences there are indeed God's gift (at least if you happen to believe in a beneficent God as I did), so there's nothing really inconsistent there. The biblical imagery is quite dispensable. The echo-chambered guitar riff and the throbbing Hammond organ are not.

I missed out on the great Ann Arbor riots, which were sort of about the War and everything else that might have been on students' minds, and which went down less than a mile from my house. I caught a momentary sight of the turmoil down one street I crossed as I was driving home from a hard day at the factory. I did not stop either to participate or to gawk, and in fact was hardly aware of them. Worse yet, I missed out on Woodstock.

And the closest I came to the free love and infinitude part was hanging out with my friend Walter and his roommates in an apartment, watching the Moon Landing, while Walter's randy girlfriend made jokes about transorbital insertions.

Partly my being in the wrong place at the wrong time was just a quick lesson in the reality of what it's like to experience a Zeitgeist: there may not be that much of a there there. (People I've talked to who *were* at Woodstock, for example, report feeling that they were in the wrong place to see or experience things properly.) But part of it was just my karma; I was not destined for that kind of summer cool. 1969 was as close as I would come. The adulthood I was rapidly reaching would have its own thrills. But not that kind.

The song that summarizes the summer for me is *What Does It Take (To Win Your Love For Me)?* as performed by Jr. Walker & the All Stars, which was a great hit during that stretch. It is *echt* southern Michigan, gutbucket soul by a tenor saxophonist from Battle Creek playing on a Detroit label. It is infused with longing, perhaps one of the longingest songs ever recorded. It is harmonious to a fault; if you only know the song from that recording, I challenge you to hum it. You really can't, and not just because of the baroque sax break line, but because of the two human voices you hear singing at places, in thirds, there is no lead. (When co-composer Johnny Bristol performed this in 1990 in Bristol, the harmony from an unbilled accompanist is, if anything, even tighter and more inscrutable. Do not, on any account, miss, however, Walker's 1985 performance of the song on David Letterman (available on YouTube), where he sings without vocal accompaniment; the melody is utterly clear there, for my money much stronger, and the playing is simply out of this world.) That song exactly chimed with my mood through much of that summer. I was lovesick, and bored, and frustrated with my family, and excited about growing up and having a car. And this is the song that evokes it all.

On Sunday, August 24, I got up at 5:00 a.m., got dressed, ate the breakfast my mom made, packed up the car, went with my mom to church (there turned out not to be a Mass at the anticipated hour), drove her home, and, by 6:45 a.m., motored away. Ahead lay a house where S. and I could live together, along with friends, and the college life I had been building for myself.

When I came back next, I would be more a visitor than a returning resident.

34

HOUSE OF SONG AND LAUGHTER

*COME TOGETHER, BY JOHN LENNON & PAUL McCARTNEY,
PERFORMED BY THE BEATLES (1969), ENCOUNTERED 1969*

*BEGINNINGS, BY ROBERT LAMM, PERFORMED BY
CHICAGO TRANSIT AUTHORITY (1969), ENCOUNTERED 1969*

*HOW CAN YOU BE IN TWO PLACES AT ONCE WHEN YOU'RE NOT ANYWHERE
AT ALL, BY THE FIRESIGN THEATRE (1969), ENCOUNTERED 1969*

PLAYLIST TRACKS NOS. 50, 51, 52

2209 RITTENHOUSE SQUARE in Philadelphia, where I lived during my junior and senior years of college, occupied a deceptively grand-sounding address (it isn't actually on Philly's famed Rittenhouse Square), but it certainly proved grand enough for me and my housemates. There were officially three of us – no, wait, there were officially two of us, one of whom wasn't actually one of us at all unofficially – but in reality there were four of us if there weren't five – unofficially. It was that confusing (as college housemate arrangements so often are).

Let me translate. Somehow it had been agreed toward the end of my sophomore year that I and my girlfriend S. and two of her freshman friends from Baltimore, Otts and Chuckie, would all figure out a way to room together. We had all done the campus thing, and were eager for the excitement of downtown. But where? We were wandering around a side street downtown with eyes peeled for "For Rent" signs when a door opened and a hippie-ish art student type came out, and we accosted her, as she looked a likely bet to share both our outlook and our limited finances. She chatted with us for a while, then offered to show us her house, shared with some other art students, as an example of what we might find.

It was perfectly sized: three bedrooms, two with bath, two with studies. And it had atmosphere to burn: erratic but carefully drawn stripes running along floors up walls and on the ceiling, a highly unconventional color scheme, and, in one room, a mural of a large harpy-like monster to which the residents had added a sculpted torso that came out of the wall at you. Naturally, we didn't want to live in a place *like* 2209; we wanted to live *at* 2209. Was there any chance this place would be coming available? we asked. Why, yes, as it turned out, there was. The caravan of artists was about to pull out. We formed an instant determination to succeed them.

We were warned that the rental agent, a man with the unlikely name of George Wallace, was devoted to enforcing the mandate of the landlord, a man with the unlikely name of John L. Sullivan, not to rent to groups of college kids. We needed a married couple as a front. S. was the only young woman in our circle, so she had to be the fiancée – and she was going to be in Philly the summer of '69 to spearhead the negotiations, but all of the guys destined to be the actual rent-payers were going to be out of town for the summer. A Philly-dwelling fiancé had to be located. By dint of extraordinary luck, we prevailed upon an otherwise sensible pre-med colleague of mine named Tom who was willing to complete the charade and put his name on the lease. Of course Tom insisted (as did George Wallace) that a bona fide responsible adult put his name on the lease, and so my poor father Emile stepped up with a guarantee; I think he was supposed to be Tom's step-dad. Could George and John possibly not have seen through this? If they didn't, they were idiots. And if they did, why bother with the charade and not just rent out in the open to the college boys who after all were going to be the rent-paying tenants? Not our problem: Tom (who never set foot in the house, so far as I know) and S., who barely knew Tom, were the happy engaged couple, and my father, who never met Tom, was Tom's father – and the proprieties were preserved.

I'm glad to say that neither my dad nor Tom ever lost a penny by this rickety arrangement. But it was a harbinger of the generally lawless lifestyle we were to pursue at 2209. We started with that ridiculous fraud and went on from there. It wasn't just that we were drinking underage or having sex without benefit of clergy. Kids, don't try this in your home: LSD was literally kept in the fridge for consumption by – one or more of us – but let me hasten to say it wasn't me. I was one year older than pretty much everyone else who passed through our door, and held down the grownup role, and abstemiousness was in keeping with the role. But I had no problems with anyone else's bliss. It was the Sixties still, even if Nixon had won. And I may have been the designated grownup, but I was a Sixties grownup.

The four or five of us grew quite close, even vacationing together. I can remember borrowing my dad's Saab station wagon in New York and taking the whole crew up to the mountains together with someone's girlfriend from Barnard.

We may not have been art students like our predecessors in phony lease-hold, but we did expand on their period style. We found some red carpet and some green carpet, and covered the stairs in alternating colors. S., who was handy with a sewing machine, ran off curtains with fabric of the era, pais-leys and wild hot floral prints and such. They were hung by simple rings from wooden dowels, but they covered the windows and gave us the atmosphere we were looking for. The material came from Otts' dad, who wholesaled paper products, especially psychedelic-style writing pads, many of which were covered with these fabrics. In his line of pads, the fabrics were laminated in plastic squares and held in place with spiral binding. In our windows, the fabrics hung free.

I'm sure we pained the neighbors. Rittenhouse Square, even the street bearing that name three blocks from the actual grand square, was for grownup achievers, not for the likes of us. We knew that full well, and felt looked down on. I recall a moment of pushback, when Chuckie grabbed a ball (I think it was on a sedate Sunday morning) and led us all out onto the street, yelling "Every-body out for volleyball, rich people!" (No one else came out to play.)

To be fair, the neighbors we actually dealt with treated us pretty well. The couple next door, a dentist who sang opera, and his wife, had a cute French au pair we were close to (though the wife told us firmly no one was to seduce the au pair). Behind us across the alley was a gay alcoholic landscape archi-tect or interior decorator (I can't remember which) who spent much of his leisure time, over my nearly two years noticing him through the back window, arranging and rearranging the bricks in his driveway to some fantastic degree of perfection, but he spoiled the effect somewhat by driving home plastered lots of nights in a big station wagon, terror of the narrow alley's garbage cans.

He was truculent when drunk, friendly enough when sober. A New Yorker cartoonist, a reserved family man, had the big house to our east.

We attracted an interesting crew. There was Carol, a sweet young lady so in love with us and the house she moved from bedroom to bedroom as time progressed, playing girlfriend to each of my roommates in turn (including my substitute after I graduated and moved out). There was a guy we knew only as The Freak, a true drug casualty, who had had some kind of connection to the departed art students but never noticed that they were not in residence any more, and so turned up from time to time. He'd come in, harangue whoever was home with tales of how he was playing now in the Rolling Stones (once it was The Doors), serenade us with an air guitar solo while singing tunelessly, and end up pulling various illegal substances out of his bloodstained socks and dosing and/or injecting himself with them. Thus fortified, he'd wander back out on the street. There was our summer substitute roommate, Jodie, who used dill in everything she cooked (I grew to despise dill and her other favored ingredient, internal organs), and who was proud of her enterprising mom who had reentered the workforce as "a professional astrologer."

The Freak wasn't the only music fan in our environment. You could encounter music all over the house, coming out of the stereo in every bedroom, and sometimes the basement. Probably the first specific memory I have of us all together in the house was of the four of us sitting in my and S.'s bedroom listening to *Abbey Road* which I had purchased the day or the day after it came out. Someone, I think it may have been Carol, came in and tried to say something, and Otts shushed her, saying we were having a religious experience. And he was right. (In honor of which I've picked the lead-off number from the album, *Come Together*, as a Theme Song for this chapter.)

I was first and foremost a Beatles man. As readers of these pages know, my loyalties had been cast in the forges of 1964. Otts may have been more open to the very newest stuff, being a year younger and music editor for the then-new arts-and-commentary supplement to our campus newspaper, meaning that he received all the hot new albums as they came out. But even for him this was a religious experience. At that point, though, it would be fair to say, Otts was a Chicago man.

Their awe-inspiring first album, *Chicago Transit Authority*, had just been issued in April: two big LPs of jazz rock. While I and probably most fans were taken with the brass section, what apparently got Otts most was the drumming of Danny Seraphine. And if you listen to just the first number, *Introduction*, and if you know anything about what rock drumming sounded like back then, you can tell that the tempo changes, the polyrhythms, the very un-rock-like tempos, were all remarkable: disciplined, erudite, mostly from a world more sophisticated than rock. Otts hankered to reproduce that feel. So in short order we had Otts' drum set assembled in the basement, and frequently the house, and no doubt the neighborhood, would resound with Otts attempting to make like Danny Seraphine. So there was never a question I would also be enthusiastic about Chicago.

Abbey Road was, though we couldn't know it yet, the end of something, the last artistically successful Beatles album. *Let It Be*, the chronicle of and testament to their breakdown and breakup, would not be released until the end of the academic year. But *Abbey Road* itself, even as one of the Beatles' successes, was rather labored going. *Come Together*, for instance, came together mostly on the basis of John's nonsense poetry, delivered in a distortion of his now heroin-addicted voice. ("Hold you in his armchair, you can feel his disease.") It feels exhausted; a man as great as Lennon should be doing more than second-hand Dylan, however great a man Dylan is, and however apt the homage. Meanwhile, *Chicago Transit Authority* both was and felt like a bolt of new and promising lightning. The Robert Lamm song *Beginnings* makes that quite explicit, repeating the phrase "only the beginning" time and again.

It would be a mistake to make too much of this. Every age, every year, every moment, is a transition between something and something else. There are so many things out there to wax and wane, that you can always pair up a couple of them headed in opposite directions. Still, this exemplified the kind of transition to which the house on Rittenhouse Square bore witness. The early 60s, the high 60s, if you will, led by the Beatles, full of a certain kind of youth and fun, were giving way to something powerful and worthwhile, but without the careless rapture.

There was plenty of fun left, of course. There's always plenty of fun. One of the things that made for fun was the unique comedy of Firesign Theatre, four amazing Angelenos. They were so *sui generis*, I am almost at a loss to describe them. Though they had their roots in radio, their real medium was the LP. They created densely-layered experiences in which, for instance, a character might be listening to the radio and then find himself inside the program he was listening to, and grow old or young during the experiences inside the program. You would quickly lose track of which experience was the frame and which the "real" world. The whole would be accompanied by outrageous wordplay, references to Joyce or Shakespeare or Conan Doyle.

Firesign had just come out with its second album, *How Can You Be In Two Places At Once When You're Not Anywhere At All*. We rapidly committed the entire first two albums to memory, doing the voices, capturing the rhythms. Firesign turned out to be as full of phrases applicable to any occasion as were Shakespeare and the Bible. We competed to see who could find the most applicable Firesign phrase for any given situation, leavening it with the occasional Dylan or Beatles quote. Otts in more recent years, before the Firesign members started dying, reported to me that he had seen Firesign in concert, and for some of their routines there were, in effect, "sing-alongs," where everyone in the audience knew the words, just as we'd known the words.

So this was what life at 2209 sounded like.

It wasn't perfect (too far off campus, for one thing). But it was our first toehold in urban living. Not one of us came from a big downtown. Not one of us had lived away from both home and campus before. Not one of us regretted it. With all its imperfections, it was a house of song and laughter, a great first experiment in the independent lives we were getting ready to lead.

35

THE AGE OF DROSS BEGINS

THE KING MUST DIE!, BY BERNIE TAUPIN AND ELTON JOHN,
PERFORMED BY ELTON JOHN (1970), ENCOUNTERED 1970?

ICARUS, BY RALPH TOWNER, PERFORMED BY
THE PAUL WINTER CONSORT (1970), ENCOUNTERED 1971

PLAYLIST TRACK NO. 53, SUBSTITUTE TRACK NO. 54

THE ALBUMS PILED up in the room of my housemate Otts, who acquired them in his capacity as the music editor of the arts supplement to the campus paper. In fragmentary but decided fashion they told the tale: The three-minute song was growing obsolete. Singer-songwriters were now artistes, prey to all the pretensions that went with such a role. Monaural AM was no longer a reliable place to hear the good new stuff.

The musical Age of Gold in which I had grown up was just about over. Whatever the merits of whatever was coming next, it wouldn't be the gold I still wanted. Wanted so badly, in fact, that I was willing to squint extra hard to see it in all the new vinyl that came sluicing into our house. But of course when you squint, you are apt to see things that aren't strictly speaking there.

One artist who turned up on Otts' floor at this juncture in whom I ended up trying hard to see the gold was Elton John. And he was, to be fair, some kind of gold isotope: he had the voice and the mannerisms to deliver a song, as well as the ear to compose catchy melodies. The trouble was his lyricist,

Bernie Taupin. That is sort of like Beethoven trying to be a great composer while limited to writing for the kazoo.

When John's eponymous album came out, I really tried to look past the lyrics. That opening number, *Your Song*, as a melody, was everything a pop love song could be. But the awful lyrics were right there:

> If I were a sculptor, but then again no,
> Or a man who makes potions in the traveling show

"No," what? Or is the "no" there just to rhyme with "show," which itself caps off a verse referencing a skill (potion-making) completely irrelevant to the singer's aspiration to show the beloved how much he loves her? If not, name the task for which sculpture is inadequate but for which potion-making could be considered an improvement. If Taupin were a lyricist, but then again no ...

I could go on. The thing was, I was still listening to the album a lot because of John's magnetism as a singer. And it still kept not being utterly wonderful.

The song that ended the album was the one I played the most: *The King Must Die!* To a student reading Chaucer and Shakespeare as I was at the moment, the medievalism and renaissancery of the lyrics, not to mention the dramatic central situation suggested by the title, was enough to hook me. Yet I kept not loving it as much as I wanted. Coming back to it 50 years later, it smacks me in the face: Who's talking and who's listening? Stanzas 1-4 seem to be addressing a "king," although there's a strong hint he may simply be an everyman. Stanza 5 sounds more like a response by the king. But there are no clues in the music or the delivery. In any case, the king seems to be in an ominous (in the literal sense of the word) situation. But the omens seem wide of the mark: "Tell the ostler that his name was / The very first they chose." Well, so what? Ostlers aren't kings, and usually aren't even addressed by kings. What's so bad for the king that someone chose the ostler? Chosen for what? And why are mercenaries singing in cloisters? Shouldn't it be monks? And if you must worry about mercenaries, isn't it actually more reassuring to have them singing in cloisters than besieging your towns? In any case, the dramatic gravity of the music, underlined by Paul Buckmaster's masterful arrangements, is utterly unearned.

At this point it would be a reasonable objection that Dylan did lots of the same thing. I admit it, it's true. It's just that Dylan was a genius who could get away with that sort of thing. And for that matter, Chaucerian touches worked well for Procol Harum in *A Whiter Shade of Pale*, even though there, as here, they didn't add up to much. But then that song was deliberately mysterious and impenetrable; that diverting talk about millers and hosts was meant to be disorienting, along with psychedelicisms about the ceiling flying away.

As I say, I listened to the album a lot, but interestingly, when I look back, I see I wrote at the time that "with big new stars, like, say, Elton John, it's impossible to determine, from their albums alone, whether they deserve their status or not, after you take into account the hype and arranging in back of them." So I guess I never quite convinced myself, even though now the source of my discomfort has little to do with the hype.

The comment I just quoted came from a review I wrote (at Otts' suggestion) of the Paul Winter Consort's *Road* album.

Today, Paul Winter and his saxophone and his ensembles, to the extent anyone regards them, are shelved with the New Age musicians. I tried to write about them as if they were to be considered along with rockers, likening the album to *Sgt. Pepper*. My license to draw the comparison was the strong use of classical music elements in both, and the willingness of both albums to draw inspiration from anywhere. But I tried to sell Paul Winter to my audience as if he and his consort were some kind of act to compare with, for instance, other acts mentioned in that issue of the paper: Laura Nyro, Richie Havens, the Youngbloods, Seatrain.

I wasn't smart enough to take in that there were things out there besides classical, jazz, and rock – and that eclecticism didn't necessarily lump an act with rockers. This was my introduction to a new flavor, but my musical taxonomy wasn't up to it.

I wasn't wrong, though, about finding it fascinating, powerful music. My Theme Song from the album – which has become Paul Winter's own theme song, even though it was written by the guitarist in the Consort, Ralph Towner – was *Icarus*. The mythical Icarus, the fabricator of wings, flew too near the sun and paid with his life for his presumption. Towner's Icarus, so far as I can make out from the song, just discovers how intoxicating it is to fly. The music is all about soaring, not the falling. There are wistful minor chords, to be sure, but just to make your breath catch as he upshifts into the major.

It is one of the great melodies, and covered in subsequent years by artists of all stripes. I am particularly fond of a cover by Towner himself with a couple of other guitarists, and a cover by jazz pianist Stef Scaggiari.

A wonderful thing, but not rock gold, because not rock. Maybe the reason, apart from my naivete, that I tried so hard to sell it to my contemporary 1971 readers as some kind of rock substitute was that if I had acknowledged it was something different and *sui generis* (at that time, anyhow), I'd have to acknowledge I was getting somewhat to one side of the popular tastes of the day, going back to being a bit of a wonk, as I'd started out. Maybe, except for this: there is nothing wonkish about that sublime melody. Listen to it, and you'll want to soar too.

36

FINDING THE MAIN LINE

REASONS FOR WAITING, BY IAN ANDERSON, PERFORMED BY
JETHRO TULL (1969), ENCOUNTERED 1970

PLAYLIST TRACK No. 55

A HYMN WHOSE tune I like better than I do its lyrics contains the unfortunate line: "We are the young, our lives are a myst'ry." I think what the versifier had in mind (other than a rhyme for "history") was the notion that young people cannot know what life will have in store for them. But most of us use the word "mystery" to denote not an unknown outcome but rather a known set of facts that calls for an as-yet unknown explanation.

Yet when you're young, there are times when the word "mystery" as most of us use it almost fits. The facts of your life feel as if they should tell you what to do next, but you can't make out what they're saying.

The gorgeous Ian Anderson song *Reasons for Waiting* infallibly calls to my mind a moment of such frustration in my youth. Or, more accurately, a time-out from that frustration. When I hear it, I see myself sitting on a train. Let me tell about that moment and that trip.

It was a beautiful morning, and I was traveling in a two-car train from Phila-delphia to Harrisburg. I had to take the trip on account of my car, that priceless gift from my dad within the previous year (Chapter 33). The only problem was that my dad and the car came from New York, and I didn't. I was a Michigander attending college in Pennsylvania. So the time had come – and passed – for me to go to the Department of Motor Vehicles about re-registering it. I'm pretty certain I'd neglected switching the car's registration until the New York registration had lapsed, and in order to get the problem fixed I had to go at once to the only office that could deal with the problem immediately – in the state capital. Hence Harrisburg, rather than Philly. Hence train, rather than car.

Why had I neglected it? OK, start with the fact that I had no more judgment and maturity than your average college student. And like an average college student, I had to do a reasonable amount of coping on a daily basis. I was holding down a very ambitious college curriculum and carrying on a serious love affair. But I was also distracted by three big questions: what graduate school to apply to, what to do about the possibility I might be drafted, and whether or not to get married. And obviously the resolution to any one of these questions was tied up with the resolution of both of the others. All of these things provoked anxiety; all of them called for grown-up powers of analysis I didn't possess yet. My mind was going in circles trying to figure them out.

And so in the midst of all this, one little bit of coping, the car registration, was allowed to slide too long. As with most overdue tasks, delay came with a price: a day of downtime to get to Harrisburg and back. If that day taught me a lesson, however, it had nothing to do with the consequences of negligence. Rather it concerned the occasional moments of grace that drop into our lives, days where downtime unexpectedly becomes time out from one's cares. There was a phrase in my old Missal that captures what that day became: *locum refrigerii, lucis, et pacis*: a place of comfort, light and peace. For one gorgeous, sunny day I was forced to stare out the window of a cozy two-car train at some of the prettiest creation Pennsylvania has to offer, and I was so entranced by the unfolding scene that I largely forgot about being anxious.

The train followed along the Main Line, that agglomeration of the old Main Line of Public Works of Pennsylvania comprised of canals, roads and rail, and more particularly of course the Pennsylvania Railroad's Main Line to Pittsburgh. Over the roughly 120 years that this rail line had been used, it had carried commuter trains for some of Philadelphia's most elegant suburbs. I passed stations named Merion, Narberth, and Haverford, Villanova, Rosemont, Devon and Paoli. And then, after a while, the suburbs gave way to Lancaster County's broad fields. As this was either advanced autumn or early spring, the vegetation was spare enough so I had an unobstructed view. And finally, after a while, the line took me along the Susquehanna banks before depositing me near the Capitol.

I have a penchant and something of a gift for finding my way around strange cities, and I located where I was supposed to go quickly, and transacted my business without much trouble. Shortly thereafter, I got on another train and reversed the route.

And through much of that morning and afternoon, *Reasons for Waiting* was cycling through my head. It's a peaceful song, despite agitated interruptions by the strings. The lyrics evoke a lover contemplating his lady, apparently asleep, perhaps in bed with him, perhaps only remembered (the lyrics grow abstract as they describe the time and the place of the lady).

What a sight for my eyes to see you in sleep.
Could it stop the sunrise hearing you weep.
You're not seen, you're not heard but I stand by my word.
Came a thousand miles just to catch you while you're smiling.

And the lyrics conclude with a hope that the beloved has "faith in impossible schemes/ that are born in the sigh/ of the wind blowing by."

Despite the mention of weeping and the "impossible" nature of the "schemes," and despite some bruising jazzy interludes where Anderson's gruff flute-work suggests conflict, the song remains serenely confident that the lady will say yes to whatever projects or commitments the singer may propose.

The optimism of the song is assured by the strings and especially by a repeated flourish played by Anderson on the flute, backed by Martin Barre on another flute. It appears at the beginning, middle, and end of the song. If you remember one thing about *Reasons for Waiting*, it will be that incurably lovely flourish, perfect for accompanying the passing of suburbs and fields in all their own loveliness.

I was really sorry for the day to end, and to be thrown back again into the less serene frame of mind in which I was spending that year. Yet I couldn't help thinking, then and now, that I was on a quest to discover the main line of my life, and that for a day at least, I had experienced what finding it might feel like.

37

WE FIRST BY OURSELVES

FOR ALL WE KNOW, MUSIC BY FRED KARLIN, LYRICS BY ROBB ROYER
AND JIMMY GRIFFIN, PERFORMED BY LARRY MEREDITH (1970)
AND CARPENTERS (1971), ENCOUNTERED 1970 AND 1971

THAT'S THE WAY I'VE ALWAYS HEARD IT SHOULD BE,
BY CARLY SIMON AND JACOB BRACKMAN, PERFORMED BY
CARLY SIMON (1971), ENCOUNTERED 1971

PLAYLIST TRACKS NOS. 56, 57

WHEN I WRITE about deciding whether to get married, a decision I was confronting in 1970, there is a clear choice: either a wealth of detail or great simplicity. In my case, discretion dictates the latter. As I've already stated here, this is my story, no one else's.

The hardest fact, then, is the easiest to tell: I suffered agonies of indecision. And this should have told me all I needed to know about whether to proceed, especially in view of how young I was, and in view of the fact my girlfriend S. was even younger. We were both good people and very nearly right for each other for the long term. But nearly only counts in horseshoes and hand-grenades, as S. herself would say in other contexts.

Harder to tell is the way the air of the times flavored the experience of going through that indecision. Marriage is such an old institution that there can be no new wisdom about it, no new thinking. Everything that could possibly be said must surely have been said. Still, every generation confronts the old questions and tries out the old answers in its own way. And certainly this was equally true of my own generation.

Consider how it had appeared to most of our parents, the ones who had Weathered the Depression and Won the War. Their identity was as a generation overcoming uncertainty and yearning to establish solid, lasting things. Marriage, the way most of them had wanted to believe in it, was one of those solid, lasting things. They could flock to its strictures and protections because they knew and were sick of the contingency of economic upheaval and world conflict. From my perspective, they didn't handle what their vows created any better or any worse than any other generation did, but I'm convinced they decided more decisively whether to take the vows in the first place. At least more decisively than my generation did.

As for us Boomers, raised amid comparative peace and prosperity, we had been encouraged to make lifelong enterprises out of exploration of ourselves and our potential. And it would presumably be harder to be continually exploring after one had made certain commitments. Marriage could only be reconciled with this aspiration if marriage itself became part of the adventure, if, instead of becoming the embrace of certainty with a person one knew intimately, it were to be made somehow the very vehicle through which the exciting though uncertain journey of life could be taken.

The trouble was, if both of you were growing in unpredictable ways, were busy exploring, what would happen when each of you had grown into someone new? After all, that you would each continue to grow, to metamorphose even, was absolutely a part of the program. Could a marriage sustain such developments? One could not know for certain in advance. The only thing certain up front was the commitment; how much the cherished exploration could persist in its wake could only be known later.

For All We Know, which appeared first in a movie all about deciding to get married, *Lovers and Other Strangers* (August 1970) (it won the Best Original Song Oscar), and then came out as a hit when covered by Carpenters early in 1971, was a perfect expression of that dilemma:

Love, look at the two of us
Strangers in many ways
We've got a lifetime to share
So much to say and as we go from day to day

I'll feel you close to me
But time alone will tell
Let's take a lifetime to say I knew you well
For only time will tell us so
And love may grow for all we know.

In other words, finding out whether (or not) you get to know the other person well – presumably if you don't, it's because the marriage failed – is part of the great exploration of life. The "great exploration" part notwithstanding, this is hardly a ringing endorsement of marriage.

The staging of that moment in the movie, with Larry Meredith singing the song in (it must be said) an unmemorable rendition, just underlines the equivocation in the feelings. Bonnie Bedelia and Michael Brandon, as the young couple whose indecision has constituted the linchpin of the plot, finally take hands, ascend to the altar, and stand before the priest. As they say their vows and exchange rings, and Meredith sings, the camera peeks around the church, lighting on various couples, their relationships in various states of array and disarray, including a hilarious three-shot of Gig Young, Anne Jackson, and Cloris Leachman, as, respectively, the adulterous father of the bride, his paramour, and his unsuspecting wife. You can read the lyrics as hopeful, but they don't have to be. And as I watched that scene at the time, I understood exactly the ambiguity the movie makers intended; I was feeling it. And then Carpenters came out with their own hit version and made the flavor last.

Likewise with Carly Simon's first hit, *That's the Way I've Always Heard It Should Be*, which came out only about a month before S. and I graduated and, two days later, tied the knot. Simon nailed the paradox of trying to make of marriage a liberation and commitment.

You say we'll soar like two birds through the clouds,
But soon you'll cage me on your shelf–
I'll never learn to be just me first
By myself.

That record stayed on the charts a long time, 17 weeks, so basically it was there whenever I turned on the radio during our first summer as a married couple. I can remember stumbling out of the house at dawn and getting behind the wheel headed for my summer job (driving a lunch truck from North

Philly to industrial locations in South Jersey) and hearing it as if it had been directed personally to me. I drew consolation from the fact that the singer concludes she should marry, doubts notwithstanding. I also drew consolation from an inability to imagine S. and me suffering in staid misery like the older generation pictured in the song. And shortly thereafter Carly Simon herself got married, to James Taylor, no less, and sang glowingly about it – for a while.

So I opted to take these basically dark and doubtful songs as omens of hope. A crystal ball focused on the singers themselves would have put matters in a different perspective. Simon, who must have been writing about herself, would see her marriage collapse at the same time as mine did. And Karen Carpenter, who wasn't actually marrying anyone in those days, married unhappily when she finally did, and, of course, met an untimely death from her struggles with anorexia. I suspect she was too damaged from an early age to make any marriage work, but certainly the one she entered didn't seem to make anything better; it looks not to have been a great adventure.

I believe the moment I finally decided to marry was during a brilliantly sunny weekend getaway, in late winter or earliest spring of 1970. Some of my friends and I, not including S., went off to the seaside cottage of one of our parents in Brigantine, New Jersey. I kept to myself, walking or sitting on the shore, staring at the ocean. I think everyone else was paired off, so no one minded when I opted for solitude.

Somewhere in the midst of staring out at the water, I decided I could see enough odds of success to undertake the adventure with S.

I cannot call my exact thought process to mind now. I do remember, however, the picture I had for myself and S. We would find our adventure in the study and teaching of literature; our metamorphoses would arise from the encounter with books. If it might seem to you that vowing to shut oneself up in the academic cloister was rather thin gruel, I have to tell you you probably weren't around in the liberal arts world of 1971. To the stimulus an elite academic setting reliably provides, the era imparted a special explosive quality. People were demonstrating, acting out, taking drugs, espousing politically radical new critical theories. Anything and everything could happen. And a lot of it had to do with books.

And one thing S. and I knew was we were talented enough to succeed at the challenge. It was a marriage of true minds. And for a good long time, to that marriage we did not admit impediments.

38

IMAGINING A LOT (TERY)

IMAGINE, BY JOHN LENNON (1971), ENCOUNTERED 1971

PLAYLIST TRACK NO. 58

IMAGINE: THE LUCKY guy has just been given his life back, and sentence has just been passed on mine.

365

Imagine: A college quad at night with someone running across it screaming "365! 365!" It is December 1, 1969, the date of the first draft lottery. The lucky screamer, born February 26, has just been given his life back. Whatever plans he's made for his future are secure, or at least secure from the threat of being called away to take part in that bigger lottery called the Vietnam War. There's no chance that a young man born on the 365th day chosen will be inducted. Not only will he be spared the certain sacrifice of two years of his life, but he is immune to the risk of the even shorter straws: killing, dying or being wounded.

Imagine: A crowd of us sitting together a few moments earlier in Houston Hall, the student union building, listening to the draft lottery being broadcast. Afterwards, I wander despondently out onto College Hall Green, where the shouter sprints by. I am filled with envy and terror. Since I was born on a July 13, my number is 42. My prognosis is the exact opposite of Number 365's. While I remain an undergraduate, I will be protected by a student deferment.

But when I graduate, as inevitably I shall in only three semesters' time, they will reach me. If the War goes on, as I know it will, and if I do not find another deferment, as I doubt I shall, it is a certainty.

42

Imagine me speaking to my parents by phone later that night. I curse at my mother, and, with rare restraint, she takes in both my anger and its untoward expression without an angry reply. Much later, after I have children, it will be obvious why. A threat to me is a threat to her. Still, little in her experience could lead her to accept my outlook.

It's no problem imagining what has formed her views. She has been through the Second World War. She is no flag-waver, but she remembers her pride in the young GIs she met in the trains in those days. Nor has anyone had to sell her on the evils of Communism – and Vietnam, they tell us, is a war against Communists. No doubt she and millions of mothers like her feel instinctively that the poet Horace was right when he wrote: *Dulce et decorum est, pro patria mori* ("It is sweet and fitting to die for one's country"). You support your church, your political party, your nation, and your nation's wars: that is her outlook. And these loyalties might call upon you to surrender up your only son. Up to this moment, I think, that conclusion has also been part of her outlook.

But now she has to imagine a contradiction to all that.

Imagine me seeing nothing sweet or fitting about dying, fighting, or putting myself at risk for Richard Nixon or his evil war. From the moment in February of the previous year, during a poetry reading by Allen Ginsberg, when I had realized that I now opposed a war I had once supported, I am growing more and more horrified at the holocaust of young men, American and Vietnamese, the War is creating. That type of sacrifice might be justified to bring about a world without Hitler, but hardly a world without Ho Chi Minh.

And now it becomes up to me to imagine ways to avoid this catastrophe bearing down on me. I try. I borrow books from my parish priest about Catholic views of war. I thus become knowledgeable. With my new understandings, I apply for conscientious objector status, but my draft board turns me down, unconvinced that I am against all possible wars, and concluding that my convictions are firm only about the current one. They have seen right through me.

I also apply for a medical deferment on the basis of back pains I've been having. I learn that I'm the third generation of my family with wretched backs, that my mother has often been in traction. I get the doctor mother of Carol, the friend who lives in our house, to write a letter supporting my deferment claim. I undergo a couple of draft physicals, one in a big tall building off Broad Street in Philly. My medical deferment claim is rejected. This time the call is wrong; I'm not malingering. (In later life my back will be operated on three times.) But the maw of Moloch must be fed, and questionable deferment claims must be rejected.

Imagine the inner dialogues, about the reality that, if I make good my escape from military service, someone else will have to take my place. Imagine me deciding that if the worst comes to the worst, I will flee to Canada, because my bottom line is I will not accept either service or imprisonment. Easy to say, but flight would mean disruption of my graduate studies and those of my young wife, and, so far as I know, I would never be able to come back to the United States to visit parents or in-laws or friends. Imagine the misery drawn out, as my deferment fights delay the moment when I am required to report for induction.

1-H

Imagine May 11, 1972, the date my Draft Board, for reasons that elude me entirely, reclassifies me 1-H. I open the envelope and see the card, and realize I've never heard of 1-H. It turns out that 1-H means not available for induction. The card looks like, and in fact turns out to be a reprieve, in a form I had not even sought. In later years I will hear rumors that it was issued to people suspected of being gay, but also that it simply meant that for whatever reason, you had not been inducted in your "year," and so the Board was moving on to the next year's candidates. (The timing would pretty much work, since when the card arrives, I have been out of college and undeferred for about a year. In which case, my sheer persistence in seeking a deferment has paid off after all, unimaginably well.) In any case, no one tells me why, then or ever.

Imagine how I feel after it sinks in. While I also understand that a 1-H is subject to reclassification as 1-A at any time, I never hear from the draft board again. And now it is my turn to feel that my life has been given back to me.

Very shortly after I know I'm probably saved, I'm driving down Light Street in Baltimore, when John Lennon's *Imagine* comes on the radio. I dissolve in emotion. It's not simply that Lennon is asking us to imagine a world without war; he sees war as part of a complex of bad things:

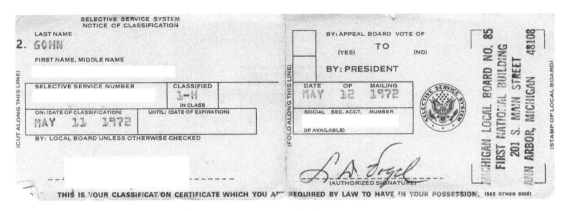

Imagine there's no countries
It isn't hard to do
Nothing to kill or die for
And no religion too

At this point in my life, I'm a very serious Catholic, but I understand the role religion has played in so many wars, so I'm not blaming Lennon for his point of view. I think it a perversion of religion to go to war for it, so I can agree with his diagnosis without signing on to his prescription.

But I'm responding to something far deeper than Lennon's words: it's the heartbroken melody, those languorous piano chords. To be sure, there's a hopeful note in there. But mostly Lennon's voice comes across as exhausted by sadness. And it speaks to me because that's how I feel after this close encounter. I could have been a war casualty; I'm not, thank God. But I tell myself I must never forget what it felt like nearly to have been one. I must not forget the months of dread, of helplessness and anger. I must not forget the way the good and patriotic motives of my countrymen were put in service of bloodthirsty insanity that threatened, among many far bigger things, my own small life and my life's plans. And I never do forget those things.

But beyond even that, I resolve never to forget Lennon's closing vision:

Imagine all the people sharing all the world
You, you may say I'm a dreamer, but I'm not the only one
I hope someday you'll join us
And the world will live as one

And I never forget that, either. If you can imagine.

39

DECONSTRUCTED

LEAN ON ME, WRITTEN AND PERFORMED BY
BILL WITHERS (1972), ENCOUNTERED 1972

PLAYLIST TRACK NO. 59

CERTAIN CONVERSATIONS CHANGE your life. Let me start with one that did, in exactly the wrong way.

It is a grey and damp March Saturday in 1971. A gentleman with close-cropped gray hair and I are walking the streets of West Philadelphia. My interlocutor is named Earl Wasserman. I'm taking part in an open-air interview for a spot in next year's Graduate English Program, which Professor Wasserman runs, at Baltimore's Johns Hopkins University.

This is a man who should be on my side, almost no questions asked. Without him, my life to this point would have been completely different, and he must know this. Back when he and my father Emile were young faculty members together at the University of Illinois, they and their spouses formed a foursome. Wasserman, an enthusiastic proselytizer for the academic program he came from, Hopkins Graduate English, had persuaded my mother to matriculate in that very program should she return East, as she eventually did. And it was there, on or around the steps of Hopkins's Gilman Hall, my mother met the man who, about a decade later, would become my stepdad, Ernie Gohn. My stepfather would earn his doctorate in that program a couple of years after he and Mother met. Wasserman knows all this history. Wasserman should be helping to write the next chapter of that history, right?

And I am the kind of student any graduate English program should welcome. Great grades, working familiarity with Old English, Middle English, and the contemporary stuff and everything in between. Earning bachelor's and master's degree simultaneously.

Yet for the moment it doesn't appear he is on my side. What do I think I'm up to, applying to a department where there are twenty trying to get in for every slot? And what is this business in my application where I say I'd like to do some creative writing in after life, along with scholarship? Am I not aware that I can't possibly do both? OK, so C.S. Lewis did it; I don't think I can, do I? Am I really unaware that scholarship consumes all a real scholar's time and loyalty? Johns Hopkins only wants real scholars who will produce great scholarly works. Am I going to commit myself to that goal, or will I skulk in, pretending that I am going to produce these works, while actually planning to go off and fritter myself away being creative, when there are so many worthy people in the world who would make better use of the opportunity?

Now, if I agreed with Wasserman's premise, I'd feel worse about trying to placate him. But I don't agree. Oh, maybe I can sense the experience that lies behind his pronouncements. But I think I'm more capable than Wasserman allows. I think that, with focus and drive, I really can do both the creating and the scholarship. But he won't let me say that, so I kind of lie and downplay parts of my ambition.

Perhaps I succeed; I am admitted two weeks later.

Have I really fooled Wasserman? I don't know, but I doubt it. My best guess, looking back, is that he let me in on account of auld lang syne, because of the connections with my mom and my stepdad – and my father. And he was probably hoping for the best, the best being that he could eventually ease me into his ascetic scholarly mold. As for me, on the strength of that conversation alone, I should have run like hell in the other direction, because even if I didn't know yet exactly what he wanted, I had been given sufficient warning that I could expect to be asked for something I could never provide. Each of us thus said yes when he should have been saying no. Call it fate.

As is always the case, it wasn't sheer cussedness alone that led me to make that choice; there were also various sensible considerations. The pattern of acceptances and financial offers I and my fiancée received made it clear we were either headed to my home town of Ann Arbor, or to Baltimore, from whence she came. And slightly better money seemed to be coming from Baltimore.

But it proved to be nothing like what I had expected. Without warrant, I'd assumed that all graduate English departments were like Penn's: lecture format (where the professor did much of the heavy lifting) with the occasional seminar. Hopkins was all seminars, all the time. We were expected to do multiple papers in each course, read them to each other, and comment (and if you think that might tend to bring out some unhealthy competitiveness amongst the tyro scholars, you're right). But those were the superficial dissimilarities. Wasserman had been less than candid too, it seems, about something even more important. Hopkins, it emerged, was all about criticism, not scholarship. And so, in our seminar papers and everywhere else, we were expected to spend more time talking about the published criticism than about the works being criticized. This brought to my mind the picture of a man bent over, playing tic-tac-toe in the dust, ignoring a spectacular sunset going on behind him.

It wasn't just the emphasis on the criticism; it was the kind of criticism. Unlike what my mom and stepdad had encountered with their band of brothers and sisters in the 1940s, the Hopkins Grad English program of the 1970s had dedicated itself heart and soul to turning out Deconstructionist critics. And what (you may ask) is Deconstructionism? Sorry: I can't tell you. There is no there there, no definition by definition. There are certain tenets: texts have no fixed meaning; we interpret them according to our sense of reality, but that sense is just another text. Criticism is therefore the creation of texts about texts, and the most creative creations of texts about texts are those that subvert the apparent meaning of the texts under discussion. Hence critical creativity dwells most consistently and most laudably in destruction. Or, as they preferred to call it, Deconstruction.

My interest in scholarship, then, was not merely different from the interests of the professors; it was an affront to the premises on which they were basing their careers. I sought to learn facts about literary works that would help us understand what they actually, objectively meant. That quest that presupposed a conviction that works had objective meanings, that these meanings were tied to authors' lives and intentions, and that lives, intentions, and meanings in many cases would be knowable. This was anathema to my professors, or something worse than anathema: belle-lettrism, literary appreciation of the most superficial, conventional and sentimental sort.

And even that wasn't the whole problem. I came to realize fairly quickly that a lot of the writers and books I cared about weren't considered worthy to be on the syllabus. So-called minor genres that I'd been able to write about freely at Penn (mystery, science fiction, spy fiction, children's literature, rock lyrics) were off-limits. A destructive radicalism in reading was thus put at the service of a conservative and snobbish selection of what to read.

You might expect that with such radicalism would come at least some kind of excitement, no matter how ersatz. Sorry to disappoint you. One day, in a fit of massive boredom, I transcribed, word-for-word, what a professor of mine was saying. I present it herewith. (Imagine him smoking his pipe.) "When…I… was…in…(puff)…(puff)…college… …(puff)…(puff)…I had… … a friend… (puff)…who wrote… …(puff)…I get tired… … (puff)…(puff puff)…Is that a sign…(puff)…of…(puff puff)…maturity?" You could go mad waiting for the end of two sentences like those, and then mad again dealing with the attitude they conveyed.

The Mount Olympus of the Hopkins Grad English universe was the Tudor Stuart Club, a paneled room on the third floor of Gilman Hall where monthly evening meetings took place. Attendance was *de rigeur*, though the Department softened the blow by laying out beer and the makings of cold cut sandwiches. But access to the fodder was in consideration of, and allowed only after, your sitting through lectures by visiting Deconstructionist luminaries. If a lecture were graspable using ordinary vocabulary and logic and common sense, it was deemed a failure. There were few failures. Instead, there would be the most impenetrable prose you ever heard. After an hour of that, the questions would start. People, mostly faculty, would pose questions, many in the same diction as the lecture, and you'd have to sit through that for up to another half hour, until dismissed.

There were those who drank the Kool-Aid, who claimed to get it, who professed to admire the Emperor's new clothes. These were the ones the professors rewarded with continued stipends and bona fide job recommendations. I felt and expressed no admiration, and the consequences for me would prove commensurate.

I caught on quickly that this wasn't a congenial place for me, writing my parents at the end of September that I hated it. Evidently the feeling was mutual. At the beginning of February, I received a letter from the department chair advising that "On the basis of the necessarily limited evidence available, we have some doubts about the quality of your work as of this moment."

My wife, who had entered the program with me, got a similar letter. In my case, the department ultimately relented, and allowed me to stay with a stipend (I was upgraded to "satisfactory" in May), but it would extend no stipend to my wife. She stepped down (and went on to better things).

In light of these developments, I wrote to a friend who'd gone to Yale:

Words have not been coined to describe the awfulness of this place.... They don't have any money and they're doing people dirt, right and left. Since there are no grades, we have no objective standards to point to in our own defense: all they have are subjective analyses of us on file with the chairman which we aren't even allowed to see.... Classwork counts for nothing, and so the phenomenal string of papers we have to turn out like sausages is the essential means the student has of establishing his worth. But around here you're expected to become somebody's disciple ... and your papers had not only better be done well, but they had better coincide in their findings with the professor's own opinions.

So I arrived at year's end battered and bruised. My value as a literary man had been impugned, my earlier-described vision of my wife and me as soaring through the clouds together sharing an academic career had crashed to earth, and I was in need of ready cash. At least there was a partial and temporary solution for that last one: My father-in-law called in some favors and landed me and my brother-in-law a summer job to split: driving a Mister Softee truck in Anne Arundel County, a marshy enclave west of the Chesapeake and south of Baltimore.

It was certainly a different experience, I'll say that.

Different, but not much of an improvement. I drove up and down neatly-platted streets of Glen Burnie and Severna Park trying to sell soft ice cream, listening to a maddening jingle played over and over again on the speaker mounted above my cab. The ice cream may have been cold, but the cab was hot, and I sweated off over a dozen pounds. I was being paid a small base plus commission, incentivizing me to sell, sell, sell. Freezers had come to these neighborhoods, though, dampening demand, and the trucks were old and prone to breakdowns, frequently killing outright my ability to meet what demand there was.

You would not have guessed the existence of either of the problems listening to the franchisee, a man named Marshall. In Marshall's imagination the sky was the limit, and mechanical troubles were to be overcome with a positive attitude, not expensive repairs. Yet ice cream trucks contained two complete mechanical systems (truck and kitchen), each with a plethora of moving parts. Old systems are apt to go on the fritz; that's just the way of it. The product was perishable, and if you couldn't turn that mix into ice cream and those bananas into splits, they had to be written off. If you had a flat tire, or the ice cream machine went down, you were out of business until further notice. Marshall thought (or at least pretended to) that if we were really committed on a deep spiritual level to sales, we could magically move ice cream irrespective of whether the trucks could budge or the ice cream machines could dispense product.

Marshall had a trophy younger girlfriend, Roxanne, who had been a beauty queen. Marshall had made her vice president of his company. It was painfully obvious to the rest of us that Marshall had mistaken whatever he saw in her for extraordinary business acumen, but that she possessed neither more nor less of that than the rest of us, and her beauty and certain degree of spunk could not change the overall direction of an undercapitalized business dependent on a badly depreciated truck fleet, peddling a product for which this neighborhood's demand was in decline. We wanted Marshall to spend less time communing with Roxanne and more time looking after the fleet. Marshall's starry-eyed embrace of motivational nostrums could not substitute for an outlay of cash, and somehow he couldn't see it. Or more likely he just couldn't afford to pay it.

While I did not share Marshall's rosy vision of pure sales karma, I did believe in getting to work on time (I'd done some growing up since working at Ford three summers before), and so, on Thursday, June 22, 1972, even though the weather was bad, I was trying to fight my way in.

I'd heard that there was a hurricane around but not exactly in Maryland. Heading out to the car, I felt a lot of rain, but nothing like hurricane winds. So I optimistically set out for Glen Burnie and the Mister Softee compound. Bill Withers' annoying April hit, *Lean on Me*, was playing on the radio as I cruised downhill on the Baltimore-Washington Parkway toward the wetlands that constitute the banks of the Patapsco River. Getting close to those wetlands, though, I realized things might be a little different today. There were no wetlands to be seen at all, just water that came up disconcertingly close to the highway – where there ought to have been at least 10 feet of grade separation. And traffic had almost stopped. As I got close to the next interchange, where

I was supposed to exit the Parkway and get on the ramp for the Beltway southbound, there were police cars with flashing red lights, waving us off.

I guessed that there was something wrong with the Beltway, but I assumed I could find an alternate route. So I not only kept on going (I had no choice about that), but also kept trying to get to work. And that was the beginning of a three-hour ordeal, in which, through increasingly powerful rain, I was seeking a way to Glen Burnie on back roads, roads I did not know, roads I was sharing with far too many drivers, roads that kept ending in roadblocks. I don't know how long it took me to figure out that Hurricane Agnes (they were calling it that even though it was no longer at hurricane strength) was simply going to keep me out of Glen Burnie altogether that day, and that, however great a sales opportunity might be presented with power out all over the peninsula and people's freezers out of commission and their dark houses driving them into the street, I was never going to get there to capitalize on it.

When I did realize it, though, I also realized that it had been my choice to put myself out here, against advice, that I was in parts of the back of beyond I did not know, getting lashed by rain, and that, by this time, the paths back to what was comfortable and familiar might be closed.

Even after two semesters at insane Johns Hopkins, I recognized a metaphor when one was rapping me on the knuckles. And I also recognized that *Lean on Me*, which was played at least once again on the radio (it would become a Number 1 hit in July) as, against all odds, I gradually worked my way back into Baltimore, was a perfect metaphor for the metaphor.

Was there ever a more ugly or simple-minded song? Starting with that opening piano cadence, an inverted C chord, followed by the hands simply moving up and down on the white keys without changing their position, and just seeing what happens. The verses doggerel, poorly scanned. A bass line that at one point is sketching out a different chord from the one being played by the piano, and not because the bass player is being inventive, but because he apparently isn't listening. And lyrics that relate two notions, though they do not explain the relationship between them, because they can't. One notion is that we need to help each other out, and the other is "there's always tomorrow." Tell that second one to the three children in Maryland whose car overturned in the floodwaters of Hurricane Agnes and drowned. They didn't get even one tomorrow. And if there were always tomorrow, then how important would it really be for people to help each other out? Wouldn't they all be assured of a tomorrow regardless of whether others lent a hand or not?

I could beat this horse for a long while, but it's dead and I'm done. The point is, that song just perfected the frustration. I knew what a good song sounded like. I knew what the proper approach to literature looked like. I knew that mysticism didn't sell ice cream. And now I was in a world where no one who ran the show cared what I knew; they thought they knew better and were going to do it their way. And I was going to have to be a part of that world for a while.

I just had no idea on that wet June day how long I would be stuck there. But stuck I was. Or, if you will, I had stuck.

40

RIDE AWAY

RAM ON, WRITTEN AND PERFORMED BY
PAUL McCARTNEY (1971), ENCOUNTERED 1972

PLAYLIST TRACK NO. 60

AT FIRST LISTEN, *Ram On* seems like an inconsiderable song from an inconsiderable album, Paul and Linda McCartney's *Ram* (1971). The breakup of the Beatles had left Paul McCartney at a moment of fooling with nonsense verse and Dadaism, purveying scraps that did not merge into a satisfying whole. This decline, one which had progressively marked everything the Beatles had done after *Sgt. Pepper*, was first and foremost Paul's affliction, and it would take him some years to bring it under control. But his ear for melody had not deserted him.

And there is much melody in this ditty, especially as contributed by a deceptively simple ukelele. Hearing that plangent instrument obsessing over a C# minor 7th chord with McCartney's sweet falsetto crooning the leading tone at the top and then swooping down through the chord to the tonic, lifts you into a sublime, solitary, and calm place.

Which is why it's a theme song for me. Year Two of our marriage had sort of felt akin to this song, and that was one reason I played *Ram On* a lot. Like the now-Beatle-less sound of McCartney on this album, everything I knew and valued was being presented to me in an unfamiliar way. Girlfriend was now wife, and our lives together were taking place in the strange town of Baltimore, not the familiar and comfortable Philadelphia where we'd met. English studies (in which I'd experienced such freedom and such a sense of exploration as an undergrad) had become abstruse, demanding and competitive, filtered through incomprehensible deconstructionist theory. And my parents who had once been too close now were far away, their space in my world largely preempted by a very-present crew of in-laws. I had felt adrift, rudderless, in my own life.

But now I found I was no longer so overwhelmed, and was actually beginning to master my new life. I liked being married, relieved to find that my cold-feet misgivings about the rigors of fidelity were misplaced, that I could after all learn to play the game in the English Department, while S., my wife, was moving on from her own disappointment with that Department.

I must acknowledge, though, that in resorting to the song this way, it didn't hurt that I misunderstood the lyrics. McCartney sang:

Ram on, give your heart to somebody
Soon, right away, right away.

But what I heard was:

Ram on, give your heart to somebody,
Soon ride away, ride away.

What I heard, then, was that you could be empowered to ride away, to move on in some good way, by the act of giving your heart away. You just needed faith in the strangeness of love to be transported in that way. And if you listened to the second part of the song (buried 8 tracks further), you could hear what I had thought was riding music. It came across all jolly and heartening. It was good music for starting the next phase of my life.

41

TRYING TO HAVE IT BOTH WAYS

HYMN AND PSALM: "A SIMPLE SONG," FROM LEONARD BERNSTEIN'S MASS, PERFORMED BY ALAN TITUS (1971), ENCOUNTERED 1972

SHARM EL SHEIKH, BY RON ELIRAN (1967), ENCOUNTERED 1972

PLAYLIST TRACKS NOS. 61, 62

WHEN I WAS a young adult, religious faith was not a problem for me. I might have tired of the nuns who'd taken me through eighth grade, but their certainty took root and proved durable. Many of my contemporaries had experienced the clerical corruption and abuse one hears so much about, and I guess I'd seen a little, but most of the nuns and priests who'd brought me along had been extraordinarily good people, and, deservedly, they'd made a great impression. I was no fool for trusting in them or what they told me. And if that were not enough, I had the example of my mother's more literary and sophisticated faith to bolster me.

As a result, at the time I got married, I had shed little of the committed, intellectual Catholicism in which I had been raised. I'd stopped going to confession, and obviously my sex life was not in accordance with the official Catholic line, but I remained a true believer, or at least one with an asterisk for matters related to sex.

This posed quite a problem when I found myself married to a Jewish woman who took her own religion seriously. (Our union had been concelebrated by a priest and a rabbi.) This led me to try to find ways to affirm both of our traditions, together if possible.

Part of it was a joint project of me and my wife, both of us bookworms, to read up and educate ourselves on the intersections between our faiths, for instance common history, both biblical and recent. It also expressed itself musically.

A prime case of the latter was my interest in Leonard Bernstein's *Mass*, a theater piece based on and inspired by the Catholic Mass. Fittingly, I was introduced to the original recording by a Catholic priest, in fact the priest who had officiated at our marriage. I knew the records; I'd taped the priest's version. I think I also knew the PBS version that aired in 1973. This is a work I've written a lot about since, but it intrigues me how much the things I found interesting about it in 1972 or 1973 differed from the things that interest me about it today.

The work follows (for the most part) the sequence of the Catholic Mass, but on that path follows the Mass's Celebrant as he and his flock move from a simple, secure confidence in God through a crisis of faith, a dark night of the soul, and thence into an uneasy return to something like faith at the very end. To me, at that point, it was the initial confidence that interested me the most.

This confidence is expressed strikingly at the outset by the first entrance of the Celebrant. As the piece begins, a jangling, atonal, modernistic Kyrie is pouring out of the sound system. The Celebrant strides into the light and dispels the annoying music by strumming a single loud G chord on a guitar, and then launches into A Simple Song.

Sing God a simple song Lauda, Laudē …
Make it up as you go along Lauda, Laudē …

Shortly thereafter, the Celebrant is quoting from one of the most serene of the Psalms, No. 121:

For the Lord is my shade,
Is the shade upon my right hand
And the sun shall not smite me by day
Nor the moon by night

Actually, however unmitigated by doubt are the words the Celebrant sings, and however directly lyrical those words may be, the music is anything but simple (just try to pick it out on the piano and you'll see what I mean), a mixture of Eastern and Western scales in keys that are constantly changing. It is a measure of Bernstein's artistry that this still seems simple.

But to me at that time that song was the heart of it. As the Celebrant's faith gradually breaks down over the course of the piece, the proceedings seemed more and more conventional and even hackneyed. The two points where I was completely back on board were the equally confident *Word of the Lord* segment, and the echoes of *A Simple Song* at the very end. I just couldn't buy into the existential angst that fuels most of the rest of the piece to one degree or another.

Today, it's reversed. Recent years have brought plenty of my own dark nights of the soul, and I've come to appreciate how well Bernstein conveys what the process feels like. It's the happy talk parts I so closely identified with then that sound superficial to me now. ("God is the simplest of all [things]"? Really?)

But harkening back to what I liked about it then, I think I also recognized in Bernstein someone who saw in Catholic ritual and faith something entirely complementary to his own Jewish spirituality.

Music was becoming more important to my religious life then in any event. I had joined the Newman community at Hopkins, and shortly found myself (without the benefit of any training worthy the name) leading the music at Sunday Mass, standing up on a platform at the front of a classroom, armed only with a chromatic harmonica. To my great good fortune, I was assisted in that effort by a number of talented musicians with enormously more developed instrumental skills. But it meant that I was constantly listening for music that might work for our Mass.

About which a word. This was the era of so-called folk Masses. That label covered a multitude of things which differed from congregation to congregation. At Hopkins Newman in that era, the folk Mass canon allowed in a lot of pure pop like the Beatles' *Nowhere Man* and Simon & Garfunkel's *Sounds of Silence*, songs which lacked a specific religious subject or vocabulary, but which raised questions that a religious perspective might be handy in framing answers to. It went nicely with the sermons by our pastor, Father Phil, a man with a remarkable facility for drawing moral and theological lessons from the latest movies.

Our congregation used an improvised hymnal of its own devising, of which I hope all copies have since vanished. I hold that hope that because it was reissued while I was there, and I made a couple of anonymous contributions to the new edition. Each song I added was a rendering into English and a religious context of songs I'd heard on a compilation album belonging, I think, to my in-laws called *Jerusalem of Gold*. Let's just say that I am not a natural lyricist.

The point at the moment, however, is that I was listening to and drawing inspiration from an album of Hebrew songs. And not just any songs, but specifically songs in an album inspired by the Six-Day War, the war that tripled Israel's land mass and gave a tremendous shot in the arm to the morale of all of my in-laws and their connections. One of the songs that spoke most to me was *Sharm el Sheikh*, by Ron Eliran, an evocation of the port down at the bottom of the Sinai captured from Egypt in 1967.

The chorus goes (in transliterated Hebrew)

At Sharm a-sheikh, chazarnu elaich shenitat belibeinu, libeinu tamid

(and in translation, so I'm told)

You're Sharm el-Sheikh, we've returned to you once again
You are in our hearts, always in our hearts

The rest of the lyrics are a poetic evocation of the town (reportedly largely a fishing village) together with a strong message that the singer and his people belong there. In other words, given the events that are implied, it is a message that Israel's being in Sharm el Sheikh was a reversion to something right and natural.

I turned this stirring music into a song about – some Christian doctrine or other, let's just leave it at that. When I listen to Ron Eliran's song today, the music continues to stir me, more now that I have a better idea what the Hebrew lyrics portend than I did then. They have to do with feeling one has returned to a place that is right and appropriate (dare I say, in the Catholic phrase, meet and fitting?).

That is what I was trying to feel about a marriage with one foot in a faith that was not my own. I think Eliran got closer to really feeling it, though, given the subsequent history of the town (restored to Egypt in 1982), one cannot help wondering. Perhaps a lot of us sing loudly of feelings that are not quite our own, assert kinships and allegiances we do not exactly feel, try to feel familiar and comfortable in places where we are not thoroughly welcomed.

42

SOMEONE MUST HAVE SENT THAT TO KEMP, OR NOT ENOUGH FRIENDS

ABADDON'S BOLERO, BY KEITH EMERSON, PERFORMED BY
EMERSON, LAKE & PALMER (1972), ENCOUNTERED 1973

PLAYLIST TRACK NO. 63

I HAVE ALWAYS loved big, long, over-the-top and slightly apocalyptic rock numbers. I was passionate about the 7-minute version of *Light My Fire*, I was intrigued by the full version of *In-a-Gadda-da-Vida*, and even more by Procol Harum's *Repent Walpurgis*, the Animals' *We Love You Lil*, and (as a later chapter will reflect), WAR's *Seven Tin Soldiers*. Take a half-hour and listen to the songs I've just mentioned, and see if you aren't blissful afterwards. There's something wonderful about a bunch of rockers casting caution to the winds and, musically speaking, saying all they really think about something, omitting nothing. But really thinking is key; one of the problems, for instance, with so much of the Grateful Dead's oeuvre was that they went on and on and not everything actually had a musical point. Their jams were great for lying down in a field with hundreds of other people and letting your mind wander – an experience I'd had in 1969 – but not for seriously listening to.

One more piece that, for me, belongs in this pantheon of truly great over-the-top rock, is Keith Emerson's *Abaddon's Bolero*, a classic of the kind of music British rockers with formal training, synthesizers, and big hair were putting together then, featured on Emerson, Lake & Palmer's 1972 *Trilogy* release. As the name indicates, Abaddon is in a musical form, the Spanish- (not the Cuban-) style bolero, suitable for classical framing. Once you hear it, you know that it's mostly true to classical form, in that the triplet-heavy melody keeps repeating itself, but every time louder and with more bells and whistles, even cranking in a phrase from the folk song *The Girl I Left Behind Me* before it's all over – a total all-in effect, what the composer William Walton called "ham, lamb, and strawberry jam." And the whole effort is carried on Keith Emerson's keening synthesizer, carrying a weird melody that seems to be constantly readjusting keys, although it ultimately keeps returning to the same place, a sort of E minor orientation. I still go nuts when I hear it.

The way I became familiar with the piece is a sort of a shaggy dog story of lonely young people leveraging what social assets they had and making do with what was available.

The natural catchment area for friendships for us when we got to Baltimore and Hopkins would have been the graduate English program. And we did make a few friends there, most notably a fundamentalist Christian couple who enjoyed our company even though they seriously believed we were going to Hell. (They belonged to something called, with no sense of irony, the Church of the Open Door.) But the husband was much better at playing the Department's political games than I was, and this, much more than theological differences, did in the relationship after a year or two. Another couple, Canadians, in a Gentile/Jewish relationship like ours that might have afforded more of a basis for sharing, were so devastated by their own problems (his Jewish parents really weren't cool with Junior dating the Gentile) that they became socially unavailable in time.

So we had to look elsewhere. Most of our other connections in this town came from my wife's family, which was local, but not thickly populated with contemporaries with whom we could have made friends. But I had a few non-contemporary contacts as well; as I've mentioned before (Chapter 39), I was a legacy of the Hopkins English program from days of old. There were still some relics around of the world my mother and stepdad had inhabited. One was Martha.

In attempting to describe Martha I find I must first describe something else: the world of what we called the Blue Hairs. This won't be easy. Let me start by saying that in its heyday, Baltimore had been a town with a very definite Society, a world of genteel, often but by no means always wealthy folk whose social lives largely took place in the area roughly running two miles to the north of the Hopkins Homewood campus. That world had largely ended before I turned up in 1971, but the survivors of it, mostly elderly women, hung on, many of them in the large and gracious apartment houses along University Parkway and nearby. Baltimore may have been (barely) a Northern town but the Blue-Haired ladies definitely had Southernness stamped on them, whether they spoke with a drawl or not. Few had bloodlines that ran North, and many had connections to great Southern families. They tended to have elderly doctors and elderly servants and elderly bankers, and memories that stretched back generations, and ideas about race relations that did the same. But they were also tough and strong and practical, and in their own way quite admirable.

I remember making my first acquaintance of one literally the moment I arrived in Baltimore, parking a U-Haul truck beside the fire escape steps to our new apartment – not leaving adequate room in the alley for her to get her car past while visiting a doctor. "What the hay-ull" she asked "do you think yoah doing?" This, the voice conveyed in only a few words, was an admonition from someone accustomed to being obeyed. I think I moved the truck.

I said that some of these ladies were wealthy, but not all. One way into the sisterhood without being rich was through Hopkins connections. Martha was of that ilk. She had been a humanities librarian at Hopkins during my parents' glory years, and had been very helpful to and close with all the graduate students of their era. My folks insisted that I look her up when I got to Baltimore. She was not wealthy, but she drank sherry with the Blue-Haired ladies who were. She had a voice cured by a lifetime of cigarettes and probably significant alcohol intake.

She took a parental interest in us as just as she had in my parents. And during the summer of 1973, after we had been two years in Baltimore, she did us a very important favor, providing a connection to Inez Malone. It was a wonderful piece of matchmaking. We had complementary needs.

Inez was the widow of the great Hopkins philologist and linguist Kemp Malone, former president of the Modern Languages Association, specialist in northern European languages, explicator of *Beowulf*, and former teacher of my mother and stepfather. "Kempie," as my mother called him, had long been retired, but had died only weeks after we arrived in Baltimore. He left behind not only Inez, but two adjoining row houses on Maryland Avenue whose double-basement was full of thousands of books. Inez had decided to convey all of those books to the library at Emory University, her husband's alma mater. Which meant she needed to have them catalogued.

Both I and my wife were literary people, and my wife, upon leaving Hopkins after one year, had gone to library school. Between us, then, we had the skills to assemble the catalogue. I think Martha was aware of my unsatisfactory job the preceding summer, as well as of S.'s librarian credentials, and put us all together.

Of course, Inez was not a friend, not in the sense of a contemporary we could hopefully grow up alongside. But she was definitely someone to know. She was a Blue-Hair who had strayed a little off-course geographically, as there were no fashionable blocks of Maryland Avenue then, and south of Hopkins was the wrong side of the tracks. But she stuck it out.

And she made a social event of our cataloguing experience. We would take a break in the middle of each day, and she had the maid put together some kind of genteel collation for us, old lady cakes, maybe tea, that kind of thing. We would come upstairs from the basement and enjoy them with her. She was entertainingly outspoken, if given occasionally to malapropism; she sometimes seemed to be losing a little control of her speech.

It was quite an experience helping S. catalogue those books. The collection legitimately took most of the summer to parse and memorialize, being in effect three collections: what must have been damn near a reference set of all important works of and sources on Germanic philology, a more general literary collection, and odds and ends.

None of the three would exist today.

As to the Germanic philology collection, there are surely still linguists toiling in the fields of Old Norse and Old English and their kin, but just as surely no one now devotes the vast resources necessary to acquiring every book, every journal, every festschrift; I'm pretty sure Malone had them all, or something pretty close. The more general literary collection, more of a reader's than a writer's collection, would now largely be on Kindles. And the odds and ends were ephemera whose time has definitely passed since then, and had probably passed already by the early Seventies: I remember city directories (which no one creates now, or at least not in hard copy) and naughty nature magazine erotica.

Of the latter, I remember thinking even at the time that leaflets with nude young ladies tossing around beach balls was the strangest way to satisfy one's pornographic needs (the word "porn" wasn't in common usage yet).

I'd grown up with *Playboy*, and when I'd started sorting the mail for Bennett Hall, back at Penn, to earn a few bucks, I'd come upon some of the professors' porn, which was of the far more graphic Tab-A-in-Slot-B variety. This stuff, by contrast, was almost too quaint to be sexy. Since we had to decide whether to catalogue the Professor's holdings of this material, we asked Inez about it, and she commented innocently: "Someone must have sent that to Kemp." Yup, in a plain brown wrapper, as I'm sure Inez knew damn well. But give her credit for defending her man.

Inez also did one other thing for us, again by way of making connections. Through her own Confederate roots (she was a Chastain of, I think, Richmond), she had been asked to keep an eye on a Southern young man whose career had brought him to Baltimore. She either had David to dinner with us or had him drop by during one of our mid-day teas. Based on that, we struck up a friendship for a while.

David was a recent graduate of Elon College, and he had taken some kind of sales job up here in northern parts. Per Wikipedia, "In the early 1970s, Elon was an undergraduate college serving mainly local residents commuting from family homes, attracting 'regional students of average ability from families of modest means.'" David probably fit that description to a T, which meant that he had little in common with S. and me, products of Ivy educations pursuing advanced degrees, products of a more cosmopolitan north. David had been a frat boy, to boot.

But his apartment was only a block away from our apartment, and he was lonely, and we were lonely, so, as I say, we tried to patch together a friendship. So we sat in his living room or we sat in his, drinking Mateus or Cherry Kijafa or some dreadful thing that young drinkers of limited means and even more limited taste drank in those days, and tried to make something happen. One time-honored way to do that was to play records together. His collection was lacking the brainy stuff, but one of the records he played us was *Trilogy*, the Emerson, Lake & Palmer album that contains *Abaddon's Bolero*. I took it home and taped it, and must have played *Abaddon's Bolero* dozens of times, meaning that I must have rewound it as many times. I really loved the song.

I'm ashamed to say that after this recollection of David, that is to say, after remembering David lending me the record, I don't remember a thing. Looking back over my subsequent legal career, I recall having represented and advised dozens of young men and women who reminded me of David, engaged in sales of medical or engineering products, constantly in conflict over territories and commissions, and very, very geographically transient. I'm guessing he was transferred or changed employers and moved along. But in my memory all that remains is David-who-lent-me-the-ELP-album. He deserves better than that, I'm sure, but it's all I've got to give him. Sorry, David.

As for Inez, her husband's library was donated to Emory University in 1974, right on schedule. She was reportedly in her glory at the reception for the collection, although with her characteristic slightly shaky diction, she started out: "Kemp Malone had a long and a happy wife." I think she had it more right than wrong. The library was a family project, Germanic philology, nature mags, and all, and she had brought the project to fruition by transmitting it to further generations of scholars. And it did make her happy.

Archibald MacLeish wrote that a poem should not mean but be. I never endorsed that view entirely, because much of poetry does mean, in fact most of it does. Actually, the proposition is more apt to be right with music than with poetry. I believe *Abaddon's Bolero* is one of those pieces that does not mean, but just is. The name Abaddon is that of an angel of destruction referenced among other places in the Book of Revelation, though his name is also used as a synonym for Hell. But the bolero does not seem to be "about" destruction or the torments of the damned. It is a cathartic thing to sit through the number to its over-the-top end. But I wouldn't call it hellish. I suspect Keith Emerson chose the name for its evocative qualities and just its strangeness. Because, really, strangeness is the key to the experience of the song.

A very pleasant kind of strangeness, I may add. Thanks to Martha, and Inez, and David.

43

AT THE APEX

DOCKLAND, MUSIC BY DARRYL RUNSWICK, LYRICS BY
LEE CRABBE, PERFORMED BY IF (1970), ENCOUNTERED 1974

PLAYLIST TRACK NO. 64

I TEND TO acquire new interests at the same time as everyone else, but I seldom abandon them when the memo goes out to move on. Case in point: as the 70s progressed and people stopped thinking of Chicago or Blood, Sweat & Tears as cutting-edge, I just doubled down on jazz-oriented rock groups (or was it rock-oriented jazz groups?) by following bands with forgotten names like If, Dreams, and The Flock. If was a group I particularly liked: a British septet with two reedmen atop a standard rock band foursome fronted by a tenor vocalist named J.W. Hodginkson.

I must have picked up If's eponymous debut album in a remainder rack. I still have the LP, clad in a silvery reflective jacket, punched in one corner: the telltale mark of a remaindered record. No surprise it was remaindered: despite coming out on a major U.S. label, If obviously was not meant for great things in the overheated U.S. record market of that era. It was too foreign, too jazzy, its members equipped with insufficiently big hair for the 70s (two of them are perceptibly balding on the jacket photos). But they came into my life at an opportune time for me, because I was attempting a self-taught crash course in up-to-date working-class-world British culture. If, and especially its song *Dockland*, were playing a lot throughout the process.

The crash course was necessitated by the decision I'd made around the same time I bought the album. I'd chosen to write my dissertation on Kingsley Amis, the British novelist and poet. I wanted to write about someone I could actually talk to; I was sick of the inability to ask questions. More than anything else, though, and more than even I recognized at the time, my dissertation choice was a declaration of independence from the Hopkins English Department. Educated people everywhere had guffawed their way through Amis' freshman effort, *Lucky Jim* (1954), of course, but it was light humor, my dear, not Joyce or Nabokov, and it was, after all, a sendup of academia, and we do have to be careful not to be too disrespectful.

Amis' offenses against decorum had then multiplied: bedroom farces, a pastiche murder mystery and a pastiche ghost story, science fiction criticism and anthologizing, a book on James Bond, an actual authorized James Bond sequel, jazz criticism, a column about drinks, television scripts, and a drift to the right politically. To be sure, the man had his respectable lit-crit side as well, and he was a published poet to boot, but in choosing Amis to write about I knew I was detouring from the approved path of giving serious attention to serious writers working in serious genres.

All that messing in popular genres did not mean Amis (born 1922) was exactly contemporary at that moment. Contemporary would have been Swinging London. One of Amis's novels, *Girl, 20*, explicitly dealt with that scene. But it was an acidulous and huffy approach, focusing primarily on an older character, a conductor who could be great but throws away his talent in a ridiculous effort to fit in with London's gilded youngsters. Amis clearly was not going to be buying his duds on Carnaby Street.

The music of If wasn't a perfect match for either the times or my dissertation topic, but a significant step in that direction. Swinging London was rock, not jazz, and If was jazz as much as rock, and its members a bit long in the tooth to be fabulous in that era's eyes. That said, its musicians were and certainly felt more contemporary than the jazz Amis had written about for *The Observer* in the 1950s (in reviews I'd photocopied and read through for my dissertation). Read the liner notes of the If album, and you can sense you're being served up a compleat blending of up-to-date rock and up-to-date jazz.

But that was okay. On the page, Amis sounded and felt like a product of the big brick walls of industrial Britain, the world of the sendup of union/management tensions, *I'm All Right Jack*. *Lucky Jim* plays a practical joke on Johns, his dim colleague, writing a threatening letter as if it came from an irate workingman:

This is just a freindly letter and I am not threatenning you, but you just do as I say else me and some of my palls from the Works will be up your way and we sha'nt be coming along just to say How do you can bet.

Don't these Works sound as if they come from the same factory neighborhoods you see in the background in *A Hard Day's Night*? Or, more to the point, don't they sound like the neighborhood conjured up in the lyrics of *Dockland*?

It's a dockland scene
Where the water runs
There's a big lock gate
And it runs in tons
While the big ships wait
While the water runs...

There's a factory wall
Where the flour-bags lie
And they're stacked so tall
That they reach the sky
By the factory wall

To be technical about it, these are all different places. *Lucky Jim* takes place at a provincial British university, reportedly based in part on the University of Leicester in the British Midlands, in an area where "the Works" were indeed to be found; *A Hard Day's Night* was mainly shot in London; and Lee Crabbe's lyrics, quoted just above, describe a canal and docklands in Ipswich, Suffolk, on England's east coast. But the slightly drab, slightly run-down world still pulsing with industrial life was common to them all.

So I felt that by playing this record and humming the melody, I was truly helping myself (in a small way at least) to get ready to tackle my subject. My other preparations, in addition to mounting a determined effort to lay my hands on everything Amis wrote or which had been written about him, consisted of writing the man himself, and asking if I could interview him.

The answer I got back was both cordial and noncommittal. He "might buy [me] a drink." Armed with little more than that level of commitment on Amis' part, I got myself and S. to London in July 1974. Amis and I agreed to meet on the 16th, at the Garrick Club. I think he wanted to look me over, to decide if I was the sort to whom he wished to extend his help. Originally he told me he would have to leave at around one. However, as I was apparently making the right impression, he then invited me to come along with him to what I later learned was a fixture in his life at the time, a Tuesday lunch gathering with various conservatively-minded writers at Bertorelli's, an Italian restaurant. The day I was there, I met John Braine, author of *Room at the Top*, the movie of which I'd seen (and I'd also read the book), and Sovietologist and Amis co-author Robert Conquest.

I was very impressed, though none of these people was what I had expected. I might have articulated it differently to myself at the time, but it was as if the entire left-wing British intelligentsia had turned right. (No solidarity with "palls from the Works," and no romanticizing "flour bags ... by the factory wall" or "big lock gates.")

At the conclusion of the lunch, Amis and I made arrangements for me to come up to his suburban home in High Barnet and do an extended interview, which occurred on July 24. This is not the place to go into the specifics of my visit to his home or our conversation, much of which turned up in my dissertation. All I need report is that Amis was a delightful host, that I met Amis' formidable then-wife, the novelist Elizabeth Jane Howard, and that I got back on the Tube sated in body and mind.

This generous helping of rubbing elbows with literati was supplemented by my going to Bloomsbury and actually doing some research at the British Museum, just like a proper scholar.

And I also had one other literary adventure on this trip. I had also produced a book-length edition (never, alas, published except for some fragments) of some Romantic-era poetry, even before I had gotten going on the Amis project. This had led me to the discovery that there was something of a fight going on over a new standard edition of one of those poets. There was a Big Name Professor in America and a Big Name Professor in England on opposite sides. In the course of a year or so, I would meet the American. But while in the U.K., I had an exceedingly odd dinner with the Briton. I think he was going senile or mad or both, but he was still in the game at that point, and trying to recruit me for his faction. This, despite my making it plain that with my newfound focus on contemporary literature, I was now somewhat *hors de combat* when it came to the Romantic poet in question. I don't think my disclaimers made the least impression on him. Nor was literary factionalism all he was trying to recruit me for; despite his denunciations of certain academic rivals as "bum-boys," I could sense a definite disappointment when I mentioned that I was traveling with my wife, and even more when I made it plain that I was headed back to her immediately after my strictly business get-together with him.

It was thrilling to be among these people of literary achievement, and it was a heady thought that I might one day be their equal. (I certainly aspired to be as accomplished and celebrated as Amis and as Big a Professorial Name as my host the editor.) Of course, it was not going to happen, but I didn't know that then. It's fair to say that, because my anticipated glowing writing career misfired so badly, this couple of weeks turned out to have been the apex of my literary life, both for whom I was associating with and for what I was doing.

I and S. were playing tourist all the while, too. In among these literary activities, S. and I traveled all over England, courtesy of our BritRail Passes: Cornwall, Cambridge, and Edinburgh, Greenwich, York and generous helpings of London.

During all those travels, I continued from time to time to think of that *Dockland* song. It is a wondrous thing, because the melody, chords, and lyrics are so tightly integrated, and they all tell the same tale in the same way: that there is a lustrous beauty and consolation ("when I'm feeling down") in these industrial landscapes, similar to what Wordsworth would have found in a natural scene:

> *See, the harbor lights are winking far and wide*
> *Hear the water lapping at the old quayside*
> *See, where the oily swans are breeding*
> *There's a morning tide receding*
> *Leaving all the scrap metal clean*
> *It's a dockland scene*

In the first two lines, the melody moves downward in a minor chordal progression to the second "See," sung at the deliciously wrong E directly above the Eb which is the key, and when the lyrics turn to the "oily swans breeding," and it resolves down to the Eb, there's a burst of rightness that mirrors the quiet, inexplicable consolation that the song is all about. When the lyrics mention someone sounding a ship horn, the band's horns not only capture the pitches of a ship horn, but the sonority, and the whole strange gamut of feelings hearing one can evoke. Throughout, the song is full of strange, jazzy, exciting chords that underline the unexpected wonder of the harbor view.

As Wordsworth wrote in a very different context – and I'll have occasion to quote again later: "Bliss was it in that dawn to be alive." I was not going to feel that kind of bliss as a literary man ever again. But I would never forget it.

44

THROUGH THE HEAT

ETERNAL CARAVAN OF REINCARNATION, BY MICHAEL SHRIEVE, NEAL SCHON
& TOM RUTLEY, PERFORMED BY SANTANA (1972), ENCOUNTERED 1975

PLAYLIST TRACK No. 65

IN THE SUMMER of 1975, S. and I faced the necessity of moving: the one-bed-room student apartment in which we had lived for four years was now going to be too small, as we were expecting a baby in September. While we'd hoped that the move would take us to some other college town now that I'd earned my doctorate, no university had yet picked up my option.

So the move was bound to be within Baltimore. We had both budgetary limitations and ideas about how we wanted to live our lives that militated jointly against doing what the in-laws would have liked and moving to their suburbs. Our idea was to stay near the Johns Hopkins campus.

But it had to be a house now. And so we went looking in various dubious neighborhoods – for a couple of months, if memory serves. For the longest time we could find nothing affordable that wasn't also grim. Eventually, I forget how, we discovered 3035 Guilford Avenue, little more than two blocks away, a rowhouse with three bedrooms and a semi-finished basement to work in as well. It wasn't in bad shape, in fact, as I wrote at the time, "it is pleasant, airy, and gas-heated." The price was right.

I wrote to my mom and stepdad on July 5 that we had the place (I assume I'd just inked the rental contract). And we moved in August. Between those dates lay much making of arrangements and then the moving itself. And when I think of that time, there is always one image – except it's not merely visual – that comes into view. In my mind's eye, I'm walking that two-block long stretch of 31st Street separating our old and new residences, in blistering, shimmering, soul-annihilating heat.

And instantly, the song that comes to my mind is a song I was listening to then, Santana's *Eternal Caravan of Reincarnation*. It's an instrumental that starts with a generous helping of chirping-cricket sounds with a saxophone behind them (played by Hadley Caliman) making strange noises like some Middle Eastern horn. One is immediately transported to a desert oasis (crickets do live in deserts, among other places). Then, at 1:45, comes swaying music marked off by a bass figure (Tom Rutley plucking away) followed 15 seconds later by a shimmering phased electric piano (Wendy Hass), making one almost see the vibration of the air with the mirage effect, and clearly we are contemplating the arrival of camels in caravan, just as the title and the cover art suggest, through a desert haze. And although Carlos Santana does play some chords, the song from that point belongs to Hass and her shimmering piano. Never have I heard a number that so vividly conveys sheer atmospheric heat.

I may have been only myself, not a caravan, but that song is me, trudging through the blast of a Baltimore summer in that season of making ready for a change, and the walk was part of it, through that heat to the new house, perhaps carrying something as a caravan would. I was clearly making progress of some kind, despite impediments, despite not finding a job, despite being turned down even by local prep schools for positions teaching high schoolers. I had finished my dissertation, and I was going to be a father (of a daughter). Those were big things.

45

BAT'S SQUEAK

BLACK WATER, WRITTEN BY PATRICK SIMMONS, PERFORMED BY
THE DOOBIE BROTHERS (1974), ENCOUNTERED 1975

PLAYLIST TRACK NO. 66

WHAT WAS WRONG with this picture?, I should have asked myself as I contemplated the events I am about to discuss. If you had asked me at the time, I would have said, sincerely enough, that I was enjoying one of the happiest moments in the life of my new family, career difficulties notwithstanding. We had a darling daughter and a house, and I was working, at least a little, teaching one course of composition at Goucher College as adjunct faculty. I had a scholarly book coming out. Journals were publishing my articles. Surely my life was, if not a completely solved problem, at least a work in satisfactory progress.

Yet what happened happened. And it showed what it showed. And surely it showed, among other things, that the work of my life may not have been in such satisfactory progress.

I had to go to MLA, the annual meeting of the Modern Language Association, held each year in the week between Christmas and New Year's. Though there was lots of reading of papers and laying down and sniffing of academic spoor, the significance for me was that it served as the main marketplace for the employment of new English Ph.D.s. Once you knew when your doctorate would finish, you knew how to time your attendance. And I had known by the beginning of the 1974-75 academic year that I would receive mine at the end of it. That meant that my first MLA would be in 1974, and the second, if there had to be one, in 1975.

And, as it worked out, there had to be one. The 1974 meeting, at the New York Hilton, had yielded nothing. While I no longer can reconstruct and contrast what I did in the first year versus what I did in the second, I know that over two job seasons I sent out over 450 resumes, to colleges and universities in all 50 states, in pursuit of the jobs listed in an MLA circular; out of those I netted 14 interviews, two of which were "cattle calls" – simultaneous interviews with about a dozen candidates. And out of the remaining 12 interviews, only two seemed like serious prospects, one each year. The main prospect of 1974 was North Carolina State, and the great hope of 1975 was the University of New Mexico at Las Cruces.

In any event, the Doobie Brothers' song *Black Water* got all mixed up in my mind with the North Carolina State job, and then, by extension, with the whole desperate process. If you listen to the song, it certainly isn't about Raleigh; it's pretty clearly a New Orleans song. But it was Southern. To Northern young men of my generation, anything from the old Confederacy was foreign enough so you could kind of lump it together as Not The North. And what the lyrics of *Black Water* tell you is that the South is a mysterious, pulsing, lively place.

Well, if it rains, I don't care
Don't make no difference to me
Just take that street car that's goin' up town
Yeah, I'd like to hear some funky Dixieland
And dance a honky tonk
And I'll be buyin' ev'rybody drinks all 'roun'

I was ever so ready to get out of Baltimore and have some adventures, even in the Confederacy. Or, as of 1975, the great Southwest.

The only problem was, I had to get invited. And it began to look as if my last plausible set of chances at getting that invitation all came through MLA 1975 or not at all. I told myself that surely it would be all right, that surely someone as well qualified as I would make it through. I told myself that, but self-reassurance, like all reassurance, is flawed because no one actually knows the future. And I wasn't taking into proper account the potential for sheer bad luck that could so easily synergize with the lousy job market.

For it was a lousy job market, a very, very lousy job market. After an entire generation of smooth riding, the great English Lit Ph.D. juggernaut, fueled by postwar defense appropriations, had hit a stretch of washboard road. And my professors were in denial, and so was I.

I have said that MLA occurred the week between Christmas and New Year's. This ratcheted the discomfort up a little, because Christmases in my family had to be spent *en famille*, and since mine (as opposed to my wife's) was the only *famille* that celebrated Christmas, it followed that Christmas would be spent with mine. This was the ninth time since I'd left for college that I'd made this particular holiday pilgrimage, but the first with both a wife and a baby in tow. The first few Christmases I came back, I was flooded with anticipatory longing. But that feeling was largely a thing of the past by 1975.

I wish I had the descriptive gifts to make entirely plain why the holidays had become so difficult, but I guess this will have to do: my mom could not gracefully accept the limits between us that should naturally succeed the closeness of a parent and a young child. This problem had become chronic with the arrival of a wife who would naturally and correctly feel that she now had the greatest claim on my intimacy, and the advent of a baby who would in the normal course of things take up a lot of my time, effort, and emotional capital. If anyone had to keep score, my mother should have been and was demoted to third place in this ranking, and she would not always acquiesce in this. Later on, S., by then my ex-wife, would comment to my second wife that my mother had spoiled many Christmases for S. during our years together. This was close to the beginning of that ordeal for her. And I know I did not appreciate what I was putting her through as much as I should, being a) callow, b) stuck with divided loyalties, and c) human. But I wasn't entirely blind to it either.

I believe S. and my daughter stayed behind visiting in Ann Arbor while I flew off. Finances were tight and we were frugal, so my flight was solo.

So, full of resolve to locate that elusive job, I boarded a plane at Detroit Metro and flew west. And that's where the trouble started. Sitting next to me was an attractive Black businesswoman maybe two or three years older than I, clearly extremely pleased by her success to that point, a success signified by a condominium she owned, simply for the fun of it, in San Francisco. It very soon became apparent that she was checking me out for the role of "the fun of it."

She let me know at once that she was just going out there to relax. I told her I was out there to go to a meeting. She asked if I were planning to do anything besides the meeting, and I told her truthfully that I was hoping to do a little sightseeing (not having been in the town since I was four), but would have to fit it around my convention-going activities. She suggested we could do some sightseeing together, and added that it would be a shame if I were to travel all the way to this beautiful city, spend the whole time indoors, and then travel home again.

As the trip went on, she pressed me at least to visit her condo, which she assured me was close to a BART station, from which I could easily get to my hotel on Union Square. I reflected that I had no definite commitments that afternoon, apart from calling up and confirming a couple of interviews for the following day, the work of a few minutes if everything went right. So, after much urging, I agreed to visit her place en route to my hotel.

There's a lot I don't remember about that day, but I do remember ending up at her apartment in the early afternoon, on the second or third floor of a new building on a hill, looking out over some pleasant watery prospect. And I remember standing at the railing of her balcony, staring out at the view.

And I remember her standing very near to me, our forearms touching. Clearly, the way things were going …

But I wasn't a good Catholic boy for nothing, at least not then. As attracted as I obviously was, and as flattered as could be by this flirtation, I kept telling myself: If you fail to make that call to the interviewer because you're here with this woman, and then lose out on the job because you can't find the interview, you will never forgive yourself. And this reflection was particularly agonizing because it wasn't as if my missing the opportunity were guaranteed or even likely if I stayed; it was merely somewhat more possible. But considering all the years of effort I had put into getting to this last-ditch opportunity, I had to protect it, even if it meant –

Well, what did it mean? I wasn't giving up going to go to bed with this lady, was I? Because that was really not in prospect; I was a happily-married man, after all. That wasn't what happily-married men did, not in my book. Having however shakily resolved on that, I began making noises about having to go, now that I'd seen her nice condo.

Not that it was quite that neat; I think I kissed her, but not the lingering kind of kiss that signals bed – and I think I did it on the way out the door. Goodbye kisses were a little better, at least I hoped so.

She tried to make arrangements to get together the next day. I told her, truthfully, that I had to get to the hotel and see the lay of the land before

I could make any plans. This clearly dissatisfied her, but she did give me her phone number.

Walking away, I wondered whether I should be depressed or relieved. The BART stop was where she said it would be, and the trip into the city was uneventful.

I checked into the hotel, I made my calls, I checked my conference schedule, and there was indeed some touristing time available, not the next day but a day or two after that. I got out the slip of paper the lady had given me, and after a few minutes of arguing with myself, dialed the number on it. But there was no answer. Evidently I had blown my last chance with the lady by not making firm arrangements before leaving. No doubt she was on her way to wherever she went to find San Francisco companionship when flirtation on the plane didn't work. (Considering that she was in the *Tales of the City* town, I'm sure she had plenty of options.)

History will record that I did keep all of my interview appointments. It will record that I did every damn thing right. I listened to papers read, scouted out the new textbooks at the booksellers' displays, buttonholed people, and did what little networking I was capable of.

In fact, history will record that I only got away to play tourist the day the conference broke up. On the morning of Tuesday, December 30th, before heading back, I went exploring on my own. Without a rental car or any useful prior acquaintance with the city, I very sensibly put myself in the hands of the Gray Line, and got driven around in a tour bus for a couple of hours. The pictures I took establish that I did see Telegraph Hill and the Golden Gate Bridge and the old Mission, and the Japanese Tea Garden and big surf on the Pacific. By then I was past mixed emotions about the lady. I was in love with my wife, and in love with San Francisco.

I believe I returned to Ann Arbor, picked up my wife and daughter, and drove back. I could look them in the eye because "nothing had happened," and I could sincerely tell myself that nothing had ever been going to happen. And yet part of me knew that there was no way to be so certain. Had the woman made a more direct move than letting our forearms touch, had she answered the phone when I called, what then?

In *Brideshead Revisited*, Charles Ryder, the narrator, encounters his best friend's sister Julia, and sees her in a new light, especially when Julia asks him to light her cigarette. "[A]s I took the cigarette from my lips and put it in hers, I caught a thin bat's squeak of sexuality, inaudible to any but me."

This experience was my own bat's squeak. I might have experienced temptation in a way that was invisible to anyone else, but I knew now that I had a susceptibility. I might or might never act on it, but I had it.

What I did not have, it soon emerged, was a job. By the following January 28th, I knew I was not getting the job at Las Cruces. By the end of March, I knew I was not going to be getting an academic job anywhere. I can vividly recall the moment I understood without qualification that there was no English Department berth for me anywhere. I was standing in the kitchen of our house on Guilford Avenue, and I burst into tears, crying on S.'s shoulder. This was no matter of a few sobs and a few teardrops. This was wrenching and long-lasting. I don't think I cried like that again until my mother's death many years thence. I wrote to a friend at about the same time that I had been "knocked on my ass."

But when you're knocked on your ass, of course, there is ultimately only one thing to do, and that is to get up. And that is what I did.

46

WHO YOU KNOW

LIBBY, WRITTEN AND PERFORMED BY CARLY SIMON
(1976), ENCOUNTERED 1976

HOW DEEP IS YOUR LOVE, BY BARRY, ROBIN & MAURICE GIBB,
PERFORMED BY BEE GEES (1977), ENCOUNTERED 1977

PLAYLIST TRACKS NOS. 67, 68

SO: WHAT DO you do when almost everything you've achieved in your life has proven unmarketable? And you're 26?

Well, at that age curling up and dying isn't an option, particularly when you have a wife getting ready to go to law school and an infant daughter. On the contrary, there are two imperatives. The first priority is to find something remunerative to do, something that earns an adult income. And then you have to rethink everything. The second requires more time; it's a process of discovery.

Task One, the job search, had me knocking on a lot of doors, especially in Washington. I remember more than one hot day near the Mall or up in the Federal Triangle, my white shoes killing me, as I walked from federal office to federal office. I had taken the federal civil service exam (a Maryland one too) and researched job openings as best I could. But no matter where I filled out application forms or left my resume, I got nowhere. To the best of my recollection, nobody ever interviewed me for anything. I also tried my hand at journalism, and had some little bits of success. But what that brought in could never have been mistaken for an adult income.

That was the unbelievable thing: I had so much knowledge and still didn't know enough about how the world worked to land any kind of job interview. I grudgingly acknowledged at last a mantra of my father-in-law's: "It isn't what you know, it's who you know." (Yes, it should be "whom," I know. But that's the way he said it.) So I started thinking about the whos I knew.

One of the "whos I knew" was an administrative law judge with the National Labor Relations Board, my mother's oldest friend. ALJ Jo lived in Alexandria, Virginia, an hour away. I called her up on a Thursday and laid out my situation. She told me she'd see what she could do, and that I should call her back the following Monday. When I did, I found Jo had come through: she could make me either a parole officer in Northern Virginia or a court reporter in Washington. I had never heard of court reporters, and asked her what they did: make transcripts of legal proceedings, she said. That sounded pretty good to me, and then too Washington was closer than Northern Virginia. So I told her I chose that one. Fine, she told me, and promised to have the contact information the following day.

And indeed she did write me the following day, with word that the boss of this court reporting agency, Roy, was expecting me to call him. Things moved quickly after that. Roy was more than willing to see me. (I soon worked out that his company had the prime contract on reporting all administrative hearings of the National Labor Relations Board, and doing favors for the ALJs was a concept he was wide open to. It wasn't what you knew …) I visited his office on Seventh Street, SW. And, on May 18, 1976, a date I vowed never to forget, I walked out of the Reporters Building with my first grown-up job offer, to start in late summer. It wasn't at all what I had expected to be doing, but it was a respectable living wage. And that was enough for the moment.

While awaiting the beginning of my training, I paid heed to another parental prompting. There I was, the son of an economist teaching at a graduate business school, and I had never had the slightest training in either economics or business. I think it finally occurred to me that perhaps my inconveniently unworldly ways might have owed something to that deficit in my fund of knowledge. So I signed up for courses in both subjects at Towson State University, as it was then called. Introductory Econ and Bus Ad rubbed my nose in how little I knew – and delighted me with a flood of new insights into how the world worked. It was also nearly my first experience of higher education at a non-elite institution – and I liked it just fine. There was something about the lack of pretension that I found liberating.

Come the end of the summer, I was ready to start my court reporter training. The technology was called voicemasking or stenomasking, a technology so passé 40 years on it takes some effort to find on the Web a photograph on the Web of the essential item: a big plastic sound-deadening mask you draped over your mouth and nose. Inside the mask was a microphone into which you repeated (with stage directions) everything that was said in a legal proceeding. A wire would carry your voice feed to a tape recorder; later you'd use the resulting tape plus a backup live tape of the proceeding itself to produce a transcript. The central skill, talking while listening, took a week or two to master. I believe I was ready to go in about a month.

It was a strange job, sometimes exciting, sometimes boring and frustrating. I never got to take a trial (there were official court reporters for those) and only got to take a deposition once (because those required notaries, and no one invested in making me one), but I got to do practically everything else one could think of.

There were plenty of the NLRB hearings (fights over unionizing or de-unionizing workplaces). And those could take you anywhere: Norfolk, Baltimore, Scranton, Williamsport, sometimes even as far afield as Canton, Ohio (that hearing canceled on me after I drove a long way in a rented car in a snowstorm). Mike, the dispatcher, would say, in a whiny drawl: "Make like a bird and go to Pittsburgh," and off you'd fly, all travel paid, with a decent per diem. If you liked travel for its own sake, and sometimes I did, that was great. Of course, if your wife had commitments that were inconsistent with childcare, it could be a problem.

But it wasn't just NLRB; we had all kinds of federal agency hearings: FDA, FCC, Treasury, Postal Service. These were at all levels: from arbitrations to commission-level deliberations. Most of those were in Washington, though I remember one FCC matter that took me to Connecticut for three days.

The most interesting matters tended to be the grand jury proceedings; in those days all felony indictments in D.C., both federal and "state," were handled by Assistant United States Attorneys, sharp and larger-than-life young lawyers. You also got to see a panoply of all different sorts of cops (D.C. Metro, Park Police, Capitol Police, FBI, BATF, Secret Service, railroad police, postal police) and all sorts of bad guys, though never the bad guys they were trying to indict. I remember particularly one pimp who must have been testifying against some other bad guy; the pimp had an utterly magnetic personality. He was funny, appealing, charismatic. You could hardly help wishing you could have him as a friend.

And the government lawyers were frequently very interesting too, particularly when they worked out that I was the product of the kind of education that made me somewhat atypical – though I quickly learned that there was no typical, when it came to court reporters. (One of my colleagues, for instance, was Joyce Carr, a well-known Washington nightclub chanteuse; I have included a song of hers as No. 69 in the Playlist.)

Also, Washington could be exciting. It wasn't all shuttling on underground trains among Union Station, the Reporters Building, the Federal Triangle, and Judiciary Square. I was a runner then, and frequently would put on my running shoes to head up to the Mall for lunch hour; I can remember one snowy weekend day when I had the Mall and the Capitol to myself, and ran up the stairs, Rocky-style, breathing the chilly air in exultation. I could head over to the areas near the National Portrait Gallery for shopping at Hecht's and Garfinckel's. And at Union Station itself there was excitement in a huge installation, just opened for the Bicentennial in the main hall, a huge pit with an array of video screens that could work in tandem or separately to hawk the attractions of Washington to arriving tourists. I remember that the music which accompanied the show (I must have seen and heard it all dozens of times) was peppy and catchy, and included plucked bass notes that reverberated beautifully in the marble halls. And of course this was the dawn of the Jimmy Carter presidency, when, for a liberal like me, all things were being made new – or so it appeared.

At times I felt like saying: "Take that, Hopkins! I may not be teaching literature, but I'm out here in the big exciting world, so there!"

At the same time, it was very lonely work. You were seldom in the same place from one day to the next. You rarely saw your fellow-reporters except back at the company offices if you were transcribing grand jury notes (you weren't allowed to take them home, unlike notes from administrative hearings). And when doing that you were in a long dark gallery where people from sister companies, not even your own company, were likely to be your only neighbors. It took me away from my wife and daughter and plunked me down in a different city, either Washington or somewhere else, almost every day. And I would always be a functionary, never a star like the lawyers who strutted and preened and growled and fought. Not even like a witness. And, let's face it, going to Scranton or Allentown or Salisbury may have had some charms, but it was not glamorous traveling.

203

So I had Theme Songs for both moods.

For the more wistful one, there was *Libby*. One day in October of 1976, not too long after I'd started, after taking down the proceedings of a Food and Drug Administration toxicology conference on new animal drugs, I found myself in a record store on the Rockville Pike, and I picked up Carly Simon's latest album, *Another Passenger*.

As I've already partly disclosed, Simon had always seemed to me like a spokeswoman for my exact cohort. Well, my exact me, actually. When I'd been doubtful about getting married, she'd been doubtful about getting married. When I'd warmed up to the attached state, so had she (*I Haven't Got Time for the Pain*). And now she was getting restive and looking for escape to new climes. Well, so was I.

You could argue that though I probably thought *Libby*, an evocation of wanderlust, was about me, it really wasn't. And on the surface, you'd be right. Obviously, for a big star with serious money to get restive and want to visit another place was different from me wishing I *didn't* have to go to Scranton. Also, the song is very feminine: a man would not have written:

> *If all our flights are grounded,*
> *Libby, we'll go to Paris,*
> *Dance along the boulevards*
> *And have no one to embarrass,*
> *Puttin' on the Ritz in style*
> *With an Arab and an heiress.*
> *Libby we'll fly anyway.*

The attitude is feminine and privileged. Finally, the song is about friendship as well as escape. As Simon wrote on her website: "The song ... is about my relationship with a woman who used to be a very close friend. The hard times became funny in our mutual observation of them. We got each other laughing over the pain." I wasn't having friendship highs or lows.

At the same time, though, the obvious experience of recent pain Simon's lyrics evoke was mine as well, and the desire to run away. And in a way, the court reporting was running away too. Maybe Scranton or Norfolk or Dover weren't Paris, but then again they were not Baltimore, the scene of my humiliation, either. And if reporting wasn't the life I'd chosen or envisioned, it wasn't always so terrible.

That kind of thinking was what caused me to glom onto another Theme Song for the moments that felt better. That was *How Deep Is Your Love*, by the Bee Gees, from the *Saturday Night Fever* soundtrack. I can't tell you exactly when I first heard it (obviously shortly after September 24, 1977 when it was released), but I can tell you with great precision the moment it was permanently associated with a picture in my mind, about 8:30 a.m. on Tuesday, October 18, 1977. On that pleasant early fall day, I was driving along the eastbound approaches of the Bay Bridge, which leaps over the Chesapeake from the military, governmental, and sailing purlieus of Annapolis to Maryland's agricultural Eastern Shore. I was headed for an NLRB hearing in Easton, MD. As you move along those bridge approaches, the Bay appears to your right, and, if you can spare a glance from your driver's focus, you can frequently make out, over at your starboard, large vessels standing in the roads making towards or away from the Bridge. From your vantage point you are going quickly and those boats have all the time in the world. For some reason, that is a pleasing and calming prospect. And this was a nice clear morning, and there were the boats – and there were Bee Gees on the car radio.

Now it's reasonable enough to argue that the lyrics are not so peaceful, and betray the singer's insecurity in his woman's love.

And you may not think I care for you
When you know down inside that I really do
And it's me you need to show
How deep is your love? (how deep is your love?)
I really need to learn.

But the music simply overwhelms all that. The limpid splotches of Fender Rhodes piano reverb and the slowly-developing quiet harmonies of the singers' voices are all about the kind of all's-right-with-the-world security you can feel when you see the boats out in their channels, and you're off about your business. Impossible at a moment like that not to think of life as a gradually-unfolding adventure. I was going to make a transcript people depended on to reach decisions that governed their work lives. I was earning some real money

It may have had some impact on my affect at that moment that I was beginning to get ideas about the next stage for me. But that's a tale for a later chapter.

47

PARENTHOOD ON THE HOOF

GONNA FLY NOW (THEME FROM "ROCKY"), BY BILL CONTI,
LYRICS BY CAROL CONNORS & AYN ROBBINS, PERFORMED
BY MAYNARD FERGUSON (1977), ENCOUNTERED 1977

PLAYLIST TRACK NO. 70

RUNNING: THAT WAS the way I summoned joy and the way I expressed it in 1977. That year saw the dawn of the great jogging era, the publication of Jim Fixx's *Complete Book of Running*, and the first *Rocky* movie (well, to be technical, *Rocky* was released in December 1976). No one who ever saw that movie forgets The Scene: the one where Sylvester Stallone as Rocky goes out for a training run through the predawn streets of Philadelphia. The scene morphs into a montage of boxing training footage, but then returns at the end to Rocky's run, memorably topping off, literally and figuratively, looking eastward into the glow from the still-unrisen sun bathing the summit of the grand staircase in front of the Philadelphia Museum of Art, as Rocky flings his arms triumphantly into the air. All of this accompanied by Bill Conti's soaring, pulsing theme song *Gonna Fly Now*, periodically propelled by swells of strings that communicate to every listener the sheer transcendence running can produce.

The Scene probably bred far more runners than Jim Fixx ever did, and led many of us who had no business lacing up jogging shoes to try living that dream for a while.

And I was one of them. I have preternaturally tight hamstrings (which I kind of knew) and a tendency to disk degeneration (which I guess I didn't). Despite my body telling me there wasn't something quite right about it for me, I was out there on Baltimore's streets, and sometimes Washington's when business took me there, three times a week. I was to pay dearly for it; I consider my three later back surgeries as mostly necessitated by it.

But at the time the immediate effect was of sheer joy. The endorphin rush was real, and I got hooked on it. No matter that my life and career had veered wildly off course; I still had a way to feel great as my feet were guiding me around, say, the Guilford Reservoir a few blocks north of our house.

And of course as I did it, my breath got all rhythmic, and mentally I was singing songs to myself that went with the ragged pace of my breathing. Later running would involve Walkmen (Walkmans?), but those were a couple of years off yet. In a time before earbuds or even headphones, my own voice was the only portable sound source. And so voice it was.

And for jogging I couldn't hum just any song to myself. Only certain songs had that power to make you run. *Gonna Fly Now* was, predictably, a regular feature of my under-the-breath playlist. In the Maynard Ferguson version, that is. Though I saw the movie when it came out (who didn't?), it was not really the Bill Conti soundtrack version I knew. Ferguson, a jazz trumpeter of formidable power and control, was never above jazzifying what was new and hot in the world of pop music. And frequently he moved as fast as the pop charts did. To choose the obvious instance, the release of his version of *Gonna Fly Now* was effectively simultaneous with the release of the Bill Conti original.

This adaptation was everything you could want in a 1970s running song: pulsing disco beat and soaring fills and solos by Ferguson that took the melody to nosebleed-inspiring heights.

I don't expect anyone would disagree that Ferguson's adaptation outshines Conti's original. Whereas Conti relied on strings and a wall of sound to add the sense of lift and elation, and this does work, Ferguson's soaring solos are simply gutsier, more powerful, and more musically inventive ways to stimulate the same emotions. They are more in keeping with the dynamic of Conti's own melody than what Conti does with it. Something about the song just calls out for a reach to the upper registers, which Conti does not do much but Ferguson does a lot – goes all the way up to three As above Middle C. And not timidly: explosively, warbling at the heights.

Of course, what Ferguson could do with one of his custom-designed trumpets was far more impressive than anything I could have sung, even if I hadn't been running, with my non-custom-designed voice. But no one else ever was intended to hear me, or did. So I was happy.

I vividly recall one run with that number on my lips, the day my first son was born in June of 1977. For medical reasons, this was a scheduled birth. We went into the hospital early in the day and by the afternoon, after a suspenseful, impatient wait in the lobby, I was holding my son in my arms. And next I left his mother to sleep for a while, drove home and – went for a run.

I'm now the father of three wonderful adults, and I've learned there's no accounting for anything in the feelings of parents. But whatever the reasons, this was the most euphoric I ever was over the arrival of a child. I felt – I don't know – limitless, transcendent, as if I were floating rather than running.

It was a very good moment, one I shall always treasure.

48

A HALF DAY

THE SEVEN TIN SOLDIERS, BY PAPA DEE ALLEN, HAROLD BROWN,
B.B. DICKERSON, LONNIE JORDAN, CHARLES MILLER, LEE OSKAR,
AND HOWARD SCOTT, PERFORMED BY WAR (1977), ENCOUNTERED 1978

PLAYLIST TRACK NO. 71

I STILL POSSESS carbon copies of the green daily report sheets I used to turn in to record my engagements as a court reporter. The sheet for Thursday, May 4, 1978 reflects a "Half Day" in the Superior Court grand jury room down below Washington's Judiciary Square. About mid-day, someone had reported there was a call for me (a rare thing), and when I got on the phone, it was my wife. "Honey, you better come home," she said. The way people say things like that, you immediately know someone has died. "What's happened?" I asked, wondering who among our vast network of family and our narrower network of friends might have left us. S. did not want to say, but eventually she let me know: it was Emile, my father. And so home I came.

I was astounded. At 28, I didn't know anyone who had lost a father, and I'd seen mine in February. In fact, I'd spoken with him in the preceding week. And when I thought about that call, my heart sank, not because of what had been said, but because of what hadn't.

I had not lived with my father since I was five. Along the way, as must happen when parents go their separate ways, someone got shortchanged on the intimacies and joys of parenthood. My father had drawn that short straw. But as I grew up and especially as I married and became a parent in my own right, my dad had begun to regain some ground. I was proud of and grateful for my father, an educated, accomplished and reflective man, endlessly able to help me understand complicated political and economic matters. I was trying to be more like him, which obviously wasn't going to happen while I was working as a court reporter. So I was putting in motion various plans to move on. (Applying to law school, buying a new house, putting a novel I'd written into the hands of a typist so I could try to publish it.)

But when I'd seen him in February, those plans were still in fairly rudimentary shape. The disparities were on display, when we'd met up at Union Station in Washington on a Friday as I was coming off work in the grand jury (taking down other people's words) and he was coming from a conference of government policy-makers at which he'd been a speaker (having people listen to his words). The two of us had ridden up to Baltimore on the last car of a train, right at the back, watching as the right-of-way receded behind us and the sun sank low in the west. It had been a moment of quiet intimacy, flavored by the half-and-half nature of my achievements thus far. I knew he sympathized greatly with me for my becalmed career, and shared my hope that I would move on. On the plus side, I had two lovely children to present to him, and a house purchase under contract. But I had not yet completed the law school application, and was still not clear in my own mind that law school was what I wanted to do.

I know he was warmly appreciative of what I did have to offer. He'd written me and my wife in early January: "Every time I am with you I am surprised how much I enjoy the parental role. It is one I've rarely exercised, and one I did

not suppose was particularly congenial. Yet I seem to get increased pleasure from it." Well, maybe you had to know him to recognize that this was effusive praise; trust me on this.

To all appearances he had been still bursting with life. After that February encounter (and it kills me that I have not the slightest recollection of our final goodbye on the Sunday after that train trip), he had gone back with my stepmother Etta down to San Miguel de Allende, Mexico, where the two of them maintained a winter home. In a late letter, he'd enclosed a trio of photos, all taken, I believe, at the Instituto Allende, the art college, where I think he was taking a class. On the back of the photo of him in the sombrero, beaming in the garden in the bright sunlight, he had written "Lush, eh?" Clearly this was a man still full of curiosity and excitement.

Yet he was also a diabetic with a related heart condition, and in the end, that was what won. On the morning of that May 4, less than two weeks after his seasonal return from Mexico, he suffered a heart attack, and died in the hospital shortly thereafter. Gone before I knew there was a problem. Oh, I knew he suffered from diabetes, but I didn't really know what that was, I was so young and ignorant.

I'd spoken with him the last time, I think, the Saturday or Sunday before. To this day, I feel terrible about that call. My offer of a place in the University of Maryland School of Law had been in hand about two weeks at that point; I had just made up my mind to accept. (I think I mailed out my intent to attend the day after the call.) But when Dad phoned in, I had been working feverishly to finish typing the transcript of an extended hearing about union issues at a company that made fire alarms and security equipment. I'd been called up to answer the phone from my typewriter in the basement and was eager to get back. I fielded it in the wall phone in the kitchen without sitting down. I did not volunteer any information about this momentous change I was about to go through, and my dad did not ask, though he knew I had an application in. I would very much have wanted him to know about all this, but I was too caught up in my preoccupations of the instant to share it, be it ever so important. And then suddenly it was too late.

That is what death is: the too-late machine; it stamps out a point beyond which nothing can be improved or made right.

We coped medium-well with our losses. Quakerdom and academia did their unimpressive best to memorialize the man, at a memorial service attended mostly by members of my parents' Friends meeting and my dad's Columbia department. No one said anything much; I vividly recall the chair of the department, a man named Boris, trying to think of something piquant to say, making some idiotic remark about the exotic airline bag my dad would carry. My stepmother and I nearly quarreled about my inheritance – friction

I swear to this day I did nothing to create or exacerbate, though I did feel I was due something. She acknowledged her moodiness in a note, but of course we were all moody then. (And almost immediately that inheritance had a major influence on my life, making it possible for me to transfer from night school to day school before the school year started.)

So I was left to mourn in my own way, in the midst of a house move and in the midst of a huge change in my life.

A record I had on loan from the Towson Library when all this struck was WAR's *Galaxy* (1977). WAR was a crew of mostly Black Angeleno musicians who had been assembled originally to back up a White Brit, Eric Burdon, late of The Animals. But Burdon had split from the group, which had gone on to forge several hits of its own, relying on such things as a weird combination of funk and Latino sound, as well as the unique combination of sax and harmonica playing together as a brass section. And this would prove to be the last album made under the WAR name by that core group. The last song of the last album by this group was a powerful 14-minute tour-de-force which for my money always seemed elegiac in the extreme.

The title is *The Seven Tin Soldiers*, and there is something a little march-y about it, and I'd assume that the Soldiers are the seven members of WAR marching along, so this seems to be a musical group portrait of them at the very end of their time together. But despite the egalitarian name, the song belongs to the harmonica player, Lee Oskar, who wrote the melodies that hold the song together, and whose solos dominate the song. The principal melody is funky and mournful – and increasingly virtuosic as the piece proceeds. And I found I could sort of play along with it. I was using a chromatic harmonica and Oskar was using diatonics (which I did not then know how to play), but still I could chime in with most of it. Our new house had a sunroom with a western exposure, and there I stood, one afternoon shortly after my father had died and we had moved in and my life was all jumbled up beyond recall, with the light of the dying day filtering in through the tree outside, tears welling up as I wailed through a requiem for my father with the instrument I knew best how to play. And in the last three minutes, the chorus of Scott and Dickerson and Allen and Miller would rise in the background and propel the song and me to a height of emotion that nothing else could express.

49

SOMETHING I WAS GOOD AT

BIRDLAND, MUSIC BY JOE ZAWINUL, WORDS BY JON HENDRICKS,
PERFORMED BY THE MANHATTAN TRANSFER (1979),
ENCOUNTERED 1979

PLAYLIST TRACK NO. 72

THE SONG BIRDLAND, which evoked the long-gone first (52nd Street) edition of a great jazz venue, was like no song I had heard before. The moment I first encountered it (listening to WEAA, the Morgan State University radio station, one winter morning in late 1979), I sensed I was in for layers of unpacking.

It was a picture of a jazz club where everyone that mattered played, and I didn't really know who any of them were:

Bird would cook, Max would look – where?
Down in Birdland
Miles came through, 'Trane came too – there
Down in Birdland
Basie blew, Blakey too – where?
Down in Birdland
Cannonball played that hall – there
Down in Birdland
Yeah

This pantheon-by-nickname evocation of Black jazz stars, most of whose names, let alone nicknames, were unknown to me then, was a challenge and a signpost. A White guy raised mainly on pop and rock (as this book attests), I could hear these words and realize I how far I still had to go in my musical basic training.

And then there was the "vocalese" aspect of the song: lyrics written and sung to follow the scattered notes of a jazz instrument. That was a new one on me too. (Later I would come to know of Jon Hendricks, the lyricist, vocalese wordsmith par excellence, and, in 2004, I would actually watch him sing and shake hands with him in a Paris nightclub, as pictured below.)

But I had to start learning about this.

I knew also that the music came from Weather Report, a jazz-rock fusion band at least as White as it was Black, and that the song was not itself the kind of jazz it praised. Much, then, to learn about fusion.

And finally, it wasn't being performed by Weather Report, either, but by this quartet called The Manhattan Transfer, who had had themselves drawn on the album cover as a series of angular tops, and photographed on the back of the sleeve as some kind of space cadets from the future. I was going to have to learn about them too, because they clearly were dedicated to reviving and expanding various musical styles I didn't even know the names for, but wanted to hear more of.

To be sure, all that homework would be fine by me. By then I was doing plenty of homework, anyhow, and none of it fazed me. I had found something I was really good at and really liked: the law. It was worth working for, just as great music was.

I had been through graduate school, and the ways it had affected me, mostly bad, have already been discussed in these pages. Law school was, for me, the un-grad school. It wasn't pretentious, it followed more or less rational rules, and the work I did was every bit as challenging to the mind as that I'd done in graduate school, but it paid off in mastery of usable concepts, concepts that worked together. One accepted metaphor for this coordination of the various branches of the law is "the seamless web." But the tight four-part harmony of the Manhattan Transfer would have been closer to the mark.

Harmony also characterized the friendships I was making. My small section was full of interesting people; the study group many of us in that section formed were like brothers and sisters, and stayed close for many years after law school.

Best of all, this exercise was heading me toward employment. No more being an out-of-work Ph.D.; this story was obviously going to end differently. They told us in the orientation session that we should avoid paid work during our first year, and I ignored them. I needed the money, and, even more, I needed the feeling of being hands-on.

My first job was reading and commenting on criminal trial transcripts for a poverty lawyer with a distinguished background as a Communist who had been disbarred in McCarthy times, and then rehabilitated as the hysteria receded. Then, sometime during or right after the second semester, I started working as a law clerk for a couple of downtown litigators, and began to learn the mechanics of a litigation practice: drafting papers, going to court, serving process, billing, office procedures. And by the time I heard *Birdland*, I had received two semesters' worth of grades, knew I was near the top of the class, and had written my way onto the law review. Best of all, I had received an offer of employment over the summer of 1980 from what many members of the Baltimore legal community regarded as the classiest firm in town.

Nor was even that all the good news. I had assembled pieces of my father's last book and just had it accepted by Praeger Publishers, and was continuing to place bits of my own writing in published locations, like my college alumni magazine. I was still a writer.

Not to mention father of two, husband of a woman about to enter law practice herself, and homeowner.

It would have been impossible and inhuman to avoid some degree of hubris at this juncture, and I was never very good at the impossible. I was feeling I could beat the world at long last. And the Transfer's exhilarating tight, jazzy harmony which had bored its way into my brain almost on contact was the perfect background music for that buzzy hubristic high.

50

AWOL

CHASE THE CLOUDS AWAY, WRITTEN BY CHUCK MANGIONE,
PERFORMED BY THE CHUCK MANGIONE QUARTET AND
AN ORCHESTRA (1978, RELEASED 1979), ENCOUNTERED 1981-82

PLAYLIST TRACK No. 73

WHEN I FELT that rush of law school success, about the first thing I did with my hubris was have my first extramarital fling.

When I started writing about this, I expected to begin with a grave acknowledgment of wrongdoing. But then I deleted the mea culpa; it wasn't true to what I'd felt then or feel now, sorry as I am for the pain it ended up causing others. The closest I can truthfully come is to say that I only behaved this way at one discrete point in my life, have not done it since, and would not do it now. And that's partly because what I did and where it took me and who it made of me taught me unforgettably the destructive power of such behavior. You want to take a wrecking ball to your marriage, screw around.

The thing was, I was then in a marriage that needed demolition. Again, I say this with no disrespect to my former wife; it was just a fact about us. And I think, though I consciously denied it, I already recognized that fact, deep down, and that's partly why I did what I did. Of course, simply being horny and in my early thirties played its role as well.

Call it my late-blooming Rumspringa. I'd largely blown my chance at the freedoms of the Sexual Revolution during my college years, and I was coming late to adultery. I knew this from the enormous body of literature and film that existed then glorifying infidelity, or at least making it seem not so bad. (See, for instance: *Portnoy's Complaint* (1969), *Bob and Carol and Ted and Alice* (also 1969), *The Joy of Sex* (1972), *Open Marriage* (also 1972), *Fear of Flying* (1973), *The Road Less Traveled* (1978), and *Thy Neighbor's Wife* (1980).) I'd read or seen it all, with increasing envy. I'd been good for so long.

And so, at the end of 1980, I gave myself permission. I didn't do anything immediately. The car stayed parked, as it were. Just releasing those brakes was enough for a little while.

But come the new year, my freedom stopped being just theoretical, thanks to a married secretary at the big law firm where I was working my last year of law school. She was the aggressor, giving me a copy of *The Delta of Venus* and telling me her panties got wet looking at me. And even with all that, I was actually kind of slow in the uptake. So we staged quite a courtship of a strange sort, mainly conducted over lunches in fast food restaurants (which is what law students and secretaries could afford), before we actually got down to business. But after one get-together she wanted no more (I believe owing to issues in her marriage, not the bedroom). I was hurt, I was frustrated, but I was not deterred.

I was not deterred because I had already crashed through the guardrail. None of my training could stop me now. I remember that at the very moment of entering the lady, I felt a sense of stepping off a diving board though unable to see any pool, of terrifying transgressiveness. Having gone ahead and stepped off anyway, and not died (for I didn't die, just got my pride bruised when she turned me away after that first encounter), it was much easier to come back and do it again, even with someone else.

Shortly thereafter I started a short relationship with someone single I'd picked up at a library but I was too married to be interesting to her for long. And then I lost my sense of discretion, and started quite publicly pursuing numerous women in my immediate environment. I became heedless of what people would think and say. I betrayed no judgment as to how my female friends would react to being hit on by me. I forever lost one of my best friends because of my persistence in the face of her gentle rebuffs, a loss I still hate to think about. Word of my indiscretions preceded me; one law school colleague, at a law school graduation party, shamed me by telling me in so many words – before I had done anything yet – that she knew I was working up to propositioning her (she was right about that), and not to bother.

In mid-July of 1981, I had a meeting with a federal district judge whose intended law clerk, due to have started the next month, had just unexpectedly reneged on his commitment. The judge, always direct if not necessarily always complimentary, told me that I was the best "blue chipper" he could get at this short notice to take the job, clearly implying that, good as I might be, I had betters who had proved their betterness by having landed offers already. This evident limited regard was to set the tone of our relationship; I still signed on with him, because he was a federal district judge, and a very well-respected one at that.

Working for the judge slowed down my campaign to go AWOL from my marriage. When, in mid-August, I reported for work at the federal courthouse on Baltimore's West Lombard Street, even I had the savvy to understand that frank and open licentiousness would be the wrong style. I guess I was worried that the notoriously upright judge would find his initial assessment of me confirmed if he learned of my loose ways.

So I think there was only one woman, a fellow-clerk, with whom I allowed myself to be at all indiscreet, and she would have none of me. (I'm old enough now so most of my colleagues only know me from my conventionally virtuous years that followed; she can still remember, and I'm sure it came to her mind when we would meet professionally, my unrequited lurch in the direction of misbehavior in the back halls of the courthouse.) There was also an assistant public defender we'll call Antonia with whom I had a friendship, but I never tried to make anything more of it.

Instead, I tried for a while to become a philosopher and theorist of infidelity. I was still at a point where I had a notion I could affirm both a marriage and departures from it, though there was absolutely no denying the tension between these apparently antithetical things. With the benefit of legal and literary sophistication, I could liken that tension to the conflicts of interest built into most legal undertakings, including the fundamental one between the lawyer's desire to serve his own interests, for instance in maximizing fees, and his commitment to serve the client, or between the lawyer's commitment to humanitarian goals and the lawyer's allegiance to the client's goals, which are seldom humanitarian.

I actually started a novel called *Conflicts of Interest* to dramatize my thoughts about these intertwined subjects. It was much better written than my high school novel or even my grad school novel had been, and I finished a first draft of it after the time I am writing of here. But I was never able to make a second draft complete. The themes did not work out; I couldn't work them out in my head — because, of course, I couldn't work them out in my life.

But Antonia, the assistant public defender, though in real life I never tried to lay a finger on her, inhabited the pages of my book, her character exemplifying a purity of legal purpose, and sexual promise and availability.

I placed the climactic sex scene between her and the hero, a married judicial law clerk, in the house of a friend of mine in Baltimore's Federal Hill. There may have been parts of my book that were inadequately imagined, but not this scene. I knew exactly, from well before I wrote it, what the characters would do, and what they would say — and what music I wanted playing when, later on, someone made a movie of it.

That song would be *Chase the Clouds Away*, performed by Chuck Mangione and his band along with a seventy-piece orchestra, the third track in a 1979 two-cassette set called *An Evening of Magic: Chuck Mangione Live at the Hollywood Bowl*. Notwithstanding all the uplifting strings, the song is really a dialogue between Mangione, playing crunchy chords on the electric piano, and Chris Vadala, a redoubtable reed man, here playing piccolo, flute, and especially a throaty alto flute, in a melody that presents half-step intervals as near-octaves as it zigzags upwards by unpredictable steps, and takes occasional brief forays from minor into major. It is a shame that this performance was not captured on film as well as on tape, but one can get a decent sense of what the dialogue at the heart of it must have looked like with a video showing Gerry Niewood holding down the Vadala role about 15 years later. What you hear, whether on tape or on video, is a song that is all longing and throb, thrusting upwards to several climaxes: true makeout music, except that somehow it conveys something stronger and more insistent than merely the passion of two people writhing on a couch, great as that may be.

In other words, it conveys that longings are important, and their satisfaction powerful and healing. It chases the clouds away.

And in 1981-82 I frequently played that song in my office on a boom box that the judge hated but mostly held his tongue about, as I typed up proposed opinions for him to issue. And as I did, I thought about the love scene I would write for that music.

What became of my own effort to dispel the clouds will be the subject of the next few chapters.

51

SUPERMAN

SUPERMAN LOVE THEME, BY JOHN WILLIAMS, PERFORMED BY
JOHN WILLIAMS AND THE BOSTON POPS (1980), ENCOUNTERED 1982

PLAYLIST TRACK NO. 74

WHEN MY FATHER died, I inherited all of his photographs, and within a few years I started trying to organize them. One summer's day I sat down with my stepmother to ask her about some people I couldn't identify in the photos. There was one black-and-white, obviously taken in the Fifties, of an attractive women in a calf-length summer dress, standing beside what looked like a driveway in the country in the bright sunlight. "Did you know who she was?" I asked. Etta, my wise stepmother, paused for a moment, and then, looking and sounding her most European, she said, "You know, Jack, when a marriage is in trouble, there are always affairs." She shared only a few more details. The woman in the picture was named Gertrude; she had been my father's translator as he drove around Austria in 1953, spreading American aid money. And evidently she had been something more as well. And, in keeping with Etta's aphorism, my parents did in fact go their separate ways at the end of that year.

My stepmother spoke truly, and the converse of her aphorism is true as well: when there are affairs, the marriage is always in trouble. Sometimes you just don't know it yet.

In 1982, I didn't know it yet. As I wrote in the preceding chapter, the judge for whom I clerked (until midsummer of that year) ran a straitlaced and businesslike chambers, and that kept my extracurricular activities in check. The firm I went to after that was exactly the opposite and would have exactly the opposite effect on me.

Things might have been a little different. Before going to work for the judge, I had been on a path to conventional BigLaw, as it's called these days; the firm that I'd clerked for between first and second years of law school had offered me a job, but we could never get together on timing and terms. Meanwhile this other firm (let's call it Funhouse, P.A.) was keenly interested in me. I knew it was different; I didn't realize how different for a while.

Many high-class firms have former Assistant U.S. Attorneys fronting their litigation departments, but mostly in those outfits, the former AUSAs have moved from prosecuting bad guys to defending big economic interests that mostly play by the rules (even if they have an alarming role in framing the rules first). A fair number of the former AUSAs at Funhouse – and the firm was stacked deep with that kind of talent – had gone instead from prosecuting bad guys to defending them. Along with more conventional, and conventionally virtuous, clients, the lawyers at Funhouse attended to the legal needs of well-off criminals, politicians with questionable lives, rich people getting divorced, psychopaths who ran businesses in shady ways and had the short temper and sense of entitlement that always went with it, tax dodgers, and people who ran savings-and-loan associations into the ground (a particularly common form of misbehavior at that moment in the history of American finance).

Of course, being comfortable with disreputable clients is no discredit; it's when their qualities begin to rub off that the problems come. And there was some rubbing off at Funhouse. (Although to be honest, looking back from forty years later, it's amazing how many of these lawyers went the other direction and grew more integrity as they went on.)

When I got to Funhouse, I think it's fair to say it was the most talented group of litigators ever assembled under one roof in Baltimore, and at the same time the largest cast of prima donnas, psychopaths – and horndogs. These distinctions were not unrelated.

For instance, rumor had it that the junior lawyer I had been brought in to replace had been let go because his sexual intrigue with a client had ended up compromising the representation in some way; I never learned the details, even though I took right over with the same client, or, more precisely, group of clients. But I was given to understand that it wasn't the intrigue that caused his departure, but the difficulty the intrigue happened to cause.

By contrast, one lawyer I was working with was known to be cheating on his wife with many of the attractive young women who were just then finally entering the profession in significant numbers. The partner's rumored play-mates were Funhouse's associates, adversary counsel, and law clerks, as well as the more traditional quarry for libidinous male lawyers: secretaries, court reporters, and courthouse personnel. Within the usages of that pre-#MeToo time, he must have treated them pretty well, because I kept track of many of them, and I never heard a single one say an uncomplimentary word about him later.

Not so with another lawyer I spent significant time working for; he was known to the women in the firm as someone to stay away from because the passes he would make at them would be pronounced, odious, and unwelcome.

An associate of mine was an open devotee of the strippers on The Block, Baltimore's row of adult bars; a junior partner was a closeted one. Another colleague of mine, a legendary cocksman, wandered into and out of a marriage while we were at Funhouse, never, so far as I could tell, altering his promis-cuous ways much.

I think the sex was not sought so much for itself as for an expression of our sheer importance in the universe. It was an era of Jaguars and trophy offices and getting photographed walking out of the federal courthouse with rich and powerful malefactors. One partner stated the philosophy very starkly one day when we were getting on a train coming back from a deposition in Newark where I had carried his bags. (We were representing some people who had sold the same hotel twice, much to the ultimate inconvenience of both sets of buyers.) We made for the club car where we ordered martinis. I tried to pay for mine and he waved his hand impatiently, saying something like: "No, Jack, the clients pay for it. They want us drinking on them." And out came the partner's credit card (and I have no doubt the charge appeared on the next monthly client bill.)

As for me, then, it was a case of monkey see, monkey do. In fact, I followed in my predecessor's footsteps and had a relationship with someone from the very same client group in which my predecessor had reportedly started the liaison that got him in trouble. I still would have said I loved my wife and wanted to protect my children, but I also wanted to walk with the big guys. For the most part, they were superlative lawyers, if not always great successes as human beings. And, smart as I was, I had begun to lose the ability to distin-guish between what I should be imitating and what I should not. I couldn't afford a Jag at that point (a yellow Corolla was more my speed) but I could have little flings, the way the big boys did.

Looking back, it seems to me these outings weren't even that much fun. The women I got involved with all pushed back against the limits I tried to set. One tried to trap me in a blizzard so I would have to be stuck with her for a day or two rather than going home to my family. Another told me pointedly on a getaway weekend that she was tired of having me talk about my home life. Another one willingly accompanied me to a night of dancing while I was away at a seminar in New York City, and then made herself so unpleasant on the train back we didn't want to see each other again. And I don't blame a one of them. They were only looking out for their own needs, and I'm sure I was no more fun than they were.

I don't think I was doing it for how good it actually felt. No, I was looking at a theoretical picture. And in that theoretical picture I was practicing law at a high level, reaping some of the rewards and prestige associated with it, and part of that system of rewards was the occasional bit of fun on the side, the sort of thing a morally sophisticated person condones.

And yes, in retrospect my rationalizations were fatuous. But while the illusion lasted, it was an ecstatic thing, no matter how miserable the realities.

There was a piece of music from that era that expressed it beautifully for me, the *Superman Love Theme*, from the Christopher Reeve/Margot Kidder epic that hit the screen in 1978. That was one of eight orchestral pieces packaged by the composer, John Williams, in a 1980 release, *Pops in Space*, featuring Williams at the helm of the Boston Pops, his home base from that year, as he succeeded Arthur Fiedler as its director. I bought the record in 1981 or 1982. I would play that record and feel good about what I was up to.

At this point, Williams was really hitting his stride as the ne plus ultra of American film composers. And this piece, an utter gem of orchestration, remains for me the best expression ever of the sheer wonder of love. It runs in the movie as Superman appears on the balcony of Lois Lane's apartment, dines with her, and then takes her for a flight. At first she is apprehensive, but soon discovers she is safe floating above Metropolis through Superman's magic. The scene in the movie is scored a little differently, heavier on brasses and strings, and definitely more playful and less languorous than the concert version. I prefer the concert version from my 1980 record; the sweetness of the music is to die for, as the theme is first introduced by the oboe and nurtured by the woodwinds before being released to the whole orchestra. In both versions, but especially in the concert version, Williams provides a musical metaphor for that wonderful dream we've all had sometime, in which we learn to fly. And that dream is in turn a serviceable metaphor for the erotic ecstasy of Superman and Lois.

That was also how I wanted to think of myself then: freed from the bonds of conventional morality, accompanying professional success with sexual release, floating high above everything.

Of course, there is no Superman and no Lois. I wasn't really having such a good time. And what I was helping to do to my family (however necessary I still believe it was) did not bear thinking of.

I was about to wake up on the ground.

52

Nightmare Time

WHO, WHAT, WHEN, WHERE, WHY, BY RUPERT HOLMES, PERFORMED BY THE MANHATTAN TRANSFER (1978), ENCOUNTERED 1983

IT'S NOT THE SPOTLIGHT, BY GERRY GOFFIN AND BARRY GREENBERG, PERFORMED BY THE MANHATTAN TRANSFER (1978), ENCOUNTERED 1983

SUBSTITUTE TRACKS NOS. 75, 76

IN ADDITION TO that wonderful dream we all have in which we find we can fly, there's another dream we all have: the one where we confidently go somewhere to do something, but then realize we haven't done it and can't find our way back to where we started. I may have dreamt that first dream, but it never came true for me. The second one did.

My affairs hadn't brought nirvana, but they (and other things not to be discussed here) had brought our marriage to a state of mutual anger. I had more than a passing disposition to anger anyway, at that age. But one thing I hadn't realized, a thing that came as a shock to me, was that you couldn't take anger off like a suit that you wanted to change. The bargain I'd made with myself at the beginning of all my running around was that anytime I wanted to I could always turn around and rejoin my life's earlier course. But when I decided I wanted to, I found anger was blocking that path back.

My mind could not cope with this. Looking today at notes I'd written to myself at that stage, I see the starkest evidence of disordered thinking, of my ideas running in endless circles that cannot be stopped, cannot reach resolution.

I was bewildered. I had come to an impasse I was clueless how to handle.

And while I was stewing, I was listening to the Manhattan Transfer's album *Pastiche* (1978). (After the Transfer's 1979 album *Extensions*, of which I've already written in Chapter 49, had made such a hit in the household, we gradually acquired and gotten to know the other, earlier albums.) There were two tracks right next to each other that nailed where I was.

One was a cover of Rupert Holmes' *Who, What, When, Where, Why*, from his 1976 album *Singles*. The singer of this song of sexual jealousy looks obsessively for what brought him and his beloved to this pass, to the roots of the situation.

You won't be my love
You won't be my friend
But won't you at least help me comprehend
What's happening to me?
'Cause after you go
My one consolation will be to know
The places and names, the reason and rhymes
The facts of the matter and points in time.
I tried for your love
But you won't allow
This guy to do nothin' but ask you how –
And – who (who)
What when where why (why)?
Who is the guy?
What made you need someone new?
Tell me
Who what when where why?
When did it die?
When'd we go wrong?
Don't you lie, tell me why —

It's not that this interrogation was precisely applicable to our situation, but it did precisely apply to my mood. I knew how things were supposed to go, and if they weren't doing that, there had to be an explanation, and I was going nuts trying to find it.

The other song, *It's Not the Spotlight* (by Gerry Goffin and Barry Greenberg), captured my sense at the time that, while my wife and I might be on paths away from each other, something might make it possible for us to reconverge at some point:

> *If I ever feel the light again shinin' down on me*
> *I don't have to tell you how welcome it will be*
> *I felt the light before but I let it slip away*
> *I still keep on believin' it'll come back someday.*
> *It's not the spotlight, it ain't the candlelight*
> *And it ain't the streetlight of some old street of dreams*
> *It ain't the moonlight or not even the sunlight*
> *But I've seen it shinin' in your eyes and you know what I mean*

Of course, this is a breakup song, and nonetheless all the talk about shining lights raises metaphorically the possibility of reuniting. But it also suggests that the reunion would be at the cost of subsequent relationships:

> *If I ever feel the light again, you know things will have to change*
> *Names and faces, homes and places will have to be re-arranged*
> *And you can help me come about, if you're ever so inclined*
> *Ain't no rhyme or reason why a woman can't change her mind.*

And we even hadn't broken up, not yet, so what this reminded me of, with awful vividness, was the cost of a breakup. And of course that terrible notion was beginning, just beginning, to insinuate itself into my mind.

It was a nightmare time.

53

A BREAK IN THE CLOUDS

CAVERNA MAGICA (... UNDER THE TREE - IN THE CAVE ...),
BY ANDREAS VOLLENWEIDER (1983), ENCOUNTERED 1983

PLAYLIST TRACKS NOS. 77, 78, 79, 80, 81

I COULD NEVER have been morose all the time, any more than I could have been happy all the time. When you're young(ish) and you have your health and you have interesting work and there are people out there who like you, you're not likely to spend all your time moping. And this held true for me even at a point when there was a big problem with my marriage.

One of the things that certainly had that benign effect on me was getting my first computer.

Things have moved so quickly in the last forty years that telling this story forces me to invoke ghosts of technology the reader may not even have heard of. But it can't be told otherwise.

Back in 1980, computers were owned by companies and governments. Working at a computer meant sitting at a terminal and interacting with a "mainframe," a very large and very hot machine that typically needed its own air conditioning system. Doing this work required extensive training that only a few people were lucky enough to receive.

For an aspiring lawyer, this meant interacting with the specially-trained women (it was mostly women) called word processors, who would sit in some central room not far from the mainframe, and would take your written or typed draft documents and input them into the computer, so that it would print out your documents as pages, either mechanically typed on glorified typewriters or buzzed onto pages by noisy dot-matrix printers.

In 1980, I was clerking at a big firm (not yet the one I've called Funhouse). In very up-to-date fashion, it had a room full of "word processors," toiling away at terminals for the firm's IBM System 6 mainframe. There were also a few terminals out at the secretarial stations.

I craved the control the word processors and the select secretaries had. All my life, being both an indifferent typist and a persnickety writer, I had found myself dissatisfied again and again with whatever I'd produced sitting over a keyboard and a platen. This led to many, many time- and patience-consuming retypings. Unlike me, these women could simply fix the problem and tell the printer to do the retyping. But of course no one was entrusting law clerks with control of one of these gizmos, let alone the training to operate them. We were simultaneously too high and too low on the totem pole. So I would hang around the word processing room just watching the women at work. I burned to know their secrets.

At last I hit on a plan. I approached one of the women and offered her a deal: I'd take her to lunch if she'd show me how her machine worked. She was agreeable, and allowed me, after the stipulated luncheon, to sit in her chair and touch the magic keys. I was entranced – and attentive. And having learned the rudiments from the lady, I embarked on a campaign of sitting at the secretarial workstations during their proprietors' lunch breaks, and writing memos, and then longer works.

The System 6 took some learning, and it could be frustrating. I remember, for instance, one delete key it was easy to hit by accident. This would spark a minor disaster, since the key would delete the entire page you were working on in a single gulp. And I don't think there was any "undo" key that would bring your page back. Still I forged ahead. I wrote an entire independent study project, later published in the *Georgetown Law Journal*, on that System 6.

I've also already written how after law school I went to work for the judge. If there was a word processor anywhere in that courthouse in 1981-82, I never met her, and I never saw any computer devoted to generating documents. But I made up my mind that I was going to push hard for my very own terminal at whatever firm I joined thereafter.

I've also written how I ended up at the firm I call Funhouse, P.A. Part of what drew me there was being told by the partner I'd report to that "we'll have a lot of fun." But part of it was being promised by the managing partner, upon my urgent request, that I'd get my own terminal. In fact, I'm sure that promise had clinched it for me.

I was to find out that that partner's promises were not always to be relied upon. I think I was at Funhouse for three years before I actually received a terminal to their system: the Wang VS. But I would sneak into the word processors' center after hours to write a novel (and occasionally do billable work) on their system. It would be easy to make fun of the VS now, but that system really was the gold standard for law firms for a while.

This all absolutely whetted my desire to own an actual computer all by myself. And in 1981, it suddenly became theoretically possible, when IBM introduced what many call the first true personal computer, known by the chip that powered it, the Intel 8080. I've written in earlier chapters about lusts of the flesh: this was lust of the machine, and it was every bit as powerful – and more reliably satisfied as well.

But not cheaply. The hardware and the software were staggeringly expensive by modern standards. After long and obsessive shopping eventually led me to buy an 8080 (two floppy drives, no hard drive) with a monochrome text-based cathode ray tube monitor, a binder containing a floppy disk with an MS-DOS operating system, a binder of WordPerfect software, one Lotus spreadsheet program, and a single frivolity, the proto-computer game called Adventure: all for the price of around $5,000 in 1983 currency – also the cost of the family car, which we'd purchased new.

The computer was installed in the converted attic of our home, and I would hide out there and romance the computer. I would write about my marital woes and hide the disks – and I would play Adventure, also known as The Colossal Cave Adventure.

In the modern era, when computer games mean handling a dedicated controller and walking your avatar down hellish galleries slaying orcs and aliens and bad guys that jump out at you with near photo-realism, it is difficult to convey the feel of Adventure, but let me try. Adventure was a text-based game in which, by typing in directions, you found a way underground through a "springhouse" and entered a cave of many galleries, in which you came upon various helpful objects, were assaulted by and killed or were killed by dwarves, and encountered many wonders, as you attempted to assemble a group of hidden treasures. For whatever reason, I never became much of a computer game devotee (solitaire games excepted), but this one did grab

me, and I devoted a lot of hours to working on it.

The fun lay, for me, not in the mathematical working through of the puzzle, but in getting to know the imaginary world, as primitively constructed as it was. And while happily embarked on this voyage, I would often listen to a cassette that made the perfect accompaniment: Andreas Vollenweider's *Caverna Magica (... Under the Tree – In the Cave ...)*, also released in 1983. Vollenweider, a Swiss harpist, together with a small collective of collaborators, created a sort of psychedelic acoustic environment that definitely was also a cave filled with adventures. The cassette starts with the scuffling of feet on gravel as a man and a woman are exploring, and then one of them exclaims (in French?): "It's a cave!" Shortly thereafter you hear water dripping from a stalactite or two, or three. The dripping slowly morphs into a jazzy rhythm, and then a mysterious whistling sound joins it, then the harp joins in, and you're off on an amazing musical adventure. Each side of the tape is designed to be played straight through, although there are definite movements, with names that may mean something to Vollenweider but don't tell us much. The movements on Side 1, for instance, are entitled: *Caverna Magica*, *Mandragora*, *Lunar Pond*, *Schajah Saretosh*, and *Sena Stanjena?*. It is bright, imaginative, and ever-shifting music.

The journey Vollenweider and friends charted out felt less sinister and dangerous than the one the programmers responsible for Adventure had contrived, but they each appealed to the same place in my head. Jointly these two creations, the game and the album, served as the perfect expression of the computer journey I embarked on at that point, one which has lasted all my years since then, and will continue doing so, doubtless, the rest of my life. You venture into mysterious places, develop new skills, and bring back all sorts of treasures from those mysterious caves we now call cyberspace.

But at that dark moment, they served a special purpose: reminding me that, outside of my private circle of misery, there was a world full of wondrous things. And if that world existed alongside the miserable one, I ought to be striking out for it, and not giving up to despair.

54

A NET IN THE NIGHT

GUITARS, WRITTEN AND PERFORMED BY
RUPERT HOLMES (1978), "ENCOUNTERED" 1983

PLAYLIST TRACK NO. 82

SOMETIMES FATE INTERVENES. In the midst of my unhappy marriage, on an extremely hot July night, at a party in a friend's backyard, I sat down next to someone. Unlike my studied seductions of the previous two years, this was unsought and unforeseen. In fact I was, uncharacteristically, trying to avoid another woman's attentions, and parking myself where the seats on either side of me were already taken so that I could not be followed. It was only polite to talk to the woman to my left.

But we did not stop talking. It seemed we had enormous subjects in common. A friend who saw the two of us at it said we seemed "intent." But there was so much to talk about with her: books and movies and shared friends.

Of course I was honest; there was no studied avoidance of mention of my wife. (I had come alone on account of the anger at home, which had by then escalated, on this occasion, to fury.) But likewise there was no disguising the rapidly growing interest I felt, an interest it seemed clear was returned.

All I knew was, I did not want to stop talking to her. She drew me in with her sparkling eyes. And heaven knows I only had eyes for her.

As the party began to break up, by rights we should have gone our separate ways, if for no other reason than that she had a tennis date early the next day. But I begged her to stay up late and have a drink with me. And my lucky stars were with me, because after a moment's consideration, she said yes. We would separately drive to a restaurant in an apartment house near the one in which she lived, also not far from where I lived.

As we walked out together, our host, who knew a good deal about the way I was living my life at this point, followed us out, his worry barely disguised. Apparently there was nothing subtle about what was happening: "Who was that woman leaving with Jack?" someone had reportedly inquired in our host's hearing, as he sprang to follow us. He didn't want the woman to get hurt.

But he was too late to intervene; the magic was already at work.

As we sat in the bar at the restaurant a little later, I was speaking of my family, and she interjected: "It sounds as if your marriage needs work." Demolition work, I thought.

It was late now, and it didn't feel as if we had begun to scratch the surface. I invited myself back to her apartment, heedless of how late this would make me coming home. All right, she said, but don't you make a pass at me. I was beginning to want her very badly, but understood that that was the price of admission, and agreed. (And I knew without even having to reflect that if I made myself untrustworthy at this moment, it might ruin everything.)

We went out into the sweltering night, and over to her sweltering apartment. And the conversation continued. At last, even I had to go. At the door I turned around, and we kissed. And, true to my promise, I walked out, down the apartment stairs, and out the front door.

Halfway down the block, I started almost seeing her face in front of me, thinking how beautiful she was, and how much I'd enjoyed being with her. Still, I got in the car, and even drove back to my house. By now, though, I was thinking, lawyer-like, that my promise not to make a pass was discharged already. If I returned ...

But more than that, I just wasn't through being in her company. I wanted to be near her.

It was only a few blocks. I parked my car quietly in front of the house, and walked back to her apartment. My plan was to ring her doorbell and then – I had no plan beyond that. I was focused on that doorbell. I would press the button and see what happened.

When I got to the apartment doorway, though, my determination began to fail. I knew this was crazy. I was afraid. The middle of the night was just the wrong time to call if I wanted to continue the relationship intelligently, but I felt that if I didn't act now, I might burst. There was a moment, maybe a whole minute, of indecision. In theory I could call in the morning, or the next day, or the next week. I could do whatever married men do to push ahead decorously with an affair. But I had a strong feeling that it had to be now, that my whole life was passing through this moment, about to be determined.

My heart pounding with apprehension, I pushed the doorbell button. I heard her voice on the intercom, and said I was back, and could I come in? And she said yes.

There was no song I was listening to at that point which brings it back for me now. A mutual friend who was there at the party later said jokingly that strains of *Some Enchanted Evening* could be heard. *Strangers in the Night* would work too for that joke. But in later years I came across the song that now infallibly calls that night to mind for me: *Guitars*, by Rupert Holmes. To understand why, you first have to hear it, and practically no one has, as it comes from an obscure 1978 album that fetches rare album prices now. So please find it on the Spotify playlist that goes with this book and hear it for free.

I'll wait.

If you've done that, you can see what I mean. I have to quote the lyrics a little:

Taut and tight, there's a net in the night.
The evening is strung with strings.
Power lines intertwine with the vines,
The telephone wire sings.
My pulse is racing.
I need to place you in this web of silver cords.
My heart is pumping in time to the theme that resounds in the stars;
I have to love you tonight while the earth is alive with guitars.
Drawn like steel across a drum,
My nerves begin to strum like a storm.
Drawn to you, I feel the pull
Of strings that ring so full and so warm.
Highly strung, we're in love and we're young;
The evening is laced with light.
Weave our way through the strange interplay
Of bodies that brush the night.
My heart is pumping in time to the theme that resounds in the stars.

The vines and the telephone wires and the guitar strings are thus all one in a dazzling poetic metaphor, all ligatures that simultaneously vibrate in a siderial harmony and draw the lovers together. And that was exactly what it felt like: that the two of us were being drawn to each other by invisible and harmonious forces.

The music too conveys the sense of it, growing from the pulse of a single guitar plucking an E note that is gradually picked up by what sounds like a host of guitars, and weaving an intricate web of harmonies, leading up to a flourish by all the guitars that sounds like a pack of cards being shuffled by a magician with perfect hands. And that is what falling in love felt like: a sight, a glimpse, something simple, that effloresced rapidly into something compound and intricate, and dazzling.

Her name was Mary.

55

HALLOWEEN

TEACH ME TONIGHT, BY SAMMY CAHN AND GENE DE PAUL,
PERFORMED BY AL JARREAU (1981), ENCOUNTERED 1983

PLAYLIST TRACK No. 83

So I HAD met someone. When she came into my life that hot July night, I was raw with the wounds of my marriage. In my moments with her, passion deadened the pain. But still I clung to some hopes of salvaging the marriage.

It was as if I had simultaneously punched two timers, one on my marriage, one on my new relationship. Time was running out on both, and I was shuttling insanely between them.

S. and I had just entered marriage counseling. Many people who have set out on that road will recognize immediately what I mean by the timer. You have only certain reserves of love and patience, and you have to save the marriage somehow before those reserves run out. (Maybe a better metaphor would be the bomb counting down towards the end of a James Bond movie.)

But my affair also began with a short and preset duration; when I met her, the woman was in negotiations to take a job far away, and that was fortunate for me in a sense, because with my baggage her sense of self-preservation would probably have dissuaded her from allowing things to proceed very far between us – had there not been a definite *terminus ad quem*. The affair could not extend beyond November 1, the date she was likely to start her duties on her new job.

Of course a condition laid down by the marriage counselor was that I had to be faithful as the therapy went forward. And so I had hardly met my new love before I had to stop meeting her. I went to her and said goodbye – and stuck by that goodbye for the rest of the summer, knowing that her job-clock was ticking away, and seeing her face before me wherever I went.

But all that this self-denial accomplished was underlining for me how miserable and bleak things felt to me at home. Suffice it to say that I was breaking my resolution and my promises by September; I was suffocating, and I needed the air for a few moments, even if there was only a small supply of it left.

Sweet as they were, those stolen moments (a date at the racquet club, a walk in the park, a drink at a bar above the Harbor) were all filled with foreboding; whatever we did or didn't do, November was coming. I think in one mad conversation I begged her both to stay and to allow me to go on with my marriage. (Thank goodness she was too sensible to give that proposition a moment's consideration.) So nothing would prevent November coming.

I started seeing my own therapist, a nice but useless man.

And the clocks went on ticking down.

The clash between conscience and longing was excruciating. There was an evening, for instance, my family went to the symphony, and the children were angels, and my son fell asleep on my arm, a living reproach to my fantasies of independence. There was the hiding of presents between me and my lover. There was lying. There was talking with my friends, who one and all gave me good reasons to fear a separation. And there was always the anger at home. Meanwhile the wonderful interludes presented me fully-realized illustrations of the alternative to all of this.

Four days before my friend was to leave, I snuck out from the children's swimming lesson to have a coffee with her. She observed that I would probably be relieved when she left. And I knew it was true, not because I wasn't in love with her, but because I was.

On what was to have been our last date, I blew my resolution (bred of counseling and of trying to make up my mind to revive the marriage), failed to keep any reserve, and just declared my love repeatedly. Having done which, I insanely bade her goodbye, went to a lecture (which was my official cover activity for the whole evening), and came home.

The very last day, Halloween, was similar in its mixture of mundaneness and heartbreak. I took advantage of an anomaly in my schedule (I actually did have to leave the car at an uptown repair shop) to pay an unscheduled visit to her on her last day of work at a midtown location. I got off the bus, found her at her office, we stood on the bus stop, embraced, and then I caught the bus the rest of the way downtown.

At 5:00 p.m., when I knew the plane was departing, I was in my office, on the 15th floor, with a western exposure. From where I sat, I could see that sun go down, all orange and lonesome. I knew that she was flying westward into it and out of my life. I was desperate, and could do nothing. Stirring myself, I tried to get a friend to come drinking with me, but he was busy. So I came home and had dinner with the family, doled out trick-or-treats, washed the dishes, and tried to act as if nothing was wrong. Distracted and trying to be bright and competent. "I don't know when or how it ends," I wrote.

As the sun was sliding down the horizon, carrying her away, the song in my cassette player was *Teach Me Tonight*, in Al Jarreau's then-recently-released version. I kept replaying it, and it made me feel a little better. Until you think about it, it might seem a strange song, both in subject and treatment, to have addressed what I was feeling then. But not when you think about it.

It's a making-out song (I've already limned two others in these pages) featuring producer Jay Graydon's brittle and bright arrangements that had so attracted me when I first heard his work with The Manhattan Transfer. In other words, a song sung by the man who's got his squeeze within reach, and it's making him as bright and happy as the shiny surface of the music. It's even playful, tongue-in-cheek as make-out songs usually are, conceiving of the beloved as a teacher, reading the singer into the love program, as it were:

Did you say, I've got a lot to learn
Well don't think I'm trying not to learn
Since this is the perfect spot to learn
Teach me tonight
Starting with the ABC of it
Getting right down to the XYZ of it
Help me solve the mystery of it
Teach me tonight

For the singer, it's uncomplicated; he wants something wonderful without reservations and he's going to get it. Jarreau conveys the feeling beautifully. The uncomplicated part was what got me, I think. Of course I wanted the sex.

But more than I knew or recognized, I wanted my life to be straight again, easily explained, simple, honest. And on that Halloween it was anything but. Still, a man could listen and yearn.

And maybe aspire to more.

56

WALKING MUSIC

ARE YOU GOING WITH ME?, WRITTEN BY LYLE MAYS/PAT METHENY, PERFORMED BY THE PAT METHENY GROUP (1983), ENCOUNTERED 1984

PLAYLIST TRACK NO. 84

AND SO THERE I was, completely alone, trying to figure out what to do about my marriage. The woman I might have relied on to distract me from the work I needed to do had left town and was gone. She soon made it clear she did not want me to write to her. What I did next was entirely up to me. I was immensely and productively lonely.

Anyone who's had a marriage fall apart will recognize the fix I was in. The person I would ordinarily turn to to help me make any important decision was the person I was contemplating quitting. In this context, my closest counselor was *de facto* my adversary. She was not – could not be – on my side in this.

I wasn't very good help to myself either, at least not initially. I kept asking myself the wrong questions, which had a lot to do with my inability to do anything other than think in unproductive circles.

But I did finally get help.

The one who finally dragged me over to the correct questions and then waited impatiently while I answered them was a new therapist. Her name was Jo. Our marriage counselor, in suspending the marriage counseling, had referred me on to her (about the only useful thing he did). Jo and I met in her Chinese-decorated office on the ground floor of a Towson high-rise that I would drive to twice a week. And there I also made the acquaintance of a therapy group who became a second family, a healthy and intimate second family with just a couple of peculiarities: no one had last names, and, tragically, one's rate of success would be measured in how quickly one was able to "graduate," i.e. to say goodbye, never to see the other family members again. The group was even firmer than Jo was in calling people on BS, which was indeed a vital talent because we all had so much of it to offer, I as much as anyone.

I'm not going to bother with the specifics of what the right questions were or how I answered them. I'll simply say that eventually I struggled past the paralysis and those great loops of thought I had not been able to escape on my own. In general, I came to three major perceptions. These were: a) the marriage was irretrievable; b) until I worked through some of my own problems, I could not be a good husband to anyone; and c) in the examination of conscience as regarded my children, I could not forget the example of the oxygen mask. (You know, when flying with children, that if the cabin becomes depressurized, you must be the one to use the oxygen mask first. Otherwise you may not be able to help either the children or yourself. Maybe you were wrong to have taken them on the plane in the first place, but once aloft, guilty or not, you still have to be the first one to the oxygen.)

Getting to that point was a process. The emotional part of it would probably be familiar to anyone who had been there himself or herself. It resembled dealing with waves of nausea. There would be periods where one felt desperate to leave, and then there would be periods of relief, when just the absence of pain felt good, and made one cautiously optimistic that the marriage could somehow be saved.

Christmas of 1983, for example, was one of those periods between the heaves. After all the hustle and bustle of preparation was done, after the cards and the presents and the tree were all in place, I took my children to see the *Christmas Story* movie, which was just out then. We drove out to an old-fashioned two-screen theater in the suburbs. We were all by ourselves in the cold before filing into the popcorn-smelling warmth of the movie house, the film was an obvious and instant bit of wonderfulness, and a feeling of peace descended on me. Maybe, I thought for a moment, we could all be happy together again.

That Christmas glow lasted less than a week. By New Year's Eve, which we saw in at a party aboard a vintage train car on a siding at the old Camden Station in downtown Baltimore, I astonished my friend the host by telling him privately: "Here's to being a free man in 1984!"

By the end of February 1984, I had finally reached the point where I no longer wavered in my realization that I needed to leave.

But acceptance, though reputedly the last stage of dealing with impending death, is only the first phase of implementing a divorce. Then you need to summon courage, logistical skill, and cash. And the greatest of these is courage. You need the courage to overcome your own tendency to back-slide into the more comfortable life you had built, the courage to stand up for yourself against the person you had up to that point been identifying as your other self, the courage to break children's hearts and brave the disappoint-ment of in-laws and friends, the courage to face a time of at least comparative economic hardship.

But courage you must have. Very quickly, in the group, I became acquainted with two people who had made themselves utterly miserable by hanging on for years in the marriages that had made them miserable, marriages they should have left. But they were never brave enough; until I graduated from the group two years thereafter, they remained stuck. And that, I resolved, would not be me. Whatever else I would be, I refused to be stuck, even if some bravery was required.

In late March I started taking some of the concrete steps one has to take (getting things out of the safe deposit box and obtaining legal representation). And, prodded by the group, I announced my intentions to my wife. The frac-turing had begun.

The day after Easter I went further and signed the inevitable apartment lease. I wrote at the time I felt like a lawyer going to trial when the facts are against him, a feeling I was not unfamiliar with. You're going to do as well as you can, whatever the outcome, but you know the experience, however necessary and inevitable, won't be pleasant. I also wrote that I was "blotting the … copybook, enrolling myself forever in the club of the sadder but wiser."

Then there remained three weeks to go, three weeks in which to finish all that had to be finished before I moved out. "As the ordeal goes on," I commented, "you lose track. You never know what's round the next curve. You lose all orientation. One moment you're cold, the next you're crying hyster-ically. There are hundreds of practical details to cope with, and you're so out of it you can't cope with any of them." The hardest task of all was talking to the children. And I will just mention that matter generally; the details are personal.

And then, eventually, blessedly, came May 15. The truck arrived and picked up my things; two friends took off from work and helped me. After they left,

I was sitting surrounded by boxes waiting for me to unpack them in a huge, well-lit two-bedroom apartment in one of the classic old apartment houses just off the Johns Hopkins campus. For my purposes of the next two years, it was perfect.

And then the ecstasy started. This was not the faintly pleasurable interstice between bouts of nausea of which I have written above; it was the fullthroated thing. Whatever had been good or bad about the marriage, it was all now in the past tense. My future was entirely to be written, to be built, piece by piece, according to my own design. And I was animated by a fixed resolve to design it far better this time.

And that's why the Pat Metheny Group's *Are You Going With Me?* is absolutely the music that comes to mind when I remember those first few days of being out on my own. From the first beat of the song almost to the ending over nine minutes later, drummer Dan Gottlieb's strutting beat (probably augmented by Nana Vasconcelos on percussion) does not falter. It is the rhythm of a determined walk. And as the walk proceeds, the scenery changes several times, and it seems as if the affect of the walker changes with it, as scenery and affect are presented through Metheny's guitar synthesizer and his collaborator Lyle Mays' synclavier. The constant is not that the walker is in ecstasy, as I now was, but that he is always in challenging minor-key environments. But despite the challenges, despite the minor key, the mood is always joyful to my ear. The melodies grow ever more complex and elaborate, the pitch rises, the volumes rise, and always the walker rejoices, striding on. Eventually, at about the 8-minute mark, the intensity becomes orgasmic, and only after that climax has been achieved do Gottlieb's drums go silent.

I was always realistic enough to anticipate that my landscape would be one of continuous, and continuously changing, challenge. But I felt now that I could be happy passing through it all.

I listened to this number many times in the months surrounding my departure. Guitarist Metheny's brilliance (like that of keyboard man Lyle Mays, whom I later grew to appreciate separately), set off by interactions with the live crowds in front of which the album was recorded, were to me the sound of a life fully lived. I felt beckoned to live as daringly, as soaringly as that song. And I resolved to try.

57

HURRYING STANDING STILL

ALONE AT NIGHT, COMPOSED AND PERFORMED BY
MICHAEL FRANKS (1983), ENCOUNTERED 1984

PLAYLIST TRACK NO. 85

I HAVE ALWAYS thought that Michael Franks was the singer-songwriter-laureate of heterosexual male desire. A big claim, considering how competitive the field may appear. But maybe it's not that competitive. There are lots of male takes on romance, and some on sheer horniness. And there are lots of caricatures of male erotic prowess, comic during the blues era, clownish and sometimes downright offensive in the time of hip-hop. But the real feeling of being a man wanting and (sometimes, not always) getting sex from a woman – a woman regarded neither as an ideal nor as a mere plaything, but as an equal partner in the fun, which I'd like to think is how most straight men experience it, at least on their best days, well, fewer people have written about that. During much of his career, it was Franks' main subject.

His greatest achievement, his *Sgt. Pepper*, if you will, was his 1983 album *Passion Fruit*, a highly varied set in which fully eight of the ten numbers dealt in one way or another with male desire. He managed to capture it winsomely and variously. Here, for instance, is part of his lyrics to *Sunday Morning Here With You*:

...[U]p on the roof we are living proof
Love's nutritious

Such delicious déjà vu
Sunday morning here with you
Your kisses made with orange marmalade
Apple blossoms toast and tea
I cannot think of any place I'd rather I'd rather be
My sleepy friend I always want to spend Sunday morning here with you
I cannot think of anything I'd rather I'd rather do
Lounging in bed Sunday papers read
Windows open
First day of spring
Hear the kettle sing
Tea for two
Lady in lace
Sunlight on your face
Quite an eyeful
Such delightful déjà vu
Sunday morning here with you

In a similar vein, try *Rainy Night in Tokyo* or *Tell Me All About It*.

The song that always makes me think of the summer of 1984, however, is *Alone at Night*. In that number Franks evokes a man who would much rather be with a lover who is sometimes there, but apparently usually not.

When I'm alone at night all I do is think about you
Especially when I'm blue I just can't do without you
I love the way you shiver my timbers
I need you here to keep myself limber
When I'm alone I contemplate every way I'd like to rendezvous you
I only hope s'il-vous plait you can respondez-vous
Your amplifier's already preset
Let's see if we can rattle the tea set
When I'm alone at night
Watching those reruns of Dragnet
Catching those rays of electrode light
Your love pulls at me like a magnet
When I'm alone at night.

246

That was me. Before the marital breakup in which I now found myself, Mary, with whom I longed to "rattle the tea set," had decamped to points west. Once my departure from my marriage had become definite, communications between us had resumed. Consequently, she was willing and able to visit me once that summer, but otherwise I was on my own. Well, as on my own as the slow onset of single-again dating allowed.

Unlike my justifications for my marital affairs, there was no contradiction between my feelings about Mary and my dating others. It was all too clear to both of us that I was hardly in a state to settle down. I was raw and beaten up, and had some healing to do in the erotic department. Not to mention that I had a lot of things to work through in therapy before I could be emotionally reliable for anyone.

Not to mention that I had a whole life to reestablish on a different footing.

I wrote in the last chapter about the ecstasy that had ensued when I first found myself in the new apartment. It was heady stuff while it lasted, a being-in-love-with-doing-it-my-own-way state in which even wheeling a cart down the supermarket aisles was an experience of happy independence. But that state didn't last long. The main experience of that summer was much more summed up in Franks' lyrics, which are a lot more dysphoric.

I spent a lot of time doing various equivalents of "watching those reruns of Dragnet."

I spent a lot of time coping with the huge number of things a suddenly single part-time father must address.

I spent a lot of time being depressed. (I dropped 20 pounds that summer with no conscious plan of doing so, no diet, no plan of exercise.)

It didn't help that the summer started with a huge fight with my therapist and my therapy group. They felt that I was committing all sorts of sins: not focusing on my children enough and showing myself too self-absorbed, too focused on sex, too willing to depend emotionally on Mary, too eager to avoid standing on my own two feet. I should be marinating in place for a while, they felt. I understand now exactly why they reacted as they did, though at the time I was just hurt and lost when they talked that way. But they did not persuade me, then or now. Time has changed my views about many things, but forty years later when I look back to that fight, I still think I was right and they were wrong.

There was no denying the power of the feelings with Mary. We were now hundreds of miles apart, but this kind of attraction, if it persisted, a love that (in Michael Franks' words) "pulled at me like a magnet," could surely bring us back together and bind us for life. I felt that everything healthy in me was caught up in that pull. And if the reason I couldn't simply surrender to it right away was that I needed to give other women a fair try and confirm that this wasn't all a stupid rebound, then I should get down to that, because I didn't want to wait until I was old to rebuild my life.

Call me a man in a hurry.

My therapeutic community disliked that hurry. But maybe I should have been forgiven my haste, considering the detours my life had already taken.

Anyway, the cumulative effect of the buzz wearing off, much loneliness, much busyness, and the group coming down on me was that I spent much of that summer in bemused solitude.

Alone at night indeed.

And yet it was an incredibly rich time. You find a married couple who take you in, who listen to you, give you wonderful advice from their own experiences of divorce in their previous marriages. You find out that single people have their own entertainments and preoccupations, and you get to take part. You learn all about budgeting. You polish up on your negotiation skills as the shared stuff a marriage accumulates is divided up. You polish up on your parenting skills too. You learn how to iron (now, yes really, one of my favorite occupations). Your personality slowly changes, as certain behaviors adopted because they chimed so well with someone else's behaviors have lost their *raisons d'être*, and maybe their appeal as well. You like to think you're a nicer person because of it. You encounter people who are lost-er than you, women too fragile to make passes at, and you let your conscience be your guide. You have really bad sex with someone else whose mind is on someone else. You learn hesitatingly how to deal with the jealousy you feel when your faraway inamorata does her own dating, because fair is fair. You discover that there have to be these little silences on this subject between yourself and the woman you love. You go back to your hometown and debrief with your oldest friends. You try making peace with your mother over the things that turn up in therapy.

Alone at night, processing a million new things. In a way, just a way, it's perfect. It wouldn't do for a whole lifetime, but for the time being, alone is exactly what you need to be.

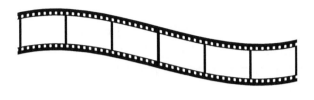

58

GLAD-EYES

MAIN TITLE - NEVER SAY NEVER AGAIN, MUSIC BY MICHEL LEGRAND,
LYRICS BY ALAN AND MARILYN BERGMAN, SUNG BY LANI HALL,
TRUMPET SOLO BY HERB ALPERT (1983), ENCOUNTERED 1984

SUBSTITUTE PLAYLIST TRACK NO. 86

SINCE I WAS newly single in the summer of 1984, you might have expected to see the odd woman around my apartment. You probably would not have expected to see this one, however. My Aunt Gladys, then 70 hard years old, was a frequent visitor, and for a time she assumed a surprising role in my life.

You can see her in a photo taken the Christmas of the following year, in ill-assorted thrift-store clothes she chose (no doubt) for their garishness, contrasting vividly with the absence of teeth and stringy gray hair, and it may be hard to conceive that she was once a great beauty and a Hollywood starlet. And yet I have ample photographic proof of the beauty part, an autographed head shot of her in those days.

And somewhere I have a still from some forgotten Hollywood picture, a large cast with Gladys off to one side, clearly not the star. But the point is, she was in the picture. Her parents, whose boys went to Harvard and Princeton, had to watch as she eschewed even acting lessons and ran off to Hollywood, maniacally assured of her future. And to her credit she made it some distance. She was in the picture. But alas, not in pictures for long. She married an actor of some note, Ted Hecht, and later she married a New York photographer, and in her own mind she was still a great actress and a philanthropist.

The story of Gladys was the story of her mind; she was a victim of what we now call bipolar disorder, in those days known as manic depression. Her family had watched in despair as her mind had driven her life out of control. When her parents died, she occupied their Central Park West apartment for a while, then lost that, as she ricocheted from psychiatric wards to the street or a shabby apartment and then back into psychiatric wards again.

Eventually she had quarreled with or driven away everyone in the family, except me. She was isolated. And as the previous chapter chronicles, in the summer of 1984 I was isolated as well. Up until that point I had pulled the same evasive maneuvers in dealing with her that most of the rest of the family did. Now, I stopped, or, if not stopped (some boundaries had to be maintained), I made sparing use of them. And I shall always be glad that I did.

One thing that Gladys may not have had much experience in doing was caring for anyone else. Mostly other people's lives were at least adequate compared to hers, and hers was so lacking and contact with her so alarming that people instinctively pulled away, ended brief get-togethers with a *My, how late it's getting!*, and kicked her out or made their escape; they certainly didn't invite her deep enough into their lives for the question of them being helped by her ever to arise. But in the summer of 1984, I needed care, and for a little while, she found her métier in providing it.

It wouldn't have worked if she hadn't been in a depressed phase. Gladys manic could be unbearable. But she was in a lengthy depressed phase.

I had a pretty large apartment. I needed to unpack things. I needed to clean things up. And Gladys pitched in. She came over and we spent, I think, two or three afternoons getting the place shipshape. She wasn't much interested in hearing my tales of woe; there was only room for one narrative in her mind, and it wasn't mine. But she did enjoy being with me and she really was a help in getting the place organized.

It was strange that someone who could generate such chaos in any space she occupied could somehow help bring order to mine. But she did.

The song I associate with our times together that summer is the theme to the non-canonical James Bond sequel, *Never Say Never Again*. Why on earth? Well, long story short:

The movie had come out in 1983, the same year as the dreary canonical *Octopussy*. *Never Say Never*, featuring the original Bond, an older but still sexy and dangerous Sean Connery, a smart and funny screenplay by Lorenzo Semple, Jr., who had brought the Batman television series to me in my golden youth, and a Michel Legrand score, was just infinitely superior. And in those days you had to wait about a year for the home video (VHS videotape) to come out. I couldn't afford much in the way of creature comforts over and above the apartment itself, but I was going to have a VHS tape deck, come hell or high water. And one of the first movies I rented to play in that deck was the then-just-released-on video *Never Say Never Again*, which I was eagerly awaiting a chance to re-view.

I wanted it so much that, when Gladys and I decided to rest from our labors, I asked her if she'd like to watch, as it just so happened that that cassette was on rental in my apartment that afternoon.

Now, Gladys was a creature of the old Hollywood, and when I say that I mean really old, *Sunset Boulevard* old. Her exposure to popular culture had mostly ended before I was born. She might just have heard of James Bond, but she certainly wouldn't have known anything about him. So I had no idea what her take on the ultimate celluloid hero would be.

Her introduction to 007 turned out to be fascinating to watch. She was dumbfounded. She wasn't given to expressions like "Well, I never …" but she repeatedly muttered similar sentiments, though I can't call the words to mind. Obviously she didn't understand most of what was going on onscreen, but it really didn't matter to her, because the whole thing was so unbelievable it was comic (even more than the tongue-in-cheek script had aspired to make it). The bottom line was, Gladys had a wonderful time.

That was a high point for me: in the midst of my chaotic summer of separation, I and my crazy aunt finding a fragile, temporary point of equilibrium, a moment in which she was doing for me what a normal kind aunt would do and I was repaying her with a treat she enjoyed, as the nephew of a normal aunt would do.

And of course the number that came from the movie to stay in my head was Lani Hall's wonderfully-rendered theme song with, as an added bonus, a soaring trumpet solo by her husband, Herb Alpert. I had been in love with Lani's voice since her days with Brasil '66 (Chapter 31). For many years I felt this was the single best Bond song, although I now think k.d. lang's *Surrender* (the end title music from *Tomorrow Never Dies* (1997)) surpasses it. (The fact that the soundtrack is obscure enough that I can't add the original to the Spotify playlist and have to settle for a cover version tells you that mine is a minority opinion, however.) However ranked, it's a really great song, and reminds me of that summer and my afternoons with Gladys.

As you might expect for someone who lived so hard a life, Gladys did not make it to age 80. There wasn't much gladness about her in the end, despite her self-appointed nickname of Glad-Eyes. My wife, who made her acquaintance a little later, has written feelingly about those difficult years that lay just ahead for her, and us in our relationship with her. (See HTTPS://WWW.BALTIMORESUN.COM/NEWS/BS-XPM-1992-11-09-1992314033-STORY.HTML for her article.)

But in the summer of 1984 there was a strange moment of ease, and when I hear that song, I remember it.

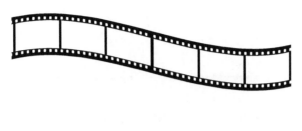

59

CATHARSIS

PURPLE RAIN, WRITTEN BY PRINCE, PERFORMED BY
PRINCE & THE REVOLUTION (1984), ENCOUNTERED 1984

PLAYLIST TRACK NO. 87

IF YOU ASKED me to name the most perfect week of my life, I would answer without hesitation that it was the one that began on Saturday, September 29, 1984. On that date, I caught a pair of flights that took me from Baltimore to Lincoln, Nebraska. And Mary, the woman who had flown out of my life on Halloween of the previous year and quite properly left me to deal with all my issues on my own, was waiting for me at the gate, her yellow Capri parked outside, ready to drive me to her new home.

Even with the occasional flashes of ecstasy over being single again that came and went, it had been a hard eleven months since that Halloween, one hard thing after another, eleven months that had left me emotionally tight as the mainspring of an overwound watch.

But on that Saturday, the hard part stopped for a while. We walked out to the airport parking lot, neither of us quite able to believe I'd made it. But I had. And so it was possible for me to do something that would have seemed inconceivable eleven months earlier: sit down in a car in a strange state, and let a beautiful woman drive me to her home. Openly, with nothing to hide from anyone.

From the parking lot, then, to Mary's apartment complex. From the car downstairs to Mary's apartment upstairs. Then the door closed behind us,

and then, to paraphrase Michael Franks, I was hers and she was mine. And the week that followed that instant is largely a blur of good things.

One thing I remember clearly is that I fell in love with Lincoln, a town that greatly (and only to its credit) reminded me of Ann Arbor, my hometown. Some events do stand out. There was a leisurely drive through truly rural Nebraska, including a visit to towns named Wahoo and Prague (pronounced with a long A). We saw the movie *Places in the Heart* at the Sheldon Museum of Art in Lincoln. We dined in and we dined out. We visited the Joslyn Art Museum and The Old Market in Omaha. We played Trivial Pursuit with some of Mary's new friends. We attended the University of Nebraska's homecoming game. We dined at Parker's Steak House, a legendary spot in Denton.

For a week, nothing intruded on the bliss. I've never experienced another whole blissful week, before or since. I've never had a week go so exactly according to plan. And a week like that does release you from cares and tensions.

Of course we talked about what the future might hold. On our last night (over dinner at Parker's, in fact), we began an indirect discussion of our aspirations, which for both of us turned out to include parenthood (in my case parenthood again). No one used the "m" word exactly; no one had to. The unused word notwithstanding, negotiations over a joint future were beginning. Only just beginning, since we lived and worked 1200 miles apart, we were each separated but not divorced, and I at least came with considerable baggage. There was no realistic way we could have done anything more than compare life objectives at that stage. And we didn't try. We knew better.

On the third night, we went to see rocker Prince's fictionalized cinematic self-portrait *Purple Rain* (out since July, but still playing). It was the perfect movie for that moment in our lives. The Kid, Prince's character, is tormented by his past, which has left him wild, angry, and hurtful to those who care for him, and prone to self-sabotage. But at the end, confronted with the emotional corner into which he is painting himself, he stops painting. You can tell he has reached that moment when he agrees to sing a song that the women in his band, Wendy and Lisa, have written, after he had been condescendingly and unproductively brushing off their proffer of the number all through the movie.

The song, of course, is Prince's big over-the-top hit *Purple Rain*. What it means exactly has been a topic of great debate, but for my purposes both on that October night and now, the answer to that question is not important. What matters is that, for the Kid, the song is a moment of both newfound vulnerability and newfound power, a fact immediately apparent to the audience on the screen, a crowd of hard-eyed youthful cognoscenti of the 1984 Minneapolis music scene. The spectators are first mesmerized and then energized.

After pulling off this triumph, the Kid explodes off the stage, dashes down to his dressing room, where he paces up and down for a few moments, in awe of what he has done, and then, in a series of flashbacks and flash-forwards interwoven with the rousing songs he sings when he returns to the stage (*I Would Die 4 U* and *Baby I'm a Star*), he sets things right, or as right as he can, with his parents (the source of his angst), and with Apollonia (Apollonia Kotero), his girlfriend whom he has been abusing.

I was tired when I saw that performance. But its cathartic quality spoke directly to me through my fatigue. I could dare to recognize then that I had been engineering my own catharsis. I had gotten single, I was doing good work in therapy, I was getting this love business right for once. And so for that night *Purple Rain* was my anthem.

When I boarded the plane home the following Sunday, we knew we were still 1200 miles apart, and all the rest. We knew there still could be no exclusivity and no promises, that each of us was wide-open exposed to the risk that one or both of us might find someone else, that all sorts of other things could also drive us in different directions. But what with the overwhelming rightness of that week, and the oh-so-tentative negotiations, we, like Prince in the movie after his breakthrough, were playing at a new level. As Mary said, it was the most adult relationship of our lives.

60

A MEASURE OF SERENITY

AERIAL BOUNDARIES, WRITTEN AND PERFORMED BY
MICHAEL HEDGES (1984), ENCOUNTERED 1984

PLAYLIST TRACK NO. 88

FIRST YOU HEAR a rhythmic pattern plucked or tapped on a guitar's upper strings, then a counter-rhythm and a melody on the lower strings. All at the same time. Then some of the notes are produced by a hand slapping the strings instead of plucking or tapping them. And no, there is no accompanist; this is Michael Hedges, somehow plucking (or tapping or slapping) with both hands simultaneously, laying down drones and sonorities with the left and with the right, playing them off against each other.

Wait: How is all that possible? We all know how a guitar is supposed to be played: one hand doing the fretwork, one hand doing the plucking. But that is clearly not happening here. There are too many notes. YouTube today reveals a small industry of guitarists trying to replicate Hedges' dexterity on this piece. He is carefully studied. But in 1984 there was only Hedges.

When, like me in 1984, you had only heard it, and if, like me, you didn't play the guitar, the virtuosity might have escaped you. There was something paradoxically simple about the overall effect, a bit like sunlight illuminating a field that seems quiet and motionless until you perceive bees working feverishly at every bud. And that was *Aerial Boundaries*, simultaneously busy and placid. This was a work of deceptively brilliant musicianship.

Aerial Boundaries was Cut 4 of *Windham Hill Sampler '84*, the other album that was part of the visit to Lincoln, Nebraska I described in the previous chapter. (I took a copy of the cassette out to Lincoln for my girlfriend Mary, and it got played a lot while Mary and I were together.) The album was an entrancing introduction to what was coming to be known as New Age Music. Later on, perhaps, the genre would come to be thought of as clichéd. But in 1984 it was fresh and new, and clean, dazzling as the sunlight.

To me, it was evocative for what it was, and important for what it wasn't.

What it was: a crystalline sound, a new way to evoke peace and thoughtfulness, things I stood in need of. Life had given me a second chance, but seizing it was not inherently a serene thing. I had to grow a real career from the little stub of one I'd achieved so far, and I still had much of the hard work of divorce to do. Peace and thoughtfulness would be great desiderata in that process.

As far as the career went, however brilliantly I may have done in law school, I was only beginning to master the basics of law office politics. Brilliant, it seemed, might not get you all that far. As had happened in graduate school, I gathered I was viewed as problematic and not a regular guy.

But suddenly, like manna from heaven, I was handed a piece of the regular guy stuff, the task of supervising the summer law clerks. By rights, it shouldn't have come to anyone at my humble level. I was only three years out of law school and four years away from any likelihood of being offered a partnership. I intuited that I would not have been given this important role had the partners at my firm, which I'll still call Funhouse, P.A., cared all that much about the summer program. Of course in a normal firm, they would have cared, a lot, and one of them would have been running it. But this was Funhouse. I figured that the way to make the most of this opportunity was to craft a summer program the equal of those being offered by the best firms in town. And I think I succeeded pretty well.

Well, more accurately, I succeeded at matching the entertainment at the best firms. Not the outcomes, though. To my dismay, at the end of the summer, only one of my charges received a job offer. By no coincidence, the offeree was the son of one of the firm's best clients. Effectively, then, my work had gone for naught.

My first response was the kind of undiplomatic reflex that had so often interfered with my chances before. I fired off a memo angrily protesting the waste of the summer program; luckily my new direct supervisor caught it before it went out, and told me not to circulate it. I followed his orders, though I didn't really understand them. Later someone took me aside and explained the dollars-and-cents reasons why the firm had trashed the summer class. But all I knew at the time was that I was being asked to suck it up when something good I had done was being ignored. And of course I had no clue then what it was like to be the boss in charge of a business and its cash flow.

Going along with this little bit of realpolitik bore fruit promptly, however. Very shortly thereafter, I found myself in a social setting with a group of the firm's rainmakers; just them and me, for some reason. They were all pleased with what I'd done. Had I given offense by bellyaching, the atmosphere would surely have been chillier. Not long after that, I was given to know I wasn't thought of as difficult any more. One of the partners told me in surprise that I'd "joined the establishment."

As another part of this "socializing Jack" effort, the new boss began to see to it that I did a lot of one kind of work for a single client, and I began to develop some real expertise.

You might have thought these weren't lessons a 35-year-old would have had to learn. But the sad truth was, they were exactly the kind of lessons I had to learn. The roots of my cluelessness in matters of diplomacy were the kind of thing I was addressing in therapy. Better late than never, I guess. And one key to addressing it was there in New Age music like Hedges': serenity.

At the same time, the emotional work of the divorce never seemed to stop; it took a million shapes.

For instance, taking my kids trick or treating for Halloween of 1984, in the neighborhood I'd left only that May, I learned that one couple I'd thought eternal were now in a nursing home. Strangers answered that door. I learned as well that a next-door neighbor had died; no one answered that door. Two families I looked on as old friends were out, and no one answered those doors either. In fact, hardly anyone was there to welcome me back during my brief return. The upshot of these little losses: I found myself greeting a strange guy I'd never liked very much, but who did answer the expected door, as if he were an old friend. But basically, I had to deal with the fact that when you move on, you move on. And many friends are not portable.

When you're divorced, the friends you do keep are apt to chip in with their perspectives on the recently ended union. I had some unpleasant discussions, let me leave it at that.

And no matter what you do, parenthood even in a good divorce can be harder than parenthood in a bad marriage. My therapist said it would take everyone two years at least to regain their footings; she was right about the "at least" part. And let me leave that at that as well.

And in other news, my mother and stepfather were proving themselves to be not immortal, as my dad had a serious fall and they both had to miss coming to Baltimore for the holidays. Nothing like a holiday without your parents on hand to force you to face up to how on your own you may be.

With all such things, as with office politics, serenity can be a help. Even when it's serenity from a cassette.

Consider the title *Aerial Boundaries*. I used to think it was a nonesuch. How can one have a boundary in the air? And then I realized that all boundaries are just imaginary lines calculated and represented by surveyors. Of course, you can depict a boundary on a plat, and you can mark a boundary terrestrially with a monument like a nail or a fence or a wall. The nature of the earth, as a (somewhat) immobile medium makes monumentation possible. You cannot mark a boundary in the air by attaching anything to the air. But that's just a matter of the monuments, not of the boundaries themselves. The concept of a boundary per se is just as meaningful in the sky as in the dirt. Perhaps the point of the title was the actual possibility of something that had seemed impossible. Like Hedges' two-handed plucking/tapping. Like a hive of activity in a field that first seems to be sleeping in the sun.

Or like finding music for myself. And some measure of serenity.

61

WORKED FOR ME

FREEDOM, WRITTEN BY DAVE MCHUGH, PERFORMED BY
CHAKA KHAN AND MICHAEL ROD (1984), ENCOUNTERED 1985

BREAK MY STRIDE, WRITTEN BY GREG PRESTOPINO
AND MATTHEW WILDER, PERFORMED BY
MATTHEW WILDER (1983), ENCOUNTERED 1985

SUBSTITUTE PLAYLIST TRACK NO. 89 PLAYLIST TRACK NO. 90

BY THE TIME I was a few months into my separation, I had made it my business to see quite a few divorce movies, a genre in which the period was rich: *Smash Palace*, *Twice in a Lifetime*, *An Unmarried Woman*, *Shoot the Moon*, *Kramer vs. Kramer*. I found them all utterly absorbing. No mystery to it: I wanted to check out as many different artistic takes on what I was going through as I could. Even though I saw them all in the theaters, I also rented and watched them multiple times, completely absorbed. This was my story up there, one way or another.

The movie in this obsessed process that affected me most, though, wasn't actually devoted to divorce. *Moscow on the Hudson* focused on a rarer subject: expatriation. Why the fascination? Well, defecting from the Soviet Union in 1984 as screenwriter and director Paul Mazursky depicted it looked an awful lot like the divorce I was going through: the longing to escape, the sense of daring and danger when one did it, the initial high, the practical problems, the unexpected new friends and allies, the bouts of missing the situation one had left, the strain on old family ties, the need to be willing to forge a new identity: all there.

When I got my hands on a rented copy of *Moscow on the Hudson*, the part I rewound and replayed the most was the end credits. They start with Robin Williams as the defector, a saxophonist named Vladimir Ivanov, as he finishes a letter from New York, where he lives now, to his family back in Russia, summing up the good and the bad, but mostly the good, of his new life. The visual behind the voiceover is of Vladimir busking with his saxophone in a park. The song he plays is the first song we got to know him with at the outset when he was a musician in a Russian circus band. In that milieu the melody (no doubt by design) sounded cheerful but superficial. Now, played solo with lots of jazz riffs, it sounds distinctly mournful and much more profound. Michael Rod (the actual musician playing for Robin Williams) leaves pauses between the phrases, which begin to be filled in by singer Chaka Khan, singing a song called *Freedom*. As the titles fade to a black crawl, Khan's song merges with Rod's, and the sax provides continuous counterpoint throughout the titles to Khan's soulful pop evocation of freedom (political and personal).

Freedom, she sings, *I just want to love you*. Possibly it's deliberately ambiguous about whether the love object is another person or just the state of being free. Nor is it clear if the freedom is personal or political. Any way you construed it, it worked for me. Note that the Playlist track substitutes the Pointer Sisters for Chaka Khan; the original is not available on Spotify, but the substitute arrangement is also helmed by arranger Richard Perry, and sounds remarkably similar, minus Michael Rod's sax and Robin Williams' voice.

Another song from that era that always reminds me of that stage of my life was a bouncy, disco-ey piece called *Break My Stride*, by a one-hit wonder named Matthew Wilder (this being his one big hit). The picture it instantly brings to my mind is of me rounding the running track at Baltimore's Downtown Racquet Club (in later years the Downtown Athletic Club, which I have belonged to, off and on, to this very day). There was a PA system there that plays hits calculated to put you in the mood to sweat, and I can recall hearing that oh-so-appropriate song as I was pounding along:

Ain't nothin' gonna break my stride
Nobody's gonna slow me down,
Oh no, I got to keep on moving

261

Ain't nothin' gonna break my stride
I'm running and I won't touch ground
Oh no, I got to keep on moving

This is not a song about exercise (though it goes perfectly with that pursuit). The above lyrics are the expression of a woman who has left the singer behind. But the singer has the same attitude:

Never let another girl like you, work me over
Never let another girl like you, drag me under
If I meet another girl like you, I will tell her
Never want another girl like you have to say
Ooooooh
Ain't nothin' gonna break my stride

In short, this is a breakup song; it's a song about two people who are moving on in both metaphorical and literal senses.

The Racquet Club was a special place to feel that way. It had opened in a disused-but-then-converted Railway Express Agency shed only a few years before, during the first flush of the Baltimore renaissance presided over by the city's great cheerleader, Mayor William Donald Schaefer, when the city seemed to have done more than recover from its 1968 riots, and to have become radiant with possibility. Young professionals flocked to the Club but also more established folks; it had quite a bit of singles action, too, at its bar. With all those atmospherics, it was hard not to feel that one was indeed getting on with one's life rounding that tenth-of-a-mile oval, while being urged on by the bounce of a song that trumpeted above all else a determination to keep on going.

Again, it worked for me.

62

SHUCKS INDEED

THE PEOPLE THAT YOU NEVER GET TO LOVE,
WRITTEN BY RUPERT HOLMES, PERFORMED BY
SUSANNAH McCORKLE (1981), ENCOUNTERED 1984-1986

PLAYLIST NO. 91

WHEN I BECAME single again, like many men in my position, after a bit of a delay to mourn and regroup, I started inviting women into my life. I was free to ask, notwithstanding the serious girlfriend off in Nebraska (and then later in Charlottesville), who like me was seeing other people too. Many of my invitations were accepted.

I had some very unoriginal things to prove: that I was attractive, that I had the maturity to deal with simultaneous relationships, that I wasn't making a mistake with the serious girlfriend. Standard recently-separated stuff.

It would have been nice not to have had anything to prove: just to have been out to have a good time and smell the roses. Nice, but not possible. I couldn't magically become someone fifteen years younger and without a history. I had children, I had burned through a marriage, and I was at least thinking about another marriage while still in my prime. I needed to know some things about myself, and I needed to know them soon. I didn't give myself any deadlines, but, objectively, I had to get a move on because there was a decision day somewhere up ahead.

So I asked out a lot of women. I would have liked to have asked them all. Sure, I knew that was absurd. But I very much wanted to try. Rupert Holmes had the perfect lyric for this thought process in his song *The People That You Never Get To Love*, which I knew at the time through a lovely cover done by Susannah McCorkle (who reversed the genders – though I reverse them back here):

You're browsing in a secondhand bookstore
And you see her in Non-Fiction V through Y
She looks up from World War II
And then you catch her catching you catching her eye
So you quickly turn away your wishful stare
And take a sudden interest in your shoes
If you only had the courage but you don't
She turns and leaves and you both lose
And you think about
The people that you never get to love
It's not as if you even have the chance
So many worth a second life
But rarely do you get a second glance
Until fate cuts in on your dance

Except I could not leave it up to fate to cut in on my dance. I had to be aggressive, and I was, for a while. I asked out a woman I frequently encountered in the lobby of our apartment house. At the Downtown Racquet Club, I chased down a woman I saw with beautiful pre-Raphaelite red hair, caught up with her at the exit, and asked her out on the spot. I drove home a prep school teacher I met in a bar. I fell in love with someone's legs in a Jacuzzi and asked her out. When our office crowd went out drinking, I slipped my arm around a colleague's waist. They all said yes. And there were others.

What happened afterwards varied. Sometimes the attraction dissipated before the evening was out. Sometimes we ended up between the sheets. Sometimes we dated for several months.

Whoever it was, though, it never lasted. Many times they lost interest in me, which I accepted without too much hurt; they were, after all, on their own scavenger hunts of the heart, pursuits I had to respect as much as I respected my own. Just as often, I lost interest.

But there were a couple of them that under slightly different circumstances might have been contenders. As Holmes put it, in the lyric I've already quoted: "So many worth a second life." I am thinking particularly about the woman with the pre-Raphaelite hair, who turned out to be kind and idealistic, one of the nicest people I had ever known. In another life, maybe I would have met her first; we could have built something lasting together. Yet in the life I was actually leading, she could not establish a lasting beachhead in my affections; that shore turned out still to be held by my out-of-town girlfriend. For me, despite honest experimenting, no one else came close. I have talked about but haven't described Mary in these pages, and I wouldn't try. I lack the gift to explain why the chemistry with one person is so much stronger than the chemistry with anyone else. But I can honestly say I was not putting my thumb on the scale when I was going through this process. My mind was truly open. Exciting as my other relationships were, though, they remained diversions for me. (Which was not to say that I was not acutely aware of and sometimes humbled by the value of the gifts I was turning down.)

The worst was the ethical side of it. That had come up with Jo, my therapist, in the first few weeks of my work with her, before I had even positively made up my mind to leave my marriage. She'd asked me what my fantasy of freedom was, and I'd said I wanted to be with a lot of women. My therapist was dismissive. *It will never work*, she told me. *I wish you luck*, she said, *but the only successful mass-womanizers are either sociopaths or narcissists who can deceive themselves into believing anything about others which suits their self-interest, and you're neither*. My face fell. *Shucks?* she suggested.

Shucks indeed. I didn't want to hurt people, but achieving what I did want ran a constant risk of trifling with people's affections. I tried hard to avoid that, mostly by being honest at all times, but I knew I was not always succeeding.

Even when I was not running the risk of breaking hearts, there was the delicate dance of not explaining to the person I might be spending Friday night with where I might be, say, on Saturday night. It can be implicitly or explicitly acknowledged that one or both are seeing more than one person, but that's still somewhat theoretical. More concrete are the silences that fall when one is discussing one's activities or one's schedule. Love thrives on accountability; playing the field thrives on its opposite.

At its best, though, and for a little while, the experience was liberating. It was tremendously exciting to be what they now call a player. I remember one moment that crystallized it for me. I was walking out of an apartment house down by Baltimore's waterfront in a brisk, sunny dawn. I had spent the night with a woman with whom there was mercifully no possibility of deep attachment, a true friend with benefits (a friend to this day, actually, over three decades later), and it had been great fun. She had been the third woman I'd spent the night with that week. And as I stood out there in the sunlight, a phrase from Wordsworth came unbidden to my mind: "Bliss was it in that dawn to be alive." Wordsworth, it's true, was speaking of far more important things than an exciting stretch in one's love life. But that was the phrase in my head.

I knew this blissful dawn wasn't going to last, that the sun was going to rise further, leaving me in some kind of workaday world. But at least I'd had that dawn. That was something.

A postscript about the role of that song in my life may demonstrate why my little experiment with casting a wide net for love was likely to succeed only in proving a negative. I had acquired McCorkle's album, also entitled *The People That You Never Get To Love*, probably within a week or two of moving into my bachelor apartment. The song and the whole album had become instant hits with me, and I had wanted to share them with everyone. Towards the end of August that summer, I went back to Michigan for a few days with my parents there, and I played them a tape I'd dubbed of the album. I mentioned that the Holmes song nicely summed up the quest I was on at that point: to find the people that I'd never got to love.

My mother was unimpressed (and I fear unimpressed with McCorkle). Isn't there anyone more important than the others? she asked. I said there was. She asked for the name, and I mentioned Mary for the first time to her. Good, she said, I'm glad. I don't think she even really heard that I was looking around, that there was a wider focus just now, and that there was a song here that spoke to it. All she heard or wanted to hear was that there was someone special. And though I would have been happier had she taken in more of what I was saying, I was glad she was glad. So I have to chalk up what can only be called a competing association for this song. Yes, even this one.

But Rupert Holmes and Susannah McCorkle could hear what Mother could or would not. They understood the sadness in the limits life places on our love lives. We can try, for a little while – I did – to break the short tether of human finitude that so restricts our access to romance, but we can never pull hard enough to snap it. We can, at best, meet an infinitesimal fraction of the people with whom we could have mated. Good things may come from crying uncle in this struggle, but let us not disguise the defeat as a victory.

We want everything. And we can't have everything. Disappointment is guaranteed: a more-than-appropriate reason to sing a melancholy song. Which was something McCorkle knew how to do, superbly.

63

BUMPY LANDING

INNUENDO, BY MICHAEL FRANKS (1987), "ENCOUNTERED" 1985-86

PLAYLIST TRACK NO. 92

LIFE'S MAJOR TRANSITIONS are often messy. When (halfway between two marriages) I finally gave up playing the field, that was a major transition. And majorly messy.

Neat would have been if I'd come to a clear-cut realization that carrying on multiple relationships was straining my integrity and imperiling my chances with Mary, the one I most cared for. Neat would have been a calm decision that therefore my wandering ways needed to stop.

Now, I did have such moments of clarity, lots of them, aided by predictable flashes of jealousy on both sides between Mary, my main girlfriend, and me. But I also had plenty of moments of the opposite sort of clarity: a clarity about the sexual freedom I'd be giving up and about my still-unsettled state (not yet being legally divorced, nor out of therapy, and certainly without a way of figuring out my long-term finances). A bit like Saint Augustine, I had always wanted an exclusive relationship; I just was having trouble deciding to have it quite yet.

So the process was messy. Let us say bumpy. Surely the biggest bump came in the fall of 1985 when I tried swearing off the other relationships – and then panicked, and begged off the new arrangement for a while. Mary, who had by then moved to Charlottesville, forgave me, but it didn't help matters between us.

So things went on until the spring of 1986. I wish I could articulate more clearly how it was different this time from the way it had been a few months before, but I have no explanations. I can only tell the story, prompted by my calendar.

As the calendar reflects, in late April I went on my last real date with someone else. By my own choice I was already down to just one someone else, and she was the friend with benefits I'd mentioned in the previous chapter; we had no serious relationship. I guess I was no longer looking for anyone who could compete with what I was building with Mary – just someone who could delay it.

Two days later, I was in Bellaire, Florida, at a national training session for new state humanities council members (I'd just joined Maryland's). Mostly I was alone; that much I recall. I don't remember much about the conference. Well, let's be honest; I don't remember anything about the conference. No doubt it was well-run and inspiring, and no doubt the company was pleasant. But nearly thirty years later, all of that is lost to my memory. What stands out – and stands out vividly – is the hotel itself, the Belleview Biltmore. Even in my contemporaneous snapshots, it is the hotel that matters, not the guests.

When we, the conferees, arrived, being humanities people, we were briefed by someone about the history of the place. It had started out at the turn of the previous century as a spot where rich folks could come down by train, park their private sleeping cars on a siding, and golf amongst their peers. The grandee market having dried up considerably after the Great Crash, the hotel had had to cope, partly, as I learned, by becoming a defense asset during World War II.

By utter coincidence, when I got there, I happened to be reading James Gould Cozzens' *Guard of Honor* (1948), a tale of the races and the sexes behind the lines in 1943, as the Army Air Corps geared up for combat. Much of the action there took place in a grand hotel called the Oleander Towers where officers attached to a nearby airfield and official visitors were billeted. The Biltmore's guests, I learned, had been attached to nearby MacDill Airfield. And much of the description of the Oleander Towers fit the Biltmore: Cozzens' wrote of "[t]he vast corridors, the old-fashioned lofty rooms with ceiling fans and slatted doors [that] were fairly cool. The high, screened balconies got some breeze … most nights.") And then I realized that the Cozzens' hotel sat on the Central Florida Gulf Coast, as did the Biltmore. And you don't have two places on that scale in proximity to each other. So I concluded the Biltmore had to be the model for the Oleander Towers! Suddenly, I could, in my mind's eye, see men in uniform striding down the hallways "down on conferences, inspections, and junkets" – in Cozzens' words, and maybe finding moments for romance, as one of his heroes sort of did.

Hence it was, I felt, a hotel that had seen everything, and if I could only be attentive in the presence of that mute historical omniscience, somehow I would receive some sort of wisdom.

What I came away with was more a feeling than a thought: a dissatisfaction with aloneness. I suspect from some scanty evidence, and again I'm revealing how messy it all was, that on the Monday night, I had a flirtatious dinner that led nowhere with someone whom I know now merely by recorded initials (the name is gone from memory). I know that after that inconclusive dinner I caught a shuttle out to Clearwater Beach, to catch the celebrated sight of the sun setting over the Gulf of Mexico from the fishing pier there. Seeing it made me wish I could share that prospect with Mary, but I had forgotten my camera. (Fortunately, my job brought me back to the area almost exactly a year later, and that time I captured those images of the sunset that had eluded me the preceding year.)

I am certain I came away leaning toward the view that it was time to bring this stage of my life to a close. But I wasn't quite there even then. Perhaps my mind was really made up two weeks later, at a group therapy session. The other members of the group did not think highly of my inconstancy, to put it mildly. One of the female members told me, in a voice that one uses to explain the obvious to a thick child, that ordinarily you put in some time being monogamous with anyone you're thinking about marrying.

Or perhaps the final turning point came the following weekend when I flew back to my hometown of Ann Arbor for a party honoring my stepdad on his retirement. I spent more time alone there, walking around, photographing my old haunts, thinking, for some reason, about being honest with my kids. Although it was no doubt a trifle optimistic to think they would be interested in their father's early years, I wanted there to be a record, an honest record, a clear and admirable one. And I knew (if only from the Group's commentary) that there wasn't much admiration for my extant way of life from those who knew the most about it.

And so I came to Friday, May 16. Early that evening, I got together again with my friend with benefits, and over drinks, looking across the room at a second-floor window revealing the fading light in an Inner Harbor neighborhood, I told her I'd decided I only wanted to see one woman now.

Don't even worry about it, my friend said. *I still want to be friends*, I said, and she agreed. We talked for an hour, we hugged goodbye, and I went home.

Not much later, Mary arrived from Virginia, and I told her I was through with everyone else. She asked me if I was serious this time, and I told her I was. I had a hollow feeling, still, though. I'd had warm feelings for the friend I'd just broken up with. But I kept it to myself.

The following evening, the two of us went to a "hat party" given by a friend – everyone had to wear a lid, don't ask me why. Two of the other guests there were women I had slept with. There might have been a day, and not long before either, that I would have exulted in that secret evidence of my prowess and attractiveness. Now I felt bad because the two other women had information Mary didn't (and, consistent with the rules Mary and I had laid down to avoid jealousy, I had not told her). I found I had stopped wanting the thrill of secret information. I was now ready for a regime of straightforward disclosure. And I felt a strong sense of relief that I would not be adding anything more to that pile of secrets. It could well be that that moment, not the isolation at the grand hotel nor the critique from the therapy group nor the introspection in my hometown nor the goodbye to the friend nor the announcement to Mary, was the real point of decision. There's no way of really saying.

Wherever it had exactly happened, though, I felt as if the train of my life had gone over a switch somewhere. I might still be running parallel to most of my old ways, but I was headed for a different destination.

The song that I hear when I think about that part of my life is actually from the following year, 1987, Michael Franks' *Innuendo*. The story the song tells bears some resemblance to the transition I was making. It concerns two former lovers coming back together, going on a date after a year off in which he's had "a few stolen kisses and several near misses" – presumably with others. He's nervous adjusting his tie in the mirror, before going out to re-encounter The One.

> *The bravado's just pretend-o.*
> *And the chic spot where we meet*
> *Is called Innuendo.*

But as they talk, as "their salads are dressing," along comes Cupid with his arrow, and though they each dissimulate a bit by resorting to innuendo rather than direct talk, eventually they finish the meal and go home together.

And this happiness we feel
As we move to the crescendo
Makes the dialogue more real,
Not just innuendo.
No more innuendo…

So, this song is about a second try at a relationship, the success of which is marked by the "dialogue" becoming "more real." That's the big similarity. The musical setting might seem distinctly less of a fit. It is lovely and placid, built around the smooth jazz guitar of Earl Klugh, who could noodle as smoothly as any guitarist in that era. So what if there'd been nothing smooth about the process of getting to this point? This record actually came out in 1987, a year after the bumpy landing, a happy year, as it turned out. No buyer's regrets this time. The smoothness of the year somehow worked backwards to make the bumpiness less bumpy in retrospect. So to me the song was a perfect fit.

64

READER, I MARRIED HER

BEBEL, WRITTEN BY ANTONIO CARLOS JOBIM, PERFORMED BY
KENNY DREW, JR. (1991), "ENCOUNTERED" 1988

PLAYLIST TRACK NO. 93

THE PACE WAS picking up between Mary and me now. At some point I would need to declare myself, and say some words in a church. But it was still hard to bring oneself to that point. Declaring that readiness and saying those words in a church are daunting things to do, when you are coming off a divorce, when you know your own capacity for folly and destructiveness, when you do not entirely trust yourself. The bumpy landing just getting to exclusivity I wrote about in the last chapter was never far from my mind.

And yet it was a season of transitions, and each one helped make the others more plausible in anticipation and easier in practice.

My divorce was final in mid-1986, and with it, certain uncertainties about my commitments were resolved. At around the same point, Mary moved closer, from Charlottesville to Washington.

That summer I also left, or as the phrase went, graduated from, group therapy. It was a tearful occasion, but Group was for people who had major things to learn that they couldn't learn elsewhere, and/or who were stuck at some critical decision necessary to their happiness, and I had learned most of what Group had to teach; nor was I stuck. It was a tearful parting, but a parting nonetheless.

And in February of 1987, I bought a house. Before doing it, I visited the place with both my kids and Mary, all together; we consciously discussed the possibility of making a nursery in the house, and indeed our plan all along was for Mary to move in in the spring.

There was an obvious direction to all this. But still we hadn't quite reached the point of making it official, even to ourselves. And then the final clarity began.

That summer, I was visiting my wise stepmother Etta at the family vacation cottage in the Catskills, and her advice to me was succinct: "Take your time, but not too much time." I think she was concerned about the bad things that might happen if I kept Mary waiting too long.

And shortly afterwards, I received what a lawyer might call a solicitation for a bid. I don't recall the exact context (some kind of joking conversation), but do I remember exactly where Mary was standing (right next to the laundry hamper in the bedroom closet, if you must know). And Mary said: "But what have you done for me lately, like marry me?"

I let the remark pass, but it was clear that the time was at hand. My serious reservations were gone. I had known her for four years. We had been exclusive for a year or more, and I had been happier than ever.

And yet – and yet. As with many another guy, the proposal itself somehow stuck in my throat for a while, even when I recognized that I was simply having nerves, not the kind of qualms I had experienced the first time around (also written of in these pages). But qualms are for listening to, nerves are for ignoring. So one night I summoned my courage and took Mary to dinner at the place we'd gone on the night we met (a different restaurant at this point, but in the same space), and over preliminary drinks, I tried to get out my question. I'm seldom at a loss for words, but somehow I couldn't quite say it intelligibly, even though I knew what the answer would be. It took a couple of indirect stabs before Mary recognized my proposal for what it was. But when she did, we held hands across the table. It was done.

From that point on, things moved with a lovely directness, at least as between Mary and me. There were external problems (completing the process of moving Mary in, finding a church that would stage a nuptial for two divorced, unanulled Catholics, dealing with my mother, a category of difficulty unto itself, and of course all the logistics of planning, which ended up taking about a year), but we dealt with them as an adult couple.

And when we got to the moment itself, in September of 1988, the ceremony was beautiful. Most weddings are beautiful, of course. But our wedding,

I'm convinced, was a classic: low-key and not marred by extravagance, but still elegant and filled with happy people.

Well, something like that needed a Theme Song. But, atypically for me, there really wasn't one to hand.

I reiterate a point I've made throughout these pages: It has been by sheerest coincidence that I've come to associate most of the songs I've written about here with important moments in my life. I just happened to be listening to them when noteworthy things happened to happen. Very little artistry, indeed, very little volition has been involved. But at this paramount moment, I aspired to come up with something more precisely right. By now I was thinking as an artist, specifically as a film director (even though that is not a medium in which I've ever tried to work in real life). I was dreaming of a movie about my recent life in which my remarriage would be the happy conclusion.

I needed a song for the end credits. I did not see the wedding itself as the last shot; rather, it would be an image of fictionalized versions of Mary and me, shot from behind, walking away holding hands along a springtime street in the twilight, as the camera pedestaled up until finally all you saw, before the credits rolled, would be the blossoms in the trees. A very specific image, in other words, conventionally shot to tell the viewer firmly: happy ending.

I knew intellectually, of course, that life never gives us totally happy endings. Even the best marriages have their rough patches, and I was sophisticated enough now to expect that. But the hell with what I knew; this was about what I felt. And even before we married, what I felt was how incredibly lucky and happy I was to have Mary. There's a sentence in George Gissing's novel *Sleeping Fires* which summed up my feelings about her: "It was the woman whom a man in his maturity desires unashamed." And there I was, unashamed after a long process.

To capture all that, the song would have be something that began in a long and hesitant fashion, but then moved from diffidence to confidence, lyricism, and joy.

I finally found that song in a music store a few years later while taking a needed extended recuperative lunch break from my job being a square peg at an outfit I'll call, in this and future chapters, the Round Hole Law Firm. There aren't so many music stores now, but this one still (as of 2020) exists, albeit in a different location, catering now as then to a mainly Black clientele. And where better to stay on top of jazz? Periodically at that point I'd wander in and ask for something new and exciting. On this occasion, I was handed a self-titled cassette album: *Kenny Drew, Jr*. Drew played a very dominant piano in front of a trio for much of the album. I'd never heard of Kenny Drew, Sr. or Jr., so the name meant nothing to me.

When I played it, I liked a lot of it and didn't like a lot of it. (Some of the boppier numbers struck me as nearly cacophonous.) But there were a couple of lovely things in there, one of which was *Bebel*. I didn't know then what the name portended (singer Bebel Gilberto, João Gilberto's daughter); for some reason I even failed to note that the song was written by Jobim, the king of the bossa nova. I just knew the song was one of the coolest things I'd ever heard. It opens with a full minute of the piano hesitantly picking a melody, two notes at a time, staggering uncertainly up and down the octaves, as if it is trying to make up its mind about a key and a register and a melody, but then there comes a moment when the melody finally commits. Then it starts to flow, smoothly, inventively and elegantly, for another five minutes, in a style reminiscent of Brubeck or Luiz Eça, each of whom I've written about in these pages.

The song was perfect, actually far more perfect than Jobim's original, which lacks much of Drew's hesitancy or dramatic contrast – another way of saying Drew adds these things. (And Jobim's voice can't handle the vocal range Jobim the composer writes for Jobim the singer.)

So this was the *Bebel* to start with. And it captures, as no other song I encountered at that time, the wonder of that moment, when, having cleared aside every impediment, I also surmounted hesitancy, and the most important part of my life came definitively together, when I was able to ask for what I needed, and to say "I do" when I was given the chance to commit to it.

Reader, I married her.

And *Bebel* was the song.

65

CUMBERLAND DAYS

THE CHAIRMAN DANCES, COMPOSED BY JOHN ADAMS,
PERFORMED BY THE SAN FRANCISCO SYMPHONY, CONDUCTED BY
EDO DE WAART (1987), ENCOUNTERED 1987-1989

PLAYLIST TRACK No. 94

BY THE MID-EIGHTIES, I had made sufficient progress as a junior lawyer that my place in my law firm seemed assured. What I'd assured, for as long as it lasted, was a work life primarily devoted to tending to one class of cases for one client. Clients are seldom forever, and case types go in waves, so my specialization was risky, but it was nonetheless a great way to start a career.

Particularly for a guy like me. I had a taste for the computer, an affinity for the library, a touch of wanderlust, and a meditative bent. And this was the job to suit all of these inclinations.

My client was CSX, the giant railroad company that was emerging in that era from the amalgamation of the Baltimore & Ohio, the Chesapeake & Ohio, the Seaboard, the Louisville & Nashville, and other roads. All of these railroads, indeed all of American railroading, had been built on the steam locomotive. A generation before, though, steam power had been abandoned; now a large part of the railroads' workforce was being abandoned as well. Really, really abandoned; there is a chart I saw that gives a sense of how thoroughly. Some highlights: from 1947 to 1986, the four decades before I got involved in this work, U.S. railroad employment had plummeted from

1,516,000 to 323,000. By the time I got out of this work, in 1994, the total was down to 234,000.

But it's an ill wind that blows no one any good. The synergy from those two abandonments nurtured my career for a while. Consider the steam locomotive: in essence a boiler laid on its side. And in the latter part of the industrial era, standard engineering practice called for doing one thing with pretty much any boiler: wrapping it in asbestos. Locomotive maintenance, in turn, called for these great beasts of machines to be lugged into back shops and roundhouses and stripped of their metal jackets, and for the asbestos sheathing to be pried away so that the machinists could get at the boilers' innards. Afterwards the process would be reversed. Needless to say, the unsheathing and resheathing would cause asbestos to become "airborne," as industrial hygienists would term it.

By 1986, there were a lot of out-of-work old men with breathing difficulties who had once worked for the railroad. From their perspective the railroad had shown them no loyalty; now it would be their turn to show none. Along with tens of thousands of former smokestack industry workers around the country, they found lawyers and took their former employers to court for what had happened to their lungs. And among the defendants were the legal shells of CSX's constituent railroads. When they were sued in Maryland, the cases came my way.

Now, at least in my view, at that time and still today, the claims of the plaintiffs in these cases to be suffering from asbestos disease were generally dubious, and the asbestos disease in those who were genuine asbestos victims was generally not very consequential. But I never thought that occupational disease was what the cases were really about. I thought of them as a sort of collective evening of the score between employees and an employer which had turned them out. Whatever the truth of the matter, the cases had to be dealt with.

The railroad almost never got sued by itself. The manufacturers of the asbestos products previously used in the railroad industry (not just boiler lagging but brake pads and gaskets) always got sued along with the railroads – at least until asbestos claims put those fellow-defendants into bankruptcy. And as much as the railroad would have liked to turn around and point the finger at this gradually shrinking pool of co-defendants or at the tobacco companies, it was also a fact that all these other companies were suppliers and shippers. So there was an odd combination of antagonistic and shared interests at work.

It was all catnip to me.

First, there were a lot of plaintiffs, allowing me to organize a lot of data, to set up a database, in other words – doing this hands-on in an era when most lawyers, even the few who had direct access to a computer, wouldn't have even known exactly what a database was. I, by contrast, was given a room just for documents and my very own computer. The software I relied on on that computer was truly primitive. About the time this work drew to a close, I started using true relational databases for other things, and it became clear in retrospect that in my asbestos years I had been trying to force a two-dimensional database (basically a big spreadsheet) to do things beyond its natural limitations. But I came close enough, largely because I was left alone and given plenty of time; any gaps that emerged I could bridge in ways that weren't strictly database queries. I don't know how much of my time was written off by the responsible partner – a lot, I suspect. But I was teaching myself database work, which has been a mainstay of my personal and professional life ever since.

There were lots of interesting legal questions, which I can't discuss, but I can say that they gave me very good reason to spend afternoons looking at statutes and cases in the library, and drafting legal memos, the lawyerly occupation above all others that I enjoyed.

Then too I was learning all about a medical field. I found out that all the expert witnesses referred to a body of medical literature comprising about three hundred articles. I painstakingly assembled those articles, read them all (indexing them in my database), and learned enough to be dangerous. Armed with this jerry-built medical knowledge, I had to develop expert witnesses. With some help from lawyers who were defending railroads elsewhere, I had to travel to various places where the experts were to make them ready to testify.

I also had to travel to the old locomotive shops, in places like Glenwood and Connellsville, Pennsylvania, and Cumberland, Maryland, to figure out what I could about the working conditions twenty to forty years earlier. (It was a sign of the times, I still remember, that at one of these shops, when the word got out I was a railroad lawyer, I was mobbed by workers asking when the next buyout would be.)

Knowing the conditions also meant knowing the products involved. Gradually I built up a book of photos of the old products, especially photos with the name identifications of the manufacturers. I figured that even if the railroad was sensitive to the perils of implicating suppliers, I had to know who they were. This took me to old repositories of dusty records, all in the process of being trashed by a corporate colossus that could not have cared less about preserving relics of its past. Principal among the places I looked was the old Baltimore & Ohio warehouse at Camden Station in Baltimore.

Baseball fans know it today as the backdrop to Oriole Park at Camden Yards; I knew it in its dying gasp as an actual warehouse. Many of its windows were broken; birds and bats flew in and crapped on cardboard boxes filled with every imaginable kind of railroad record, indexed in haphazard ways. You could get lost in that vast space, a kind of vertical equivalent of the repository where the Ark was stored at the end of *Raiders of the Lost Ark*. As indignant as I felt about this handling of the old records, veritable books about a bygone way of life if you knew how to read them, I knew that dumpsters and shredding awaited these boxes that I might be the last human ever to open.

But it wasn't just dusty places I went to. I also had to sit in a high rise office tower to go through several years of corporate minutes of the B&O and the Western Maryland boards, to learn – various things.

Beyond that, I had to get to know my plaintiffs. I know, I know, my client was the defendant. But in order to try to defend that client, I still had to know the plaintiffs, these machinists and brakemen and engineers and firemen and maintenance-of-way workers, and I thought of them as mine. I had to get to know about their individual asbestos exposures, their individual careers, their medical histories, their hobbies, their tobacco use, their families, their non-railroad occupational exposures to asbestos. Sometimes they had moved far away, and I went there after them and their treating physicians: to San Francisco, to DuBois, Pennsylvania, to Sandusky, Ohio, to Three Churches, West Virginia. But most of them had not followed that pattern.

Instead, most of these old men had aged in place, in or near the Appalachian railroad towns I've mentioned. This especially meant Cumberland, Maryland, the home of the big back shop that CSX still used (and in 2020 still uses under the name of the CSX Cumberland Diesel Locomotive Shops) to service much of its motive power fleet (all diesels now, of course). I and a group of lawyers representing the dwindling but still substantial corps of solvent manufacturers of asbestos products once used by railroads would sit in a conference room for days on end, several times over the years I was doing this work, asking the same questions over and over again of one after another railroad worker. After a couple of stabs at other venues, we lawyers came to a consensus that the place to take the depositions was the Best Western

Braddock Motor Inn in the little village of La Vale, halfway between Cumberland and Frostburg.

For me, it was a wonderful time, though it is a bit peculiar to describe. Let me start with the trip itself. Though once or twice I flew out to Cumberland (once in a private jet chartered by a defense lawyer who had far more clout and financial backing than I did), mostly I drove out on superhighways, as far as they would take me – which was not initially all the way. What is today known as I-68, the leg of the road from Hancock to Cumberland, La Vale, and Frostburg, was still being built when I started. I would roll out of bed before sunup, and after about two hours' drive be in Hancock, the narrowest part of Maryland's panhandle, about 1.8 miles wide, squeezed between Pennsylvania and the Potomac. Then the trip became more of a challenge. The old National Highway, aka Route 40, uneasily coexisted with the superhighway under construction that oft-times was usurping its roadbed. At best, a driver could expect to cope with detours, mud, and dust from the great machines that were, foot by foot, grinding mountainside into freeway. At worst, there could be delays up there in the clouds on the curve of a two-lane highway with no sightline to what was halting traffic and no intelligence about when the cars would begin to roll once more. As the months and years went by, more and more was done, so that eventually you could get right up to the brow of the valley where Cumberland sat, plunge down the mountainside, and then zoom up the hill again toward the mountain pass where La Vale lay.

It was while going through that dip in the opposite direction that my "single again" car, a sporty but truly disappointing Toyota Celica, finally died on me, when I found that I could not engage the clutch to go back uphill; this vehicular fail, along with my changing life circumstances, prompted me to buy my "newly remarried and looking forward to parenthood minivan," a black Plymouth Voyager, which is the car that mainly comes to mind now when I think of these trips.

Eventually, you'd get to the Braddock, lying just north of the new highway, adjacent to an exit. The setting was always calming after the rigors of the road. There was a babbling little mountain stream, the Braddock Run, shaded by pleasant trees that ran right past the parking lot, and the building was covered with brown rustic-looking wooden shingles. You could park your bags in your room and then go right down to another hotel room that had had the beds taken out and a table brought in, and go to work.

The depositions themselves were about as relaxed as litigation ever gets. I many not have understood why at the beginning, but I soon worked it out. Nothing really mattered. All these cases were going to be resolved. From the point of view of the corporations that sent most of the lawyers, these were exercises in putting checkmarks in the database. Did a man have pleural thickening? Did a man have a plausible claim to asbestos exposure? Those and similar questions were ultimately reduced to statistics on both sides. And periodically I would learn that a group of cases were to be dismissed, I presumed with some reference to those checkmarks, though I seldom learned much about it. Above my pay grade.

I never got to try one of these cases. Not one. But no one grudged me the opportunity to sit in a hotel room and make believe. It took me a while to figure out the game, but when I did, it certainly took the pressure off. I realized that, as Arlo Guthrie put it, "the judge wasn't going to look at the twenty-seven eight-by-ten color glossy pictures" – all the articles and the databases, and the expert testimony I had so painstakingly assembled. It was all Kabuki.

So even though I came to each deposition with a full collection of work records and medical records, even though I asked all the right questions and got into occasional tussles with the plaintiffs' lawyers over objections, basically I was free to enjoy what the depositions had to offer: an unparalleled look at a bygone slice of life. I developed a genuine affection for the railroad men, and got to know a lot about them as a community: who was married to whose sister, who had worked alongside whom, whom they had reported to in the roundhouse at a particular era.

I learned about their hobbies (a lot of what they called "feeshin'" and a fair amount of roller skating). I learned that the industrial world that had produced them had collapsed. That there had been three big employers in their world: the railroad (which had so drastically shrunk), "the Celanese" (acetate works, closed in 1983) and "the Kelly" (Kelly-Springfield tires, closed in 1987). The rug had been pulled out from under them and their friends, and their dependence on tobacco had in many cases destroyed their bodies and condemned them to invalid lives and early deaths. These were men who by-and-large had been built for loyalty, for relationships of lifelong reciprocal support between themselves and their country and their employers. And even when it all went wrong, most of them went on being the strong people they had grown up to be, survivors of the Greatest Generation, mainstays of families. I did my duty by my client, but I was glad it was so ineffectual.

As for me, the stays at the Braddock were frequent, for one day, two days, once even a week. There wasn't much in the way of nightlife or fancy dining (one first-class restaurant in Frostburg), but you could go for a dip in the hotel pool, and just luxuriate in the peacefulness of the setting. And no one ever questioned my expenditures. To the extent I desired company, I generally had it, in the other lawyers participating, on both sides. I made friends with more than one of the plaintiffs' lawyers we sat across from during the day.

So it was almost always with pleasure that I would rise early in the morning from time to time and chuck boxes of documents into my minivan, and head around the Beltway to the beginning of I-70. I used to joke that the car knew the way. Even today, over a quarter century later, if I approach that interchange in an absent-minded state, my tendency will be to move my vehicle into that exit lane without thinking about it, forcing me to correct my course when I wake up and realize what I'm doing.

While I was on those trips, the cassette in my onboard cassette player was often the San Francisco Symphony's very popular rendition of five works by composer John Adams, highlighted by his twelve-and-a-half-minute fantasia *The Chairman Dances*. The liner notes were worded in a way that made it seem, without actually saying so, that this number was from Adams' hit opera *Nixon in China*. Although I'm a great fan of the musical stage, I'm not much of an opera guy, and so I went on believing what the liner notes kind of implied until I was in preparation to write this chapter. When I acquired a Blu-Ray of the Metropolitan Opera production, I realized I'd been had. The correct way to describe the relationship between the opera and this piece is that *Chairman* makes liberal use of musical figures and themes from the third act of *Nixon*. The piece really is simply a marvelous polyrhythmic confection. The subtitle is "Foxtrot for Orchestra," but when you're talking about a minimalist composer, don't look for promises like "foxtrot" to be kept. Foxtrots are four-beat animals; this sounds as if it's written in eight much of the time, though there certainly is a quite-deliberate Fred-and-Ginger feel about a lot of it; it's supposed to evoke Mao, rejuvenated in fantasy, dancing with his "queen," Jiang Ching.

Everyone who encounters this piece seems to hear different things in it, many of them surprising to me. But that capacity to evoke almost anything is a strength. The piece soars at times; it sounds like pounding industrial pistons at others; it whispers like the second movement of *Eine Kleine Nachtmusik* at others. It covers a prodigious amount of exciting musical territory in less than a quarter hour. The multitude of the "reads" is easy to understand.

My own is what you'd expect: a vision of the territory between the Baltimore Beltway and Maryland's Alleghanies rushing up to meet my windshield. This infinitely pliable music has a motile quality most of the time that goes well with memories of the rapidly changing scenery.

Generally, all five pieces on the tape would last me most of the way to Frederick if I played it once, or to Hancock if I played it twice.

To this day, if I hear the music, I think of my Cumberland times, and if I take that drive, I think of the music. They were good trips for me, and it's a happy association.

66

LOOK, MATTHEW, IT'S YOU!

THE RAINBOW CONNECTION, WRITTEN BY PAUL WILLIAMS
AND KENNY ASCHER, PERFORMED BY KERMIT THE FROG
(JIM HENSON) (1979), ENCOUNTERED CA. 1991

PLAYLIST TRACK No. 95

IN 1990, AFTER about two years of marriage, Mary and I became parents. For me it was a third go at fatherhood, a chance to learn from experience and do it better.

I was not disappointed and, I hope, did not disappoint.

Almost immediately it was clear that our son Matthew' life was lived mostly in the sunshine. Lots of laughter, lots of enthusiasm. I have a wonderful video of Matt right after he'd learned to walk, just following me around the house, giggling with excitement. It sums up our one-year-old. Of course no child is always happy, and Matthew, our tiny son, could start that little lower lip trembling with incipient tears at the drop of a hat; any frustration would do. Still, there were a lot more laughs than tears.

His older brother accurately said of Matt a little later that his tail was always wagging. And while I know that every child brings something uniquely his or her own to the relationship with parents, I am certain that coming up in an atmosphere of palpable stability and love improves the odds of happiness. I couldn't sufficiently provide these my first two times around; this time I could.

You could see this dynamic in Matthew's efforts to learn to speak. It was a joyous thing for him. He had a "language tape," a VHS video transcription of the first three Muppet movies that I had made in the previous decade for his older brother and sister during a Muppet marathon on Baltimore's old Channel 45. It was complete with commercials and station breaks and really, really bad video, but it was perfect for Matt.

For instance, there's a moment when the Kermit and Fozzie are behind the wheel of a Studebaker en route to Hollywood, and they come upon a billboard on which the evil Doc Hopper (Charles Durning) has appropriated Kermit's likeness to sell his would-be fast food Doc Hopper's Frog Legs. "Kermit, it's you!" exclaims Fozzie in astonishment. Matt, who watched the tape a lot, and whose command of his own name was still a little wobbly, would go around saying things like: "Look, Mytoo, it's you!" He mined the three movies for all sorts of things like that.

Of course, it was more than the lexical vocabulary of the movies; Matt inhaled the sunny, madcap spirit of them, and the music. And now the music makes me think of him at that age.

Midway through *The Muppet Movie*, Dr. Teeth and his band crowd around a copy of the script of *The Muppet Movie*, reading the movie's own first scene: "Exterior. Swamp. Day. In a long helicopter shot we discover Kermit the Frog playing his banjo and singing." Dr. Teeth doesn't get around to telling us what Kermit was singing, but the audience members are not likely to forget; once having heard *The Rainbow Connection*, Kermit's wistful but hopeful little tear-jerker, one will never be free of it.

It is a song with two sides: the as-yet unsatisfied pursuit of wonder and the faith (naive or not, you choose) that we will attain it one day. It is not a religious song, because the wonder the frog aspires to find is probably earthly (though I have heard the song sung in church), but it is close to a secular equivalent.

Why are there so many songs about rainbows
And what's on the other side?
Rainbows are visions
But only illusions
And rainbows have nothing to hide.
So we've been told
And some choose to believe it
I know they're wrong, wait and see
Some day we'll find it
The rainbow connection
The lovers, the dreamers, and me.

When we get older, we know that in this life at least we will never quite find that rainbow connection that Kermit aspires to with such touching confidence. But we grownups tend not to tell our children about that letdown. Childhood should be touched by magic.

Matt's was.

67

THE BEST REVENGE

YOU OUGHTA KNOW, WRITTEN BY ALANIS MORISSETTE AND GLEN BALLARD, PERFORMED BY ALANIS MORISSETTE (1995), ENCOUNTERED 1995

PLAYLIST TRACK NO. 96

LIVING WELL IS the best revenge, they say. By the time Alanis Morissette's volcanically angry signature song *You Oughta Know* came to my attention, I'd already chosen that kind of revenge for myself, over a year before. The anger that had driven me to choose that revenge was still fresh, though, and my anger was as persistent as Alanis', too good to let go of even if one could have. And that mattered more than the obvious fact that whatever had provoked her anger was way different from what had provoked mine. Sometimes all angers are one. That's why I could drive along with the cassette of her album *Jagged Little Pill* cranked up in my car radio, singing along at the top of my voice —

And every time you speak her name
Does she know how you told me you'd hold me
Until you died, till you died
But you're still alive

— over and over again.
Paradoxically, I'm not sure I could have enjoyed my anger so much if I hadn't reached a point in my life when, overall, I was calming down. I had been

one to indulge my rages over the years, not only against the bad guys life sends one's way but against the good guys, my family members especially. By now, though, I was coming to realize the moral imperative of holding my temper better. But temper and rage are one thing; this was different: productive, liberating anger.

In mid-1995, I still had a raging hangover of that anger.

Over what? You have to go back to what I've been calling the Round Hole Law Firm, where I found myself nominally a partner, in 1993. And let me be fair. I owe that firm my gratitude for rescuing my practice group and hence me from the 1989 collapse of the law firm that in these pages I have called Funhouse. But I was a square peg at Round Hole, a lawyer whose work didn't really fit any of the practice groups, and wasn't plentiful enough so that I could constitute myself a practice group of my own. My square peg-ness became more apparent as my designated practice group's principal client began withdrawing work for various reasons.

Now when you as a firm have a square peg, you can try to make a square hole by finding that square-peg person work he or she can grow. And heaven knows, I was doing everything within my power to be a good service partner and justify receiving that kind of help, should they choose to offer it.

But they didn't choose to offer it. Basically, they went to the other extreme.

When you are hurting for a "book of business," as I then was, the one thing you naturally want most is to develop one. But at a large law firm, the chances are that almost every client engagement that might otherwise augment your book falls into one of two forbidden categories: already spoken for or conflicted out. That is, either someone else in the firm, most likely one of the people senior to you, has already laid claim to that piece of business, or no one in the firm can touch it because of some ethical conflict of interest. This double-whammy can make trying to market oneself very, very hard. I kept coming up against that problem.

Then, late in 1993, to my delight, something was offered to me that could have been profitable: a contractor's claim for unpaid work building out some mall storefronts. Since the store chain that had commissioned the contractor's work hadn't paid, my client had a claim against the chain's surety, the entity that had promised to pay if the store chain failed to do so. As it happened, Round Hole often represented sureties, but not this particular surety. So there was no direct conflict. Recognizing there was still a possibility of an "issues conflict" (where the firm might be required to make contrary arguments on the same legal issue for different clients), I carefully sought the blessing of the lawyers who did the surety work. Again, to my delight, I received that blessing. So I signed up the client.

And then I had to go into the hospital. I've previously mentioned my back problems. At that point, they had flared up badly enough that I needed to undergo surgery, be hospitalized, and take a week or so off from work as well. While this process played out, some unidentified someone fired the client without consulting me. When I arrived back at the office, no one apologized, or even explained. My assumption is that the same partners who had originally discounted the possibility of an issues conflict had rethought the matter, but that's just a guess. Still, firing my client behind my back when I was sick in a hospital, a client everyone involved must have known I really needed, and then not even explaining it to me, was simply despicable.

This was followed closely in time by the division of the profits at the end of 1993. All law firms, except those that are strictly "eat what you kill" operations, have to find some discretionary way of dividing up the profits. When you need an exercise of discretion, someone has to exercise it, and in most firms, the partners vested with the discretion are the partners with the clients.

The ritual at Round Hole was that each partner would sit down with the committee and justify his or her claim for a share of the firm's profits. This was an exercise I am sure I would have found humiliating even if I had possessed a large "book of business." But I tried to keep up my dignity and my hopes as I participated in that ritual. I was truly proud of my record as a service partner.

When the numbers came out, though, I could see that the members of the Committee had (in my view) paid themselves and their friends remarkably well at the expense of people like me. I had been screwed.

So there I was, screwed because I didn't have a book of business, and screwed in trying to develop one. Just generally screwed all around.

I realized then that I faced a fundamental choice. No one had said a word to me, but I had been told remarkably clearly where I stood. I could see how the firm's command structure felt privileged to treat me. There was no reason, given these cold realities, that I should expect anything better, if I stuck around. It may seem incredible that sticking around even appeared an option. And it may not actually have been an option. In light of things that happened at Round Hole later on, I doubt I could have hung on forever. But the option seemed real to me then.

Real – and horrible. I had seen what sticking around looked like.

One illustration was a partner I'll call Tim. At one time, he must have had some self-regard. But he just didn't have the business, and got by on hand-outs from others. By now, however, he was treated as a joke by his partners, even by his wife. And then he died. He died without having experienced dignity anywhere in his life for quite some time.

Then there was an "of counsel" I'll call Lou. The firm had taken his one big case, his dowry, milked it, and then given him nothing back. Consequently he was coming in to work each day and doing nothing. And as he told me confidentially, "There is no harder work than doing nothing." Unlike Tim, he was rescued when an old colleague in another town invited Lou into his practice. The last time I saw Lou, he had a spring in his step and a smile I had not seen in years.

So was I going to resign myself to being a Tim (a man without hope) or a Lou (whose hope consisted of waiting for someone to pull him out)? The answer might seem obvious: I had to do something else. But actually choosing anything different was a hard decision. True, I had been flirting with variations on the theme of escape for a few years. I had quietly interviewed with other firms (always coming up against the same barrier of having no book of business, despite my credentials). I had tried to draft a business plan for going out on my own (but always running up against that same barrier). I might be willing to make a bet on myself, even though I had practically no "portables." But I had three kids for whose education I was paying at least a share. Making a bet on myself would be forcing a lot of other people to make a bet on me as well.

I could very well have stood poised on the edge of the diving board forever, or, like Tim, walked sadly back to poolside. What decided me to jump? The anger, of course.

I was coldly furious at many of the people I was constrained to be polite to as I met them in the office, day after day. They did not deserve my cheery greetings, which were sticking in my throat. I had to take these two incidents as a sign from God; I reflected that Moses could never have had a business plan when he left Egypt either. You had to be crazy enough to count on some parted seas and columns of fire and manna and burning bushes and water flowing out of rocks. But the Israelites had made the right choice.

As a wiser Jiminy Cricket might have said, Always let your anger be your guide.

So, at the beginning of January, 1994, I announced that I would be resigning effective the last day of February, and starting my own practice the following day.

Having done one bold and risky thing, I then spent the next two months trying as hard as I could to be careful and provident. I rented space, had stationery designed and printed, bought malpractice insurance, acquired a computer and staged it with carefully selected software, borrowed some starting capital from my stepdad and my father-in-law, ordered office furniture, etc.

As the day approached, it got scarier and scarier. But the anger kept me going. I was damned if I was going to stay subjected to people who had treated me that way. And the way the upcoming division of my work was being handled didn't do anything to cool me down. It was made very clear that, even though I was the one who had been for years in nearly sole charge of the railroad asbestos business described in an earlier chapter, I could have that over their dead bodies. (Nothing like someone else's greed to keep the blood boiling.)

Of course I got no work done on my last day, Monday, February the 28th. Much of my stuff had already been moved to my new quarters. At the end of the day, a colleague helped me haul the last couple of loads to my car. It all came to a very quiet conclusion.

The next day, in my new office, with the new furniture not yet delivered and the new computer somewhat balky, it was not until my landlord, whom I want to thank by name for his many kindnesses towards me – Nevett Steele – called me into the library of his suite where I was subletting space and presented me with a sheet cake showing me climbing a wall and making a jailbreak, that I suddenly began to have a conviction, not merely a hope, that somehow things were going to be all right.

And then the phone started to ring. Former colleagues at the big firm referred cases. Old clients turned up with new business. Friends sent friends. People I'd never heard of referred other people I'd never heard of. People I'd applied to for a job sent cases. One lawyer who had formerly been my adversary in a number of matters asked me to represent him personally. To my delight I was making ends meet, and doing better work, too, simply because I was happier than I had been in a long time. I had not budgeted to turn a profit at all in the first year, but I was into the black in only fourteen weeks. I started repaying the parental loans. I and my family never missed a meal. The State Bar Association started responding to my oft-expressed wishes to be involved in committee work. Friends from big firms were asking me about my break for freedom, and I could hear a wistful note in their voices.

March 1, 1994, the date I inaugurated my practice, the date I was first entirely on my own, turned out to have been the beginning of the happiest years of my professional life. It was the best revenge.

68

IN THE DARKEST PLACE

IN THE DARKEST PLACE, WRITTEN BY BURT BACHARACH AND
ELVIS COSTELLO, SUNG BY ELVIS COSTELLO (1998), ENCOUNTERED 1998

PLAYLIST TRACK NO. 97

THE CALL INTERRUPTED a happy moment. On a Veterans' Day evening, I had just come out of an enjoyable dinner meeting of the county bar association. My cellphone rang. I don't even remember who was on the other end – maybe Mother, maybe one of her friends. My stepfather had fallen and was in the hospital. This time he was in serious danger.

No great surprise there. He'd been in awful health for years, especially since a fall he'd had in 1977. He had the classic health threats of his generation, too, alcoholism and tobacco addiction. Still, he had beaten a lot in his 76 years, and even, recently, tolerated an amputated foot (lost to diabetes he didn't acknowledge at the time but I'd suspected). He had remained grimly optimistic, notwithstanding. "I expect to die an old, old man," he'd told me. "Never in good health, but old."

I'd always been skeptical. When the foot had come off, his emphysema had been so bad, he couldn't draw the air into his lungs necessary for the exertion of getting around on a prosthesis. The house my parents lived in had stairs at the front and back doors, and likewise stairs to go between living room and bedroom. So the loss of his foot was a catastrophe for his mobility. And it was a catastrophe in the delicate synergy by which he and my mother had managed to stay independent. Her cognitive powers and hearing were fading, but even with his physical strength being none the best, he had still been able to do various things for the two of them. Now he was essentially an invalid; their friends had stepped up and become far more involved, bless them. Still, my folks were no longer really getting by.

I had done what the adult kids always do in such situations: begged them to move to a senior living facility where they would have support and company and no stairs, preferably somewhere near me, their only child. I had been stonewalled by both of them. It wasn't a matter of money; they could have afforded it. I never received a satisfactory explanation, but I suspect the root cause was a realization by both of them that my mother lacked the mental and my stepdad the physical ability to pack and tackle the logistics of a move. But probably there was also just some codger cussedness at work.

In any case, coming off the call, I promised I'd make my way to Michigan the next day or possibly the day after (my calendar and my memory both fail me on this point). And then I let myself feel it a little: that vertiginous "this is really happening" alarm that comes when you realize that things are going very badly, and in a life-changing way.

Whichever morning it was when Mary dropped me off at the airport, I was oppressed by that feeling. By now I'd had some experience in shooting life's rapids, but it wasn't entirely helpful in maintaining my composure here. What I'd learned from experience was to tell myself things like *nobody's dying* as I confronted whatever lesser crisis I encountered. The trouble was, on this occasion, I was pretty sure somebody I did not want to lose *was* dying.

My instinctive mode of first aid for myself in these situations throughout life had been to get myself some kind of treat, to cut life's bitter taste. I did that here; there were a few minutes before the flight, which I took advantage of to stop by the music store on the airport concourse and buy myself a CD. (In those days one traveled with a tiny portable CD player.) I selected *Painted from Memory*, the recent if unlikely album collaboration of Burt Bacharach and Elvis Costello. (I'd seen the movie *Grace of My Heart*, a song from which, *God Give Me Strength*, was the germ of this album, and I'd loved it.) The album proved to be an excellent choice for what I was about to face, though not in the way I'd been expecting. Instead of making an effort to cheer, the songs almost unremittingly take you to the dark place where relationships end.

And that was indeed exactly where I was about to go in my life: to the place where relationships end. Admittedly, this was to be an ending of a different sort from the kind Bacharach and Costello were making music about. Nobody had cheated on anybody, which seemed to be a frequent theme in these songs. My stepdad, Ernest Gohn, had been extraordinarily faithful to me, as best he could be with his addictions and other issues, in the forty-four years we had been family. It had not my choice to dispense with my much loved birth father's last name, but I could never be ashamed of acquiring my equally loved stepfather's. When I used the word "Father" as a name in conversation, Ernest Gohn was the person I was referring to. I shall do so now.

I was extraordinarily fortunate that one of the friends who had rallied around my parents so kindly during my parents' last years together was Kathleen, a nurse, formerly their next-door neighbor. I knew I could not count on Mother to give me a useful accounting of Father's medical status. But when I got to Ann Arbor, I met not only with Mother but also with Kathleen. Briefly, what had happened was that, while trying to shift himself from his bed to his wheel-chair, Father had fallen and was unconscious on the floor. As near as anyone could tell, the fall was the result of his unconsciousness, not its cause. Apparently his brain had largely shut down. He had awoken briefly in the hospital to which he had been taken, to observe to my mother: "They do things very well." (Probably meaning the staff at the hospital; if so, as a veteran of so many medical interventions there, he could speak with authority.) Then he had lapsed into unconsciousness again.

Kathleen warned me that Father was being kept alive by machines and artificially fed. I was going to have to help Mother make a decision. And I knew immediately what kind of decision I was going to have to help her make.

Shortly thereafter, I drove Mother to the hospital to see for myself. When they ushered me into Father's room, I found him lying in bed with ugly tubes covering his face, looking fatigued even through his unconsciousness. Monitors were relaying information about respiration and heartbeat. I believe Mother said something about our needing to pray really hard, and my immediate reaction was that we were well beyond prayer already. I also had a visceral reaction against the tubes covering his face. Although I thought it extremely unlikely that he was sentient enough to mind them at all, I minded them. They struck me as an affront to his dignity; I know it makes no sense, but that's what I felt.

My recollection is also a bit hazy about whether we met with the doctor that day or the next day or even the day after that, but if I had to bet I'd say it was that day. Whenever it happened, the meeting with the doctor was one of the things that stands out most vividly. He was wearing a brown suit and a bowtie, and was tall enough that he loomed over Mother and me. He was struggling to describe Father's situation in layman's terms. Cirrhosis, kidney failure, diabetes, emphysema, and brain damage were the principal things I grasped. Father was not going to emerge from his coma.

Mother, who could be thick, if pardonably so on this occasion, and who also with all literalness believed that miracles were commonplace, seemed not to be taking in what the doctor was obviously telling us. At last she blurted out: "Is there no hope?"

"No hope at all," the doctor said, with maybe a hint of irritation in his voice. Mother had been making it hard for him to get the message across, and he may have been taking the slightest bit of pleasure in twisting the knife in the wound.

That silenced Mother. I asked what our options were. As I'd figured, they were to keep Father going in a vegetative state or to pull the plug. And having confirmed this, we left, agreeing that we would talk it over and come back on the morrow.

I remember going back to the house and cleaning up the blood from where Father had fallen in the study-turned-bedroom. Unfortunately, this was not my first task of this nature connected with his care. I'd been back on another occasion (before he'd been stuck on the ground floor) when something in his gut had ruptured, and on that occasion there had been blood all over the upstairs bathroom. My mother, in her not-quite-there way, had not been able to undertake the cleanup, and it had fallen to me. But now I was thinking this was enough.

Was I thinking about myself? Partly, of course. I didn't want this repulsive work anymore. But mostly I was thinking of Father. Even if it could have been possible to bring him back, this was no life for a former world traveler and a great dancer. Whether it was God or oblivion that awaited him, either alternative beat what he could expect here.

The one for whom Father's death would be an unmitigated disaster would be Mother. Their relationship was a peculiar one in many ways, but no one could doubt her devotion to Father, or his to her. What she would lose when she lost him would be profound and incalculable.

When I left Mother that night to return to my hotel, I left a woman who was heartbroken but holding that heartbreak at arm's length for one more night. We agreed, I recall, that we would put off any decisions until the next day.

I left for a hotel rather than staying at the house, for two reasons. First, unless I wanted to bunk down with Mother or in the alternative sleep in Father's bed, there was no bed for me. Second, I had for some years avoided sleeping there when I visited. Mother's degeneration had left her hostessing skills in tatters. She could not reliably provide sheets and towels, and break-fast preparation would predictably take an hour. Nor was this a matter of me lazily demanding service when I could do it myself. Where all the sheets and towels had gone was a mystery I could never solve, and Mother would not hear of me going into the kitchen to fix breakfast. In pity for my children and Mary – and myself – I had decided everyone's sanity would be served by my staying at a hotel I liked. And that always had continued to seem like a wise choice.

I know I played the Bacharach and Costello disc later that night in my hotel room. The mournfulness of the music felt like a relief. I might pray as my mother was praying, but I already knew what I had to do the next day, and I knew that God was not going to spare me from doing it.

Nor did He.

The next day, back at the hospital, I found myself in a conference room with Mother and others whom I cannot recall. Even with the doctor's advice, Mother couldn't wrap her mind around the dilemma facing us, the dilemma that really wasn't a dilemma, since there was no hope of reviving him.

I can't think of many things more wretched than to tell someone that yes, they really do have to pull the plug on the person they love best. And tell them and tell them, because they are mentally challenged, in denial, possessed of religious beliefs that question worldly science and logic in such matters, and desperately frightened. But sometimes you have to keep at it, even so. Was I persisting because I needed my own relief from this dilemma-that-wasn't? Oh, yes, I know I was. But I trust Mother's welfare was uppermost in my mind. And Father's too. He needed to get on with the business of dying; I knew he did, though he could neither feel nor know that need. It was time for his poor tired body to shut down.

I cannot tell you the words any of us used. But Mother eventually relented. I think she asked for one more night, but the fight had gone out of her.

I believe it was the following day we came back, just Mother and I and Kathleen, to finish it. I think they'd already taken the feeding tube out, and we could see Father's face properly. Then Mother, sitting across the bed from me, launched into one of the most amazing goodbyes I have ever heard.

Talking directly to Father, in the conviction he could still in some fashion hear and understand, she told him all the things about their marriage that had been wonderful to her. I would give a great deal to have had a recording of that speech. I remember her mentioning the parties they had given and the trips they had taken together, and the friends they had shared. It went on for a long time, a very detailed list, unique to Mother's and Father's experiences, almost a history of their lives together. At the end, it was evident that in saying goodbye to all of that, Mother was saying goodbye to her own life in most ways. With her dementia, she wasn't that clear about much, but she obviously grasped that nothing much good was ever going to happen to her again, and she would never have anyone to share it with as she had with Father.

Then the nurse undid some other connection, and very soon the monitors made it clear Father was sinking. I think it went on for about an hour and a half. Eventually he flatlined.

I burst out in tears, embraced Kathleen and my mother, and went out into the hall to call Mary. I know I spent some time crying on the phone to her.

Yet even then, to be honest, I was holding some realization away from myself, using my misery to hold off even greater misery. I had had to do that, to begin with, in arguing with Mother that we had to let Father go. And I had to go on doing it now, in all sorts of ways. The Bacharach and Costello CD was a lifesaver in that regard. The music beguiled the ears: spectacularly lush, vintage Bacharach orchestration with lots of the signature Bacharach staccato flugelhorn licks. Costello's voice and lyrics perfectly combined to chart various courses of romantic misery. I could focus on them, suck out the pleasure, and feel subtly, not overwhelmingly miserable.

In the Darkest Place was an excellent example:

In the darkest place
I'm lost
I have abandoned every hope
Maybe you'll understand I must
Shut out the light
Your eyes adjust
They'll never be the same
You know I love you so
Let's start again

I was starting to see that I would never be the same, but that I could never start again, having been exposed here to some kind of loss I was not going to recover from entirely, although there was still a large part of my mind that was youthful enough still to reject the notion of my own vulnerability. And paradoxically, this music, by embracing misery but not too much, helped on both sides of the dialectic.

I got through the next two weeks that way: the arranging a mausoleum-site, putting together a funeral Mass service, helping to hold Mother together. I could not have done it without my family, without my parents' friends and my own, and without this music.

69

TEACHING WAR

LOVE THEME FROM THE WINDS OF WAR AND WAR AND REMEMBRANCE,
COMPOSED BY BOB COBERT (1983), ENCOUNTERED CA. 2000

PLAYLIST TRACK NO. 98

KIDS GROW UP. Lucky parents get to have fun with them as they do it. In the case of me and my young son Matthew, the route to shared fun was quickly identified: we gorged on movies and television together. Many weeknights after schoolwork we shared one or another TV series; on Friday nights we'd often frequent the multiplexes together. And this was still an era when we could patronize the neighborhood video rental store (now long gone) to fill in nights when there was nothing on. Today, Matt having inconsiderately grown up, those nights are now among my most precious memories.

Our sharing didn't mean we always gravitated towards the same things. Matt, for instance, could not get enough of special effects-heavy extravaganzas where a lot of things blew up and bad guys and good guys would shoot it out. I cared more for character-driven small films. More often than not, when our aspirations diverged, we went his route. But not always. And there was a lot of ground in the middle.

Probably the most beckoning middle ground was the area of war movies and TV. Lots of spectacular stuff there, things blowing up, and shooting. But then too lots of room for stories that plumbed the depth of the human heart and touched on big themes, not least of which were war itself and the tides of human history

Of course with a youngster, you can't make just anything available. *Saving Private Ryan*, for example, is not appropriate for a 10-year-old. But a lot of the best material is in a gray area. I did want us to share early the long, somewhat rambling *Winds of War* and *War and Remembrance* series, based on Herman Wouk's novels. They were then freshly out on videotape. Yeah, there was some very grownup Holocaust material in it. (I think I may have initially skipped some of the most graphic parts.) But the more conventional war story stuff in it (sailors and soldiers getting ready for and fighting a war) carried its own challenges.

Those of us who grew up as I grew up, those for whom Vietnam was the specific war we'd defined ourselves against, were bound to have problems with the tone. Herman Wouk was certainly not an unqualified admirer of the military, witness his book and play *The Caine Mutiny*, which ultimately excuses the tyrannical Captain Queeg, but not before showing that his actions have provided much that requires excuse.

Still, by and large, the American sailors and naval officers presented in the shows are decent types, and even the German general staff officer we get to know is more admirable than not, though of course the SS people are appropriately loathsome. But to a child of the Sixties the tone was still too worshipful. I was fully prepared to concede that World War Two was a "good war." But.... But it remains true that even the best war will provide even the best countries with opportunities and excuses to act badly, and none will completely resist those opportunities. Very little of that came through. So there had to be a discussion of that.

On the other hand, the series did pretty well present the Holocaust, both the brute facts of the extermination and also the way it had appeared in real time to Americans who heard only rumors and largely disbelieved them, and whose own genteel anti-Semitism may have facilitated the killings. This was important to teach my son, whose forbears may have included my Jewish grandfather from Lithuania and Jewish grandmother from England, but whose cultural exposure to the horrors of this particular genocide would nonetheless likely be limited by the predominantly Catholic background and milieu in which he himself was being raised. So we certainly had discussions about that.

Also, as vast as the scope of the *Winds of War* series was, it did tend to focus on the "Great Men" a bit too much for my taste. You know, Roosevelt and Hitler and Stalin and Churchill. Wouk's storyline gives its hero, Pug Henry, access to each of them, and even when Henry isn't dealing with them, we get privileged glimpses of what they're up to. Not for Wouk the Tolstoyan view (shared by Victor Hugo) that the Great Men are actually history's puppets. In Wouk's book, these are leaders of great consequence whose decisions were determinative. While greatly enjoying the glimpses *Winds of War* gave us of these privileged leaders, Matt and I also talked through the opposing view.

At bottom, though, we must have surrendered emotionally to the Great Men stories, whatever our intellectual approach. How could we not, when their faces were presented to us at the outset of every episode, peering out of the giant letters of the title, set against a background of roiling clouds, while Robert Cobert's majestic *Love Theme* rolled in the background and the opening titles rolled with it? Cobert, a journeyman who also wrote much game show music, may not have been a John Williams or a Hans Zimmer, but this was his moment of greatness. The music tells us that this is a great story, epic in scale, and full of emotion, full of heartbreak and love. Strings sing the theme over a bed of growling trombones; it is irresistible.

So we found ourselves idolizing FDR and Winnie along with the brave Henry and Jastrow families whose stories were the primary focus.

Winds of War is also incurably old-fashioned – was old-fashioned even when it was being produced, and not just because it presented us Americans as the good guys, good with the merest trace of the kinds of shadows Vietnam had shown must have been there even in the "good" Second World War. It was old-fashioned because of the "newsreel" introductions, with the voice of William T. Woodson announcing facts the way newsreel announcers had done, authoritatively, unhesitatingly, conveying far more effectively by their tone than through any assertions that there is only one perspective to consider – that of the omniscient White male. Again, this needed to be unpacked, and we did that together.

Perhaps the most old-fashioned thing about it was the rampant chastity at its heart. We are supposed to believe that married Pug Henry, the naval officer we follow for five years, who has an affair with a delectable British lady throughout most of that period, never beds her through all the wrack and ruin of war until he is divorced from his faithless wife and married to the Brit. Roosevelt is not a randy old goat, and he and Eleanor seem to have a fine marriage. We are supposed to disapprove of a flyer's widow having an affair to hold at bay the misery from her loss. We are meant to pardon the aforementioned

British lady having a fling with an old flame only because: a) Pug isn't ready to marry her yet; and b) the old flame is slowly dying of a tropical disease, so it's mercy sex. Meanwhile, we are supposed to believe the hot British lady is desperately in love with Pug even though he's portrayed by Robert Mitchum, who was twenty years too old for the part. All very interesting discussions to have with a ten-year-old.

There was technical old-fashionedness too; if you view the DVD transfers available now, you can see how much less satisfying the low-density narrow-screen productions of that era were. More visual information on the screen is just more interesting. And for all the huge budget, the kinds of *trompe l'oeil* that any digital effects shop would endow any war movie with today are simply missing.

In short, we were looking at an artifact together, Matt and I, one whose flaws were as instructive as its achievements. So much to talk about. Now, when I hear those sinking cadences of the main title (which I still play for myself occasionally), I remember those evenings of discussion, and wish I could go back. I'd like to think my son, who grew up to be a maker of videos and blogger and podcaster about movies (and beer), and a very sophisticated media consumer, feels the same way from time to time.

70

LITIGATION ISOLATION

CARUSO, BY LUCIO DALLA, PERFORMED BY
JOSH GROBAN (2003), ENCOUNTERED 2004

PLAYLIST TRACK No. 99

FOR A COUPLE of weeks in 2004, I was about as alone as I've ever been in my adult life, before or since.

As the two weeks came closer, the prospect of the isolation gradually morphed from a threat into a certainty. From 2003 going into 2004, I had two big cases going: cases which, if I wasn't able to settle them, would end up in jury trials that could last a week each. One was in Philadelphia, the other in Annapolis. The trials had been scheduled a few weeks apart, so I figured, between the likelihood that at least one would settle and the fact that they were supposed to go down at different times, I could count on dealing with them separately and sanely.

But counting on those likelihoods turned out to be like hoping everything works out okay in a Greek tragedy. The cases didn't settle; and though it seemed to me my clients had the stronger hand in each case, in neither could I get the other side to see it that way. And then a pregnant lawyer on the Annapolis matter, the one that had been set to go earlier, gave birth a little sooner than expected, delaying trial of that case to the Monday after the Philadelphia trial.

In consequence, I suddenly found myself looking at trying cases in two consecutive weeks of August. Out of town. (Annapolis is just far enough away from Baltimore that you don't want to commute when you're putting in the kind of effort that a full-on trial requires.) I asked the judges to accommodate me by moving the cases further apart again, but it was "no joy" on either of those requests.

There are lawyers who do over and over what I was doing then: handling cases that are geographically dispersed, with witnesses all over the country, putting forth on the fly the required intellectual effort and organizational skills and oratory and writing and witness preparation to the extent that for extended periods there is nothing else in their lives. Lawyers like that are called trial lawyers.

I, on the other hand, was what's called a litigator, which counterintuitively meant that I seldom tried cases (but rather handled cases that could go to trial but ordinarily were disposed of in other ways). So, while I was holding my own, barely, in the logistics of my struggles with these adversaries, all of whom had larger legal teams than I did, I found myself far outside my comfort zone in terms of impact on my life.

By now my older children were grown, but I had a teenager at home and a wife who was busy enough with her own career that my leaving so much of the day-to-day family business to her was causing friction.

But I had no choice. I felt like a swordsman in a fight for his life; you may want to attend to other things, but if you allow your attention to waver, you die. And so you focus on the one big thing to the exclusion of all the others, even the ones which are in the grand scheme far more important to you.

My posture, then, was simultaneously liberating and constricting. Good trial work requires great concentration; being both freed up and forced to narrow one's attention in that fashion is in some ways a wonderful thing, an intellectual and indeed spiritual adventure of the first order. But there were reasons I was a litigator rather than a trial lawyer. I was a homebody by nature, a wool-gatherer, a nurturer, a man of many avocations. For a couple of weeks, I couldn't do any of those things.

All I could do was keep putting one foot ahead of the other. I kept trying to assemble a calendar of all the tasks I had to complete in order to present or defend against two solid weeks of testimony, and no matter how I manipulated the agenda, I could never fit everything in and still leave time to sleep. So inevitably, like every other litigator in every other trial, I approximated the effort required for some tasks, and gave myself unstintingly to others. And yes, of course I slept. On a battlefield triage and occasional oblivion are both necessities.

As I have said, the Philadelphia trial that should have been second came first. For five days, almost without break, I shuttled between my hotel room in Center City and the courtroom a couple of blocks to the east in Philadelphia's Beaux Arts-style City Hall. In my memory it was cloudy or rainy the whole time; this probably wasn't quite true, but if not, it was nearly so. Local counsel, a charming woman who lived in a restored downtown townhouse, had me over to dinner one night, but apart from that one act of mercy, I was socially on my own. I have no recollection of dining with anyone else, nor do my charge account records contradict my recollection.

I have forgotten a great deal about the ordeal. But not all.

What I remember most is a brief shopping expedition I treated myself to as a break on the second day of the trial, and bought a CD at a nearby Borders. Yes, Borders, now a feature of America's commercial past but at that moment a shining and wonderful distraction, one with which I had a small personal connection.

Readers of these pages know that I hail from Ann Arbor. So did Borders, although by 2004 it was a huge international chain of book and music stores. In the previous couple of decades, my parents, both great bibliophiles, had become big fans, as the tiny store grew and came to purvey an astonishingly wide stock of books. Philadelphia's Center City branch of the store was located in the space left by a defunct department store. Borders had brought the space back to spacious and vivid life. I wanted to borrow some of that vividness for my mentally if not physically drab hotel room, and a new CD was the best way to import it.

The album I hit upon was Josh Groban's *Closer*, which I bought largely on the strength of the jewel box cover art, and the awareness that he had become a Big Thing while my back was turned.

After bringing the disc back to my room, to play as I continued to prepare for the trial, I soon realized that I had picked an exceedingly contrarian choice for my situation and my mood.

You might call Groban's genre "popera." The young man had an operatically-trained voice applied in an operatic way to pop material. Even the cheerfuller songs came across as dramatically gloomy, the way opera tends to be. Don't take my word for it; here is part of Aaron Latham's review on AllMusic:

The best tunes bookend the disc as the atmospheric opener, Oceano, sets an ominous tone while the mysterious Never Let Go is a welcome collaboration with Deep Forest that allows Groban to successfully move away from the saccharine ballads and grow as a vocalist. However, there is still plenty of romance included for the PBS crowd as When You Say You Love Me painfully cries out like a rejected Celine Dion cut and the Celtic-infused bombast of Secret Garden's You Raise Me Up plays like the sequel to his debut's most famous song, To Where You Are.

"Painfully cries out" – yeah, that's about right. Somehow, even when it was happy, it was sad.

The song that spoke most to me in my isolation was *Caruso*, Lucio Dalla's song. I couldn't translate Italian to any great extent, but I got the gist: the legendary opera singer, standing alone beside the water, mulling his regrets. I didn't have that many regrets at that point; the loss of a marriage, and of a father and step-father (all written about in these pages) were about the worst, and far fewer and less painful than what some of my contemporaries were racking up. Still, in my isolation and subject to the incessant responsibilities of the trial, the gloomy melo-drama of that song and indeed the whole album, were just the thing.

My legal efforts bore fruit. I had been right about having the stronger case in both matters, though I'll take some credit for steering them in the right direc-tion so that the juries in both cases saw things as they should have. We ran over on the first trial, and I had to go back to Philadelphia on the Monday that I should have been in Annapolis picking a jury. The Philadelphia judge got on the phone and made my excuses to the Annapolis one, and in consequence I gave my closing argument to the Philadelphia jury, warning them with regret, that I would not be there to hear their verdict, but that local counsel would have to take over for me. I told them truly that I had enjoyed their company. (When you're effectively by yourself for so many days, the silent interchange of looks with a jury passes for companionship.) And then I hopped in my Hyundai and headed south on I-95.

I got the phone call with the good news on my cell before I was out of Delaware; it had taken the jury less than an hour to reach its verdict. But there was no time to rejoice, no time to process it at all. My partner was in Annapolis picking a jury for me, and the judge wanted me there as soon as humanly possible either to start the trial or at least go through pretrial motions. And I was encountering serious traffic congestion and worrying about making a bad impression on both the judge and the jury by getting there late and inconveniencing everyone.

In short, I never left the litigation cocoon. En route from one trial to the other, I drove within a mile of my home in Baltimore and never veered off course, just kept on going.

There are far worse forms of isolation. To go from one luxurious hotel room to another, from one courtroom where you are first chair to another courtroom where you are first chair, is in many ways a not inconsiderable pleasure, especially when you are winning, and sense it, in both proceedings. And yet it was lonely, and that loneliness cannot be gainsaid either.

As I write these words, past the end of my litigating career, I am very grateful for those two weeks, which certainly were its pinnacle. Yet I am even more grateful that my life did not repeatedly force me into situations like that, as it might have done had I been a different kind of lawyer.

Still, play that music for me, and I am cast back instantly into the complex feelings I had when, for two weeks, my mind had room for the thrust and parry of two trials, and very little else.

71

TRAVELS: TRIP HOP

IN THESE SHOES?, WRITTEN BY KIRSTY MACCOLL AND PETE GLENISTER,
PERFORMED BY KIRSTY MACCOLL (2001), ENCOUNTERED 2005

JIM THE JINN, WRITTEN BY PIT BAUMGARTNER,
PERFORMED BY DE-PHAZZ (2001), ENCOUNTERED 2005

PLAYLIST TRACKS NOS. 100, 101

IF YOU'RE LUCKY, you'll spend your earliest years in a fine flush of rapture in which everything seems new and memorable. Later on, unless like Peter Pan you make up your mind never to grow up – and are more successful at it than most of us – you'll have to look at things differently. Having begun like Miranda, marveling at the brave new world around you, you'll end up voicing Prospero's dismissive rejoinder, Aye, 'tis new to thee. You'll recognize that most of the time, most things will appear "bleared, smeared with toil," to use Gerard Manley Hopkins' phrase. Yet even then, life affords the occasional wormhole moment, when gaps open up in your mental cosmos and allow you momentary trips back into that earlier state of mind. In late February 2005, I stumbled on one of those wormholes.

It was time. After various struggles that had predictably done their best to blear and smear things for me, I had reached a non-ecstatic, if comfortable, adult moment. I was eleven years into being my own boss. I was writing a newspaper column (see Chapter 75, below), and receiving some respect in my profession. My mother and my wife's mother were both in one stable environment where we could keep an eye on them. Our son was in the last throes of childhood. Mary's writing was going well still; the great destruction the Internet was about to wreak on freelance journalism was a year or two in the future. Everything was sufficiently under control for the moment. But there wasn't much contact with what Hopkins called the "dearest freshness deep down things."

And it was time for some fun, the perfect moment for me to encounter Trip Hop. And Trip Hop is ...? Let me acknowledge immediately that there's a complete lack of unanimity in what that label means. But for me it was captured in two CDs I had ordered from Amazon the preceding month, and fell in love with immediately.

I was playing them on the day our son Matt and I drove the 110 snow-covered miles from Baltimore to Berkeley Springs, West Virginia. We were making the drive to join Mary, who'd traveled there the day before, to be a judge in a water contest.

That's right, a water contest, i.e. a showdown among various brands of bottled spring water. This simple combination of hydrogen and oxygen molecules, among the commonest and most homogeneous stuff in the universe, was competing and being judged, fundamentally, on minute differences amongst the chemical impurities its bottlers were compelled to purvey, a bug treated as a feature. And Mary, by virtue of her travel writing, had been made a judge. The whole enterprise evinced a happy frivolity.

How appropriate, then, were the two CDs in the car's player! One was *Death by Chocolate*, a collection of collage-like songs full of sampling and turntablism by De-Phazz, a German collective with at least a couple of Americans sprinkled in, all performed in English. My favorite was *Jim the Jinn*, which I'd first encountered as the music (speeded up) for the opening titles in the romantic comedy thriller *The Truth About Charlie*, and been so enthusiastic about that first I'd bought the soundtrack album, and then, in January, the source album, *Death by Chocolate*. The song was all about shape-shifting:

> *You might just be a poor tailor's lazy son*
> *I don't mind, rub the lamp and the show goes on*
> *I can make you travel in time and space*
> *I can change your sex, I can change your race*

If that weren't enough, the song begins and ends with the throwaway phrase "Daddy was just a girl in disguise." The movie was about shape-shifting, too, being a remake of *Charade*, both movies full of sinister people who keep turning up in different contexts, and an apparently wholesome guy whose claimed name and job keep changing. De-Phazz's music is irresistible, from the first upsweep of a harp to the bouncy, trombone chorus-propelled fuselage of the song. You cannot possibly take any of it seriously.

The other album was Kirsty MacColl's *Tropical Brainstorm*, an extended exercise in sublime frivolity with a strong Cuban accent. Come to think of it, its mambo flavor was itself a form of shape-shifting for a quintessentially British pop songwriter and performer. The standout song, *In These Shoes?*, is a upbeat tale of the singer being propositioned by three different men. She cheerfully accepts each overture in principle, but she has to evaluate the specifics of each proposed tryst relative to her shoes. Two of the guys are told that "in these shoes," the idea of making her tramp somewhere else or ride a horse to get it on is ... not on. The shoes aren't described (and you never see MacColl's own shoes in the official video, where her own appearance is almost as fleeting and disguised as one of Alfred Hitchcock's), but it seems likely from the description of the third encounter that shoe fetish styles may be involved. All to the sound of Cuban trumpet breaks and a somewhat inconsequential chorus sung in Spanish by a female chorus.

It was perfect background music for that day, the whole of which was just for fun. We picked up Mary at the bed-and-breakfast where she'd stayed the preceding night. We walked around the park in the heart of town, taking in an apothecary and a print shop. We drove Mary up to the Coolfont resort, where the judging was to be, stopping to admire the nearby valley. Then Matt and I drove back and treated ourselves to a Roman bath in the heart of town, fed of course by the eponymous Springs. Matt and I had never had a Roman bath before, and found it a wonderful distraction from the cold weather outside. We also drove off westward, exploring, and ended up in Cumberland. I wanted to show Matt the locomotive shops where I had spent so much time two decades before, as I've written in these pages. We came back and took pictures of Mary in judging mode, before going to dinner with her and driving back to Baltimore.

Somewhere along the line, maybe while I was uncharacteristically unwinding in the baths with my son, it came to me not merely that I was happy, but that everything around me seemed wondrous. As we drove through the woods in the chilly afternoon in the direction of Cumberland, that feeling persisted. The way the winter sunlight cut through the denuded trees and blinked upon our car seemed a revelation – of what I cannot say, but maybe that's merely because words were lacking, not because nothing was revealed.

Even when we got to the Cumberland shops, which Matt, it must be said, found massively unimpressive, and which seemed even to me to have lost some of their grandeur (perhaps along with some grime), the feeling did not go away, perhaps owing to a perception that the diminution of the mundane, workaday shops only highlighted the lasting magnificence of the surrounding hills, the works of God almost always overshadowing those of mankind.

So what then was the connection that day between the frivolous fun of the music and of the water-judging competition on the one hand and the more serious sense of Hopkins' "dearest freshness deep down things"? Again, impossible to articulate in any way I find convincing. All I can say with confidence is that there was a connection, that light-hearted fun is sometimes a gateway, likely sometimes the only gateway, to something much more profound. There are those who scorn fun as a distraction from the proper objects of our attention. Days like that February day assure me they are wrong.

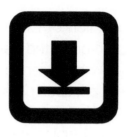

72

COMMEDIA

WINE SAFARI, WRITTEN AND PERFORMED BY
ROLFE KENT (2004), ENCOUNTERED 2006

PLAYLIST TRACK No. 102

SHE'S OKAY, YOU KNOW, the nun said, speaking of my mother who had just died a day or two before. We were sitting in the retirement community where my mother had spent her last, confused, unhappy years. The nun meant, of course, my mother's soul, in the hands of God. She spoke confidently, and I told her confidently I was sure she was right. Her struggle with dementia was behind her; her good times had begun.

I was not to be so sure for very much longer. An uncertainty, very unfamiliar to me, was about to arise.

Nowadays, I look back with nostalgia at that confidence and the way it affected my outlook.

I had passed fifty-six years believing essentially what I had been taught in grade school by other nuns: that there was a God who gave both existence and meaning to life, a God who would preserve us from the death trap of our bodies, and even from the larger death trap of our universe. I knew that this was what most of us desperately wanted to believe, but I also knew that merely wanting to believe something is no proof of its falsity. We also desperately want to believe there's food and sex, for instance, and we can say, on the basis of overwhelming evidence, that such things do exist. The proofs for food and sex are more empirical than the proofs for the presence and agency of a Deity, but still: wanting something to exist is no good reason, standing by itself, to disbelieve in it either.

And at the moment I'm speaking of, I had both sense and reasoning to persuade me affirmatively in my belief. I felt I could sense God's immanence in various things: a shiver down my spine at the moment of the consecration, a frequent exposure to beauty and goodness in all sorts of places including the persons of my fellow-worshipers, and the sheer authority with which Jesus spoke. Nor was I unpersuaded by at least two of the philosophical proofs of God: the various perfections in the universe which made our corner of it such a suitable cradle for humanity, too convenient to be the plausible outcome of random events, and the inconceivability of there not being an uncaused cause at the start of the chain of events. I was well aware that neither my subjective senses nor the philosophical proofs were unassailable, but they were enough for me.

So I went on believing even after most of my contemporaries had given it up. I don't think I was ever a grating bore about my somewhat passé point of view, but I wasn't embarrassed of it either.

And in that conversation with the nun I still was not. I still looked at life as a comedy in an older sense of the word, Dante's sense: a progression from a world familiar with discord and pain to one from which these things will be banished.

That sense of life as comedy was far-reaching and had many roots, including my sense of the fundamental accuracy of the world-view of comedies in the modern sense: narratives intended to make us laugh, and to reassure us that in the long run all manner of thing shall be well.

One comedy-in-the-modern-sense that became emblematic of my viewpoint at that time was 2004's *Sideways*, an aptly-titled road story about two middle-aged guys on a tour of California's wine country. Every generic hurdle was surmounted – as must happen in road comedies – but in off-kilter fashion. One of the two travelers, Jack (Thomas Haden Church), is on a mission to find some pick-up sex notwithstanding that he is engaged to be married in a few days, and consequently the trick can only be pulled off by concealing the engagement from the women involved. The other traveler, Miles (Paul Giamatti), is unable to detach himself from his feelings for a wife who has not only left him but divorced him and remarried as well, even when a woman who is both appropriate and available slides into view. In unforeseeable and quirky fashion the universe seems to dispense happiness to them each, together with appropriate punishment for their respective sins, by the end.

I was able to enjoy it with my son, a budding cinéaste who was now (just) of an age to appreciate sex comedies, but I know he thought my enthusiasm for the movie excessive. The truth was, I was responding to the Dantean comedy in it, to the way everything moved toward the good and the beautiful, as much as I was responding to the comedy-in-the-modern-sense. It was important to me that the way things worked out for the best was unfathomable in advance, and full of moral ambiguity.

It chimed with my updated Dantean thinking. Clearly, if there was a God at the helm of the universe, He was a devious Bastard. All the bad things there were, all the pain and sickness and terror, all the death, somehow – or so my faith urged me to believe – were unimaginably transfigured into agencies of providential good. And I believed they were.

The film score for the movie, by Rolfe Kent, was absolutely a part of this. If you listen to any track of the soundtrack album for a spell, you'll come to realize that the cheerful and agreeable surface of the cues is a bit deceptive. You keep hearing things that are wrong, that aren't what your ears expect. I'm not saying that Kent was a full-fledged disciple of Thelonius Monk, the high priest of unexpected turns of melody and harmony; I am morally certain, however, that Kent was familiar with Monk's oeuvre, and was very happily borrowing Monk's line of attack.

What I had, then, when the movie came out, even when my Mother died, was a confidence that the universe made sense, that when the inmates were running the asylum, God was running the inmates, and that despite all the evidence to the contrary, the God running those inmates was benign. Like a confidence that Monk's (or Kent's) dissonances made sense, which in the end they always did.

That album was close to my first legal download, in September of 2006. By the moment I authorized Napster, the original music file sharing service, to fire the tracks to me over the telephone lines, Mother's death, as I'll discuss further below, was already wreaking unforeseen havoc in my psyche. I stood flummoxed, grasping hard for the old certainties and ways of looking at things. The *Sideways* album, purchased over a year after I'd seen the movie twice in theaters and some months after I'd bought the DVD, promptly became a sort of touchstone for me, an aural reminder of the careless confidence I had enjoyed but a short time before. Call it a musical boundary line.

Commedia on one side, then, and something a lot less fun on the other.

73

STILL CHILLED

IN THE STILL OF THE NIGHT, WRITTEN BY COLE PORTER,
PERFORMED BY CARLY SIMON (2005), ENCOUNTERED 2006

PLAYLIST TRACK No. 103

IN THE STILL OF THE NIGHT suffers from the overfamiliarity that plagues too many songs in the Great American Songbook. We don't really hear it. There's a prettiness on the surface that belies its rawness and insecurity, its desperate plea for an impossible reassurance.

Think about it.

The lover asks this loaded question:

All the times without number,
Darling, when I say to you
Do you love me, as I love you
Are you my life to be, my dream come true
Or will this dream of mine fade out of sight
Like the moon growing dim, on the rim of the hill
In the chill still of the night?

And how could the beloved could ever make a satisfactory answer? Beloveds, no matter their devotion in this moment, can't know the future. Humans change over time, and beloveds are only human, and hence, with the best will in the world, they cannot issue unqualified guarantees. And worse, even the beloved's present sincerity is not totally knowable.

Nor is the lover's question just about the beloved's constancy. The beloved's survival also enters into the question. Every affair or marriage, no matter how devoted the parties, will end one day, and (barring what lawyers call a common disaster), at least one of the parties will have to live with the loss.

In short, the lover's insecurity is not unreasonable. But it can easily be unreasonably extreme.

My mother felt such extreme insecurity more than anyone else I ever knew. In retrospect I recognize that I was the truest love of her life, and that my infantile adoration, while she received it, was the sweetest feeling she would ever experience. And she received it for a long time, probably longer than she'd had any right to expect; most boys my age seemed to move on quicker than I did. Yet, eventually I saw my parent's limitations, and the need to adjust my previously uncritical response, as all children eventually do. To her dying day my mother could never accept this inevitable nuance. Nor could she truly accept my subsequent commitments to lovers, spouses and children, friends and work, which were all experienced as deep wounds and neglect, even at times apostasy and treason.

And this became the great tragedy of her life. My mother could neither understand nor consent to a mature love from me, and, try as I might, I could not propose to love her in any other way. Her demands grew increasingly strident, and my resistance increasingly cruel-seeming to her, and sometimes to me.

Yet I was not blind to what underlay her insistence: that all-too-human fear of the oblivion of love of which Cole Porter wrote.

After she died, I had occasion to ruminate bitterly on this, largely while I was on the road. I did some traveling in her wake. Though she had passed her last couple of years at a senior community in Baltimore, we had decided years earlier that her ashes would be immured next to my stepdad's in Ann Arbor. So there was a visit home for a funeral and a memorial service. And then there were two more visits, because I wanted to write about the re-encounter with my home in the middle of my life, to use Dante's phrase, and wanted to do some research, as well as to mourn in the place that felt most appropriate for this particular siege of grief.

On the road, I was frequently playing Carly Simon's previous year's album, all standard love songs, called *Moonlight Serenade*. One of the cuts was

In the Still of the Night. And when the lyrics came around to that lover's question, I realized it was the central question of Mother's life, for many years and certainly towards her sad end, an end rendered heartbreakingly solitary by the dementia that had shredded continuity in most of her relationships.

But now that question had become my question. I did not, could not, love Mother as she had loved me, but that is far from saying that I did not love her. Of course I did, difficult as she had been. And now she was not there. So what did that mean? Had she and our relationship just faded out of sight, as Porter so aptly phrases it?

I'd felt differently somehow when I lost my father and when I lost my step-father. With Mother there was no sense of assurance, none of continuity. And I was feeling exactly as the lover in Porter's song dreaded to feel: left "in the chill still of the night."

It's hard to overstate what a shock this "still chilled" feeling was. I had always been a cheerful person, an optimistic person, no matter what difficult or sad times I might be passing through. Now, though I had hardly lost the ability to be happy, the default setting of reflexive cheerfulness had disappeared. I could not shake and – to this day fifteen years later – have still not shaken the opposite reflexive sense, one of isolation and doom.

I had to conclude that, unbeknownst to me, and with all the difficulties between us, my mother had somehow been the indispensable prop of my sense of well-being, and that there was nothing to replace her. In saying this I do not slight any of the others who were close to me, my wife, children, or colleagues. I depend on them even more now. But still something essential to everyday happiness had to my astonishment departed.

And as I was quickly discovering, and will discuss in the next chapter, other things had departed with it.

74

PANTHEISTIC CONSOLATIONS

THE SONG OF PURPLE SUMMER, LYRICS BY STEVEN SATER, MUSIC
BY DUNCAN SHEIK, PERFORMED BY THE ORIGINAL BROADWAY
CAST OF SPRING AWAKENING (2006), ENCOUNTERED 2007

PLAYLIST TRACK NO. 104

THE LOSS OF my mother in 2006 not only tore me loose from my emotional moorings, but from my religious ones as well.

I'd not seen it coming.

Mother's death – yes, that I'd foreseen, of course. And I'd anticipated it as a blessing; Mother had been ill, demented and lost. But I realized after the fact that I'd been operating on a barely articulated conviction that I would somehow feel her presence, and that I would also be comforted by my faith. But nothing of the kind occurred. It proved to work the other way around. Not feeling her presence challenged my faith.

After you lose your equilibrium, you naturally fight to regain it. But because you know how badly you want it back, you suspect any sign you think you see of its return. And that was my situation. Every time I thought I might be hearing either Mother's voice or God's in my mind, I was driven to consider rigorously the likelihood I was just talking to myself. So I veered back and forth. Enough of that will soon make you wretched.

Sometime not too long after Mother died, I had a lunch with my older son, who spoke, not disrespectfully but quite definitively, about his view that there was nothing to religion or its consolations. And I realized that he was speaking for the majority of educated opinion – that somewhere between my youth, when probably the majority of serious grownups held sincere religious beliefs, and now, the balance had shifted. Somehow I had gotten quite out of step.

Confidence is always easier when you're in step than when you're not. And I had lost mine. I regrew some of it eventually, after much struggle, a struggle which of course is still ongoing.

This was the synthesis the struggle has left me with: I could never again deny the substantial possibility that my faith was completely in vain – and I have to acknowledge that, if so, there could be little reliable basis for an equanimity based on faith or on anything else. On the other hand I still feel that I'm on the right track going to church, and I plan to keep on, holding fast to my perception that some things, like human decency and the existence of existence, still seemed more plausibly explained in a universe with a God in it than in one without. My certainties have fled, but I have at least decided on my course.

Big questions, to be sure. I've always looked to art to help me tackle big questions. This time was no different.

In January 2007, in Manhattan on an overnight stay before a court appearance, I attended a performance of the previous year's Tony winner for Best Musical, *Spring Awakening*. This adaptation of a scandalous Expressionist 1890s play about the difficult sexual and social maturing of adolescents also takes up the existential challenge of death in a putatively God-less environment. Melchior, the youthful hero, confronts that challenge after the losses of his love Wendla (victim of a botched abortion) and of his close friend Moritz (hounded to suicide by the small-minded martinets who run the village school). What good is Melchior's life under these new circumstances?

The musical at the end proposes two answers to the problem. First, in the number *Those You've Known*, Melchior is visited by "ghosts" of Wendla and Moritz, although these are evidently emblems in his mind, not actual beings. The point is, he has internalized them through his intimacy with them, and they will remain valid sources of inspiration to him. Secondly, in the inspiring closing number, *The Song of Purple Summer*, a kind of pantheistic solution is suggested. Though the lyrics of the show that I and most audiences have heard differ from those on the CD (recorded before the show was "locked" in previews), the CD's lyrics were the ones I learned by heart, and they state the issue more expressly than the song as now sung:

And all shall fade–
The flowers of spring,
The world and all the sorrow
At the heart of everything…
But still, it stays –
The butterfly sings,
And opens purple summer
With a flutter of its wings…
The earth will wave with corn,
The grey-fly choir will mourn,
And mares will neigh with
Stallions that they mate, foals they've borne…
And all shall know the wonder
Of purple summer…

The message, it seems, is that there may not be any Wendla or Moritz now, and there may be a permanent "sorrow at the heart of everything," but there is still the eternal, unconquerable beauty of summer. That beauty can give meaning to life, to everyone's but also to Melchior's specifically. The meaning with which God was once thought to have imbued Creation, and which, succeeding Him, Wendla and Melchior symbolized, is now to be found all around, in the butterfly, the corn, the "grey-fly choir," and the mares and the stallions and the foals. These things amount to a pantheistic replacement of the Lutheran God whom the youngsters had been brought up to look to. And the power of the message is driven home by the heart-rending harmony with which the cast always delivers it.

Even with the softened lyrics, I was sent out of the theater reeling, a freshly-purchased copy of the CD in my bag. I played that song several times on my laptop when I got back to the hotel, before dropping off to sleep eventually.

Yet I soon realized that that kind of consolation was not for me. The lyrics (the original ones, the ones on the CD) did not promise that nature's beauty could wipe away every tear or fill the God-shaped hole. All they promised was that it would help.

I appreciated help, but I was still looking for a cure. I would go on to see the show several times in several productions, but I always recognized the correct limits of the consolations it offered. Accurate or not, the Christian promise at least identifies the one thing that actually would constitute a cure:

a world in which the Wendlas and Moritzes truly survive death, in which the Melchiors can actually be reunited with them. I wish I were more confident that that promise is accurate, but I know it's the only thing that would truly make me feel better.

And so, though I flirted with pantheistic consolations and was grateful for them, I went on past them. I am still getting further away from them. I keep revisiting my beliefs constantly, and time has blunted grief over my mother (though as I age, the accelerating toll of deaths among those I love keeps adding fresh causes to grieve). I am sufficiently worldly to take pleasure in many things, but, however worldly I may be, I am no pantheist, and I do not confuse the things that give me pleasure with the things that impart meaning or value. There may be a God and there may be meaning; I believe these things are possible. But if they exist, they do not reside in the world around us.

75

AND I KINDA LIKE IT

NOT READY TO MAKE NICE, BY DAN WILSON, NATALIE MAINES,
EMILY ROBISON, AND MARLIE MCGUIRE, PERFORMED BY
DIXIE CHICKS (LATER THE CHICKS) (2006), ENCOUNTERED 2006

PLAYLIST TRACK NO. 105

"AND I KINDA LIKE IT."

Those who remember the pop, country, and political scene in 2003 to 2006 will recognize that tag: the affirmation by the group then known as the Dixie Chicks (Natalie Maines, Emily Robison, and Marlie McGuire) of Maines' costly but liberating decision in 2003 to state her views on the run-up to the U.S. invasion of Iraq. From the stage of the Shepherd's Bush Empire Theatre in London, Maines commented: "Just so you know, we're on the good side with y'all. We do not want this war, this violence, and we're ashamed that the President of the United States is from Texas."

At that time, the Dixie Chicks were about the most popular country music act. Their resultant loss of status in that community was instantaneous. Their then-current hit *Landslide* fell from No. 10 down to 43 on the Billboard Hot 100 in a single week. Country is and does a lot of things, but no one is likely to dispute that among them, it usually serves as the house music of the religious, socially, and politically conservative among us. For these audiences, country music fits into a constellation with evangelical identity, football, and the military – and in 2003 all of them were aligned behind George W. Bush's war in Afghanistan and incipient war in Iraq. The reaction to the Chicks' apostasy against this cultural combine was fierce: death threats, denunciations, a demonstration where their CDs were destroyed. They rethought their identity, stated they no longer considered themselves part of the country music community, and rebranded themselves as rock-n-rollers.

Three years later, the Chicks came out with a powerful meditation on what they had done, what the reaction had been, and how they felt about it. It is an anthem of anger at the anger directed at them, acceptance of the consequences for them, and affirmation of the course they had set out on: they kinda liked it. And if you go to the Chicks' website today, you'll see their "Causes" listed, and you'll see that they have gone right on with the liberal course: Planned Parenthood, democracy, LGBT rights.

As the Chicks proclaimed, it is always liberating to shake off constraints and speak one's truth.

I'm not ready to make nice
I'm not ready to back down
I'm still mad as hell, and I don't have time
To go 'round and 'round and 'round
It's too late to make it right
I probably wouldn't if I could
'Cause I'm mad as hell
Can't bring myself to do what it is
You think I should

This song spoke to me about as directly as any chronicled in these pages.

From sometime in the previous decade, I'd been part of the Lawyers' Editorial Advisory Board of the Maryland Daily Record, a business and legal newspaper. This was a group of fifteen or so lawyers who collaborated to write op-ed pieces in that paper on matters of legal interest, sometimes intramural within the Maryland community, sometimes broader. I served as principal author of a number of the pieces, but was finding it an increasingly frustrating task. I wanted to say some things that were startling and direct, and collegial authorship was making that close to impossible. There were always colleagues who disagreed with my point, or who counseled what I considered mushy compromises. Some wanted us to focus on municipal boosterism, while I wanted to talk about the big political issues, public policy, constitutional legal issues, and things that affected me as a practicing member of the profession.

But our controversies went beyond subject matter. I was spoiling for fights that not everyone on that board wanted to have. And as long as I had to work with the board, I wasn't going to have most of them.

Thank goodness for our handler from the newspaper, Barbara Grzincic. One day in 2003 after a meeting of the board she pulled me aside and offered me a monthly column of my own. I think I said yes on the spot. You can see the entire result in my old blog, still available: THEBIGPICTUREANDTHECLOSEUP.COM. I have republished all my columns in the Big Picture section of the blog.

Of course, it took me a little while to find my feet. One of my early pieces, for example, I later had to retract: I had addressed the Intelligent Design debate with insufficient facts. I also focused more than I should have on being a lawyer. My pieces were too long – something a colleague eventually poked gentle fun at when we were presenting a continuing professional education seminar together, and he assured the audience that in my segment, which came next after his, I would speak for several hours.

But I knew I had something to present, and a way of presenting it that I had to work out.

I began to hit my stride when I started to write about Afghanistan, Iraq, surveillance, all the lies pouring out of Bush's White House, and the history of presidential constitutional violations and dishonesty that had enabled the current abuses. The core material was some research I had done nearly twenty years earlier, for a talk to the League of Women Voters, during the Reagan years. Bush, I now saw, was a logical extension of the Nixon and Reagan lies and the Johnson and Reagan overreach. That earlier work gave me a grounding, and my anger at the way things were going pushed me forward. Eventually, my War Powers, War Lies series within my column came to twenty-five columns, a small book.

Over the two years I was producing my War Powers series, I started having fans. People I met on the street, some of them strangers, mentioned that they read me regularly. I also acquired a few detractors, most of them being, however, opposed to what I said, not to me personally. I'm pleased to say that I never had anyone challenge my facts, however. I tried really hard to get them right.

Of course my little brush with local fame had at least one drawback. I knew from the start that any ambitions I had ever had to become a judge would vanish because of my outspokenness. The people who choose judges generally shy away from those with controversial viewpoints, particularly controversial ones from my end of the political spectrum. Luckily, I had never been prey to that ambition in anything but the vaguest daydream.

The ambition I had had, I'd already achieved: I was a name partner in a good law firm. Better yet, as I quickly realized, neither my clientele nor my partnership was going to put any appreciable crimp in my ability to be outspoken. I did not alienate any clients that I was aware of by what I said, nor did I confront what lawyers call issues conflicts (where a position you take in some public context is inconsistent with an argument you're making on a client's behalf), forcing me to silence myself or even moderate my views.

The greatest gift, though, was finding my voice. I was expressing my distrust of the powers that were, my awareness of the evils wrought by the powers that had been, and my bitterness about the whole situation, with all the honesty and erudition at my disposal. I had never heard myself talking that way before. And I kinda liked that sound.

The first time I heard *Not Ready to Make Nice* I snapped to attention. The Chicks were singing exactly what I was feeling. Of course they had been playing for much greater personal and business stakes than I. But the exaltation at breaking through, at saying what they felt, at liking how they sounded: that was what I was feeling. That song was my anthem.

Even now, a decade and a half later, I still get a glint in my eye when I hear it.

76

TRAVELS: ELSEWHERENESS

DANZA DEL PIRINEO, TRADITIONAL, PERFORMED BY
ANA ALCAIDE (2005), ENCOUNTERED 2009

ROSARIO-RETIRO, WRITTEN BY MARTIN DELGADO, PERFORMED
BY SAN TELMO LOUNGE (2007), ENCOUNTERED 2011

NO PLAYLIST TRACK FOR ANA ALCAIDE. PLAYLIST
TRACK NO. 106 FOR SAN TELMO LOUNGE

THE SPANISH HAVE NO CULTURE!, my mother once exclaimed in the middle of some argument, neatly betraying a number of her shortcomings at one fell swoop. For all her Boston Girls' Latin School/Radcliffe/Cornell/Hopkins cultivation, or perhaps because of it, she maintained a firm Anglo-Saxon snobbery. In her view of the world, certain nations were respectable for their literature and music and art, and the rest, apparently including the Spanish, were irredeemable also-rans. As a result, for all of her travels, I don't believe she ever set foot in a Spanish-speaking country. I was never persuaded by Mother's dismissiveness, and had long harbored a rebellious ambition to go where my mother had never trodden.

After she died, and after our son went away to college in 2008, my wife and I found ourselves the following year with the leisure and means to check for ourselves whether she was right. Ironically, in doing so, our first significant musical adventure was an encounter with a performer who has herself maintained in an interview that Spain has no culture, in effect disproving my mother by agreeing with her, since her own very Spanish music is nothing if not cultured.

We had spent five rapturous days in Barcelona and surroundings, places so laden with great architecture and art and history that to deny one was in the presence of culture would have been ludicrous. Then we had taken the swift AVE train to Madrid, staying there two days, and then went on our first excursion out of town, to the extremely hilly city of Toledo, El Greco's town. To get to it, one walks uphill for a long way from the train station, and even in September, it's hot and thirsty going, but, as we found, once you get past the city wall and through the gates it's much pleasanter, because the streets are mostly narrow and fronted with high buildings and walls that minimize the direct sunlight.

As we approached the Cathedral, we came upon a young woman in a flowing lacy white dress, seated on a card chair, playing an extraordinary instrument the likes of which neither of us had ever seen. She was busking with

this strange object. And the sound she was making was enchanting. Despite our limited time in this unknown town, we had to stop for awhile and just take it in. Naturally, I came up with the ten Euros or whatever it was for her CD, and learned her name was Ana Alcaide, and that the name for the instrument was "viola de teclas," i.e. "key viola," so-called because one does the fretwork with the left hand pushing keys beneath the neck. (I later learned that this was a Spanish coinage, and that the instrument's "native" name from Sweden, where Alcaide had first encountered it when she was there as a graduate biology student, is "nyckel-harpa," i.e. "key harp.")

Building on this instrument and her voice, Alcaide has since become a name to conjure with in the world music movement, but at this point she was still launching her career. Her repertoire then was focused on Spanish, and more particularly Sephardic precedents, and that was what the album largely provided.

The liveliest song, *Danza del Pirineo*, a "Dance of the Pyrenees," is described in the liner notes as a "traditional melody of Huesca," a town in the northern mountain region of Spain. Clearly a folk dance, it served as the catalyst for my later reminiscences about all the high places we visited in Spain, including the valley whose prospect one can appreciate from the plaza in front of Toledo's Alcazar. (Others would be the long down-mountain panoramas glimpsed a few days earlier from the front of the cathedral in Montserrat, and the view from the top of the Santa Barbara castle overlooking Alicante, which I visited nine years later.)

If *Danza del Pirineo* became a touchstone for places visited, *Rosario-Retiro* was something less usual: a touchstone for places not visited, or more accurately not yet visited. The year following the Spanish trip, enthralled by a Yo-Yo Ma recording of *Libertango*, I chose to download a sampler of Argentinian music, and this instrumental cut, a product of a group called San Telmo Lounge, was on it. The music was snappily-syncopated, each phrase ending somewhere slightly unexpected, each phrase rhythmically deceptive to expectations, and it was all, not a tango exactly, but tango-orchestrated and tango-inflected. I loved it. I'd never been to Argentina; I didn't know then that Rosario-Retiro was a Buenos Aires transit line; I had never heard of San Telmo. But I learned all these things from my researches. (They were like my much-earlier researches about Rome recollected in Chapter 12.) As a direct result of hearing that record, though, I knew I had to get to Argentina, which I did, finally, in 2017. So this was a theme song of yearning for the unknown, not of nostalgia for the known.

Both songs, however, were signposts of a traveling imagination; I was beginning to develop a bad case of it, as this book will bear further witness.

77

PROTESTING TOO MUCH?

O COME, O COME EMMANUEL, TRADITIONAL, PERFORMED BY
THE CAST OF ROCK OF AGES (2011), ENCOUNTERED 2011

PLAYLIST TRACK NO. 107

IN 2009, I had been invited to start reviewing Baltimore-area theater for Broad-wayWorld.com, a pursuit that soon became an important part of my life. Not long thereafter, I was also asked to write about theater for *The Hopkins Review*, a journal of the Writing Program at the Johns Hopkins University. I had reviewed theater before, both for my college paper and briefly again in the 1990s (for the *Baltimore Business Journal*'s Arts and Leisure page, when there was one). But this was much more serious and absorbing. I began to feel a part of the actual theater community, and began to entertain the notion that I might write plays myself.

As part of my newfound seriousness about this connection to an art and a community, I wanted to get up to New York and check out the scene there more often. So I began roughly quarterly forays to take in multiple shows. One of the first happened in October of 2011. And that was when I first became aware of Broadway Cares, a fund-raising program to provide services for people with AIDS and other serious diseases. Their marquee project was *Carols for a Cure*, an annual compilation of holiday music that was promoted and sold at Broadway shows during the lead-up to the holiday season and in the season itself. Each year, each participating cast of a current musical would put its own spin on one piece of holiday music, and the resulting recordings would be accumulated and dispensed in two-CD sets. I bought a set most seasons after that. I believe I purchased my first in the year I'm speaking of.

This event marked a kind of transition in my approach not only to holiday music, but to the holidays themselves. By this point I was more involved in the Catholic observance of the season than I had been in earlier years, owing to my also having joined the choir at my church, in the role of harmonica player (the flautist and I, who played as a unit, made some marvelous sonorities together). At the same time, however, as I have discussed in Chapter 74, I was continuing to struggle with my actual religious faith, in the light of the loss of my mother among other things.

So I was simultaneously participating more in the forms of faith and perhaps less in the substance, one might say. Somewhat in keeping with this shift, I began changing my holiday music purchases. To be sure, there had always been those purchases. I was raised not only with *Pussycat's Christmas* (Chapter 1) but with 78 shellacs of Fred Waring and his Pennsylvanians, and Bing Crosby and Dinah Shore warbling about Christmas. And later, I started ritually buying one cassette of holiday music each season, typically from Hallmark where I would also buy the seasons' complements of holiday cards to send. I liked these cassettes, which imparted a high gloss to what was often very enjoyable kitsch. Then I started craving something hipper, and started buying CD compilations of jazzy and/or classical takes on holiday favorites from Starbucks, when Starbucks was still in the music business. Starbucks quit selling CDs in early 2015, so I suspect my purchases from them overlapped my Carols for a Cure habit. But Carols for a Cure soon became the main deal for me.

This new transition to the melding of Broadway entertainment and piety intensified my ambivalence. The heart of theater is fakery, as Shakespeare was often at pains to point out. When Hamlet observes the actor emoting about Hecuba at the fall of Troy, he observes:

> *Is it not monstrous that this player here,*
> *But in a fiction, in a dream of passion,*
> *Could force his soul so to his own conceit*
> *That from her working all his visage wann'd,*
> *Tears in his eyes, distraction in's aspect,*
> *A broken voice, and his whole function suiting*

With forms to his conceit? and all for nothing!
For Hecuba! What's Hecuba to him, or he to Hecuba,
That he should weep for her?

Theater is called a mimetic art, one that imitates life. But as Hamlet sees, it can as appropriately be deemed a mendacious art, feigning emotions, concerns – and belief. If the faith of all the artists singing about Christmas or Hannukah on a Carols for a Cure album were bona fide, it would, in my estimation, be a powerful testament to the verity of their subject. But it is hardly to be believed that in every case the songs were sung from religious conviction.

If I were a cast member, particularly one fund-raising to counteract the ravages of AIDS, I might well be gay, for example, and I would know how wrongly and cruelly organized religion has frequently dealt with homosexuality. And yet I would sing. And if I were a cast member without religious convictions, I might still, out of sheer solidarity with my fellow cast-members, wish to hold up my show's reputation in the tight-knit Broadway community. Or I might have been so focused on my craft from an early age that I had never made room in my heart or mind for the struggle that a serious mature faith probably requires.

So as a consumer of these performances, I knew I could not treat these performers as bona fide witnesses to faith, let alone reliable ones. And yet I did hear them as such. And I think I was right to do so. Regardless of how one conceives of the act, one does not sing a religious song without entering into some kind of dialogue with faith.

Along these lines, one carol in particular struck me in the year we're speaking of, a rendering of *O Come, O Come Emmanuel* by the cast of *Rock of Ages*. The musical was an affectionate pastiche of 1980s pop and rock hits set within a ludicrous story of clueless youngsters coming to Hollywood to become music stars. (It may have been at a performance of that very show that I bought the CD in question.) I started listening to that song, and immediately got the feeling that this rendition was not all it seemed.

At first blush, it comes across as a plea grounded in faith. Most conventionally-raised Christians know the carol, which in one form or another seems to date back to the 8th Century. It begs Emmanuel to come, Emmanuel being a name associated with Jesus, relying upon imagery from Isaiah 7:14: "Behold, a virgin shall conceive, and bear a son, and shall call his name Emmanuel." Jesus is not here yet, and that's okay. As Christians celebrate Advent, Jesus not being here yet is the whole point, almost part of what we're celebrating. But it must be noted that as generally intoned at church, *O Come* is a song of serene expectation.

This version of *O Come* is not the one generally intoned at church, however. The melody has been changed, for one thing. There are echoes of the ancient melody in this version, but it isn't the same. This is a rock-inflected power ballad delivered by performers who know how to belt, Broadway-style. And the resulting emotional tone is both unsettled and unsettling. After an opening stanza with solo voices and otherwise unaccompanied acoustic guitar, there is a repeat with more voices and a slightly fuzzy guitar, and then a repeat with a more powerful drum beat, a chorus and soulful descants, and all of a sudden there is unmistakable emotional turbulence. This chorus really wants Jesus to come, with noisy intensity. And then with gospel-singing intensity. "Sing it like you mean it," one of the voices interjects.

Well, do they mean it? I can't tell, especially if by "meaning it" one indicates confidence as opposed to mere desire, no matter how urgent or profound. I think I hear despair there as much as the confident hope Romans 8:25 calls for. And there's no telling which of these feelings the makers of the song thought was winning.

But there's a winner in my mind, in my sensibilities. To me it feels as if the singers are protesting too much. It's the sense that what the song's singers really mean is they wish Jesus would come, but are close to losing hope for that to happen. And I find myself singing along, emphasizing that desperate tone, when I play it in the car. The only time I can feel God's immanence nowadays is when playing and listening to music. But as this song subtly betrays, I'm not safe even there.

Still, even if all I'm doing is responding to a God-shaped hole, that response remains a religious-adjacent experience I must continue to pursue. And so I do.

78

OTHER WORLDS

SAMBA NO. 2, WRITTEN BY DAVID CARBONARA
(2010), ENCOUNTERED 2010?

MAIN TITLE TO GAME OF THRONES, WRITTEN BY
RAMIN DJAWADI (2011), ENCOUNTERED 2010

HISTORY IS MADE AT NIGHT, WRITTEN BY MARC SHAIMAN
AND SCOTT WITTMAN, PERFORMED BY MEGAN HILTY
AND WILL CHASE (2012), ENCOUNTERED 2012

PLAYLIST TRACKS NOS. 108, 109, AND 110

OF COURSE, THERE'S more to life than staring into a void of existential doubt. I could no more focus fixedly on the thought that there might not be a God than I could previously have focused at all times on the God whom I was once taught needed to be the object and the measure of every action. All dogmas notwithstanding, our attention sometimes needs to be diverted. Worldly fun will sometimes be good enough, or, if you will, God enough, for us.

And what better fun than what TV was providing at this point? Along with everyone else, I realized around the time of *The Sopranos* that television was getting much, much better, especially in its long format, the scripted drama and/or comedy series. In time, the phenomenon came to be known as "peak TV." This wasn't a reference to quality but rather to the sheer unprecedented number of scripted shows, which caused John Landgraf, the TV executive who coined the phrase in 2015, to predict that the number of scripted shows available had reached its peak and would have to decline. (Landgraf later admitted that his prediction hadn't come true as of 2019.) Still, "peak TV" seems just as apt as a descriptor of quality as it is of quantity.

Long stories, rendered with high performance values, full of complex plotlines, intriguing writing, and surprisingly original characters, enacted by performers with big names and without, kept me coming back to the flat screen, even as my interest in live theater was also growing. I was asking myself what made this moment in the medium so exciting, and what I kept coming back to was that I was being transported to different worlds.

Case in point, a series about the advertising trade in the 1950s and 1960s. In a world full of doctor shows and detective shows and lawyer shows, no one had ever taken us into that milieu, or shown us its tragic underbelly. Or one set in a grimly reimagined Middle Ages in which magic and dragons are real, as is a complex dynastic struggle so fierce that no character seems immune from being unexpectedly butchered and written out of the show. Or a series about the people who make today's musical theater, in which the show-within-the-show is almost as fully realized as the story about the producers and the performers. I could cite many more examples, but these three will prove my point.

In each of these instances, I found the music captivating as well, frequently to the point that I would experience instant Pavlovian delight at just hearing the title song.

There were mostly two different kinds of music on *Mad Men*: bona fide period recordings (chosen not only to trigger nostalgia but to comment, frequently mordantly, on the action) and cues written expressly for the show. The latter were David Carbonara's work, principally employing Carbonara's chosen instrument: the jazz orchestra. The pieces he wrote for the show were simultaneously of the time-frame the show covered and of an earlier time. Henry Mancini, a film- and television-scorer of that period, could have written many of them: sinuous, with sonorities that often harkened back to hot jazz of the 30s and the big bands of the 40s, but also the popular dance of the 50s and 60s. I've chosen here to focus here on one of the latter, *Samba No. 2*, which equally could have been played at a nightclub in Don Draper's New York or at a hotel in pre-revolutionary Havana. A piece of uncertain mood but confirmed minor key and unfailing elegance, it evokes both the everyday, somewhat cosmopolitan prosperity of the ad men and women, and the emotional indeterminacy of their lives. Maybe one might envy the prosperity and style – and it's hard to imagine not being fascinated by it, but, as the entire series makes clear, there is little to envy in their personal lives.

By contrast, the martial, cantering drum figure that underlies most of Ramin Djawadi's main title music to *Game of Thrones* unmistakably evokes the war of all against all which the series is devoted to chronicling. It is a savage game played out on an immense board, illustrated by the opening titles, which take the viewer on a geographic stroll among those locations important to the individual episode. Wherever this show will take us – and we soon understand it will be lots of places, from deserts to frozen wildernesses – it will be very little like any world we are familiar or comfortable with.

By a further contrast, the songs and vocal performance styles of *Smash* summon up pure escapist fantasy: a dazzling showbiz world unspeakably tempting to the exhibitionist in each of us. We would all like to inhabit it: to be talented and magnetic, to prompt applause from the crowds, no matter what the state of our personal lives. The music to bring it out must be nowhere near as monochrome as, say, the Carbonara score for *Mad Men*. *Smash*'s songs are deliberately all over the place: anthems from the pop music of the Aughts and Teens, recastings of hits from bygone Broadway eras, and ersatz contemporary Broadway music. For instance, *History Is Made at Night*, a kind of makeout song from the musical-within-the-show sung by Marilyn Monroe and Joe DiMaggio with a heavy choral infusion of doo-wop and powered by rock-n-roll double-triplets on the piano, is not exactly character-appropriate for those figures nor that much like what Broadway would actually provide for those figures. But it's sexy, smart, and harmonically fun. I probably played it dozens of times after I downloaded the soundtrack album. And the thing about escapism, whatever the genre, is exactly what the name implies: liberation from the world of the everyday.

It was like my dad and stepmom's yellow country placemats. When I would visit the family cottage in the Catskills growing up, there they lay, beneath our plates, salvaged from an ancient Renault promotion (from the *Mad Men* era, come to think of it), featuring the catchphrase of the ad campaign: *Vivez un jour loin de tous les jours* ("Live a day far from every day"). That summed up what, in my sixties, I found peak TV doing for me: allowing my imagination to visit places that were far from everyday, at least my everyday. And via dramatic vehicles so worthy of attention that I felt no embarrassment at being captivated by them.

And of course the music was a big part of it.

79

TRAVELS: WIDE OPEN SPACES

MAYBE NOT TONIGHT, BY GLEN HANSARD (2012), ENCOUNTERED 2012

PLAYLIST TRACK No. 111

I PICK UP Irish singer Glen Hansard's album *Rhythm and Repose* on a whim at an Oklahoma City Starbucks on October 10, 2012, as I'm progressing westward along the roadbed of the legendary old decommissioned highway, Route 66. I've started 66 at its eastern terminus on Lake Shore Drive in Chicago, and I'm following it all the way to its opposite end at the Santa Monica pier. In the city where I've acquired the CD, the road still is headed through the middle

American farmland, flat, but not so flat the road was seriously straight. Up ahead, though, lies something else. As I cross southwesterly into the Texas panhandle, it becomes a land of long and straight, if slightly boring, vistas. I don't mind at all; it gives me time to think. (A photo is below.) As I make for Amarillo, the late afternoon ahead of me, I experience the straightness of the road as profoundly calming. And it is then that I first grasp the musical fitness to the scene of Hansard's song *Maybe Not Tonight*.

It's not that the song is about anything like the experience of being at liberty driving west into a sunset; it takes a long time for me to unpack what the song is actually about. At first, I think the lyrics, in which a man is clearly trying to lure a woman back into his bed, present a flirtation in which one or both of the parties is spoken for. But somewhere after the third listen, I realize that what I am actually hearing is what might call a failed breakup song. When the singer suggests repeatedly that he and the woman both "just do what's right/ But maybe not tonight," the criterion for "what's right" is the fact that they have taken "vows" to break up, not to stay together. Maybe later they will actually keep their hands off each other, but "maybe not tonight."

Not a song about straight roads and wide open spaces at all. But it fits, in fact it's a beautiful fit for straight roads and wide open spaces. The lyrics, fortunately, as we've seen, a little bit obscure, aren't nearly as important as the music, which is sonorous and languid, played at a slowly ambling pace. Many of the guitar and piano chords are so sustained they seem to stretch to infinity. And often Hansard's voice seems as much an embellishment of those chords

as any of the instrumental notes. I'm experiencing the background of the song as the foreground, and I think I was meant to.

And this moment will repeat in various ways for the next three days.

The next day will bring my nearly constant companion, the BNSF rails, up to my right, a straight line accompanying a straight line, and the rails will seldom stray far from me as I cross the pink-accented deserts of New Mexico and the lava-strewn grazing lands of Arizona. Of course, further west, the roads will bend somewhat to accommodate canyon outlines and mountains. But basically the road will keep being straight and direct, and will cause me to confront sunsets head-on for three days, before I reach the deserts and declivities of California on the way downhill to the Pacific. Lots to keep the eyes occupied as I drive.

And as I make my way through this stage of the journey, again and again I play *Maybe Not Tonight*, not for the lyrics, but for that incredible leisurely sound. I have been engaged for many years in the struggle to make my way in the world, to establish a law practice, to raise children, and now that struggle is behind me, and I'm free to coast awhile. Freer than I've ever been, simply to marvel at the world, to drink it in quietly.

It is an intoxicating time.

80

TRAVELS: NEW OLD WORLDS

DOVE STA ZAZÀ?, TRADITIONAL, PERFORMED BY
PIETRA MONTECORVINO (2004), ENCOUNTERED 2013

OYUN HAVASI (DANCE MOOD), WRITTEN AND PERFORMED BY
HÜSNÜ ŞENLENDIRICI (2005), ENCOUNTERED 2013

PLAYLIST TRACKS NOS. 112, 113

IF YOU'RE AN American with a taste for the exotic, and you want to look locally, it will have to be modern exotic. Apart from archeology, the age of things here tops out at about four centuries. And that's okay; my 2012 Route 66 trip mentioned in the last chapter was not just a quest for landscapes but for roadside attractions (historic structures and graveyards) and follies (a blue whale mockup, dinosaurs, teepees, cars parked atop buildings, antique auto museums), all of which can be called exotic. But one has to look further afield for exoticism based on deeper history. And that was what Mary and I were looking for in 2013.

Thus, for our 25th anniversary (yeah, it had been that long), we bought ourselves tickets for a Mediterranean cruise, by definition a foray into parts of the world associated with the very roots of our civilization. Barcelona to Istanbul, with lots of stops in between, areas we had mostly not visited before. And before we even departed, I was assured that we'd see, on that single trip, St. Peter's, the Parthenon, and the Hagia Sophia. For the more ancient exotic, it's hard to beat that sort of itinerary.

In the year or so before we left, partly in anticipation of our trip and four days of port calls in Italy, I'd happened to purchase an anthology of 100 Italian hit songs, mostly pop. It was eye-opening to make a first acquaintance with the variety of talent on display there, including the likes of Mina, Fausto Leali, Lina Sastri, Orietta Berti, and on and on. The one that impressed me most, though, was Barbara Dalessandro, known professionally as Pietra Montecorvino.

There were three songs by this extremely hoarse-voiced singer, and what fascinated me was that no attempt was made to render her voice conventionally beautiful, or to fit her renderings into the kinds of molds that most of the other singers had adhered to in Italian pop. Instead, I was hearing distinctly North African drumming, and distinctly non-Western harmonic modes. The effect was dazzling. I soon ascertained that all three numbers featured were from her album *Napoli Mediterranea* (2004). And so of course I had to have that album. And after I'd gotten ahold of it, as I discovered in playing and pondering the album, I could see that it was not merely a showcase of Montecorvino's strange voice, but of the malleability of conventional Italian songs (traditional and folk dance songs and ballads). They could be remolded to fit new time signatures and harmonic modes, and could be accompanied by non-western drums and instruments, to be married to African musicianship, in effect.

I was later to learn that Montecorvino was particularly influenced by Libyan music, in retrospect a predictable source in light of Italy's colonial history there and the geographic proximity of the two countries across the Med.

Take, for instance, *Dove Sta Zazà?* ("Where Is Zazà?"), a traditional song. As I checked out other versions (of which there are multitudes), not one was close to Montecorvino's. There's quite a bit of ambiguity to the lyrics, but this much meaning is evident: The singer, named Isaiah, has been accompanied by a woman named Zazà to the Feast of San Gennaro, a big holiday traditionally marked with parades and crowds, and somehow amidst all the participants, Isaiah and Zazà have become separated. The body of the song is the singer's expression of woe at the separation – and perhaps resourcefulness, because by the end of his lament he seems to be turning his attention to Zazà's unnnamed sister, who seems to be with him. Is Isaiah supposed to be the object of fun, a dolt making the best of a bad situation after Zazà has given him the slip? I don't think the song is conclusive on that.

In listening to the many other versions, one finds they vary widely in their emotional hue. Many, for instance, lay an emphasis on the patter-y parts of the lyrics, and make the song come across like an excerpt from an *opera buffa*, which does not, as a rule, lay serious emphasis on distressing emotions. Others, like Montecorvino's, make much of Isaiah's distress.

But no one delivers the distress like Pietra Montecorvino. She has at least four videotaped performances of the song out, each musically a little different. But in all of them she comes across as a woman on the verge, tossing a huge mane of tousled hair, croaking out the lyrics while dancing, bending over to share a prominent tattoo in her decolletage and waving tattooed arms, flirting with a skirt (sometimes flowy, sometimes a little black dress that seems more like a slip). There is never a note of irony when she channels Isaiah's suffering. But she stays on the verge – she does not quite go over it. Her Isaiah is angry, not berserk. If Isaiah is making moves on Zazà's sister, this may well be an act of revenge, not desperation, in Montecorvino's rendering. And Montecorvino can be comic in other contexts; if she withholds comedy here, it's because her Isaiah is not a fool and should not be the butt of any joke.

Obviously, then, I found richness in the cultivated exoticism of Montecorvino's performance.

And that performance and that album were very much in my ears and on my mind when we went on that cruise, and especially on the September day we clambered into a dockside bus in Naples (the town that was the album's namesake) and toured the Amalfi coast. Those who have visited Amalfi know that it is one of the most picturesque places on earth, with sweeping vistas of the Mediterranean swooping down cliffs to little tourist-and-fishing towns. Even without having researched the matter, I felt in my bones I must be not only in Montecorvino's Naples, but also in her neighborhood, that I was close to the spiritual home of that strange, pulsing music she purveyed. And later, I discovered that I had been on the money.

Pietra Montecorvino's stage name, I learned, was the name of her home town, a walled village called, naturally, Pietramontecorvino, which was at more or less the same latitude on the Italian boot as Amalfi, if closer to the Adriatic than to the Med. But Montecorvino's album title had specified Naples and the Mediterranean. So I knew I was close to Ground Zero. And what made it all so especially piquant was that I could imagine Montecorvino in this part of the world where I had never been before, a place which definitely counted as exotic for me, seeking out rhythms and modes and sonorities that were exotic to her, and mastering them, bringing them into her life. To one who was beginning to dedicate part of his life to travel, to broader horizons and stranger places, she came across as an inspiring example.

Not that I could ever be her; my creativity ran in other channels. But I could acknowledge a master.

When we later arrived at Istanbul, where we spent four nights, we found ourselves in a world of minarets and harem enclosures and calls to prayer and strangely-attired marching bands and spices and the gorgeous blue of the Sea of Marmara outside our hotel room window. The very embodiment of exoticism, in other words. We did so much: the Grand Bazaar and the Spice Market and a ferry ride across the Bosphorus, and a visit to the underground cisterns and tours of the Harem, Hagia Sophia and the Blue Mosque, and long walks through the souks. Having been raised on *Murder on the Orient Express* and *From Russia with Love*, and having recently watched James Bond race a motorcycle along the roof of the Grand Bazaar in *Skyfall*, we reveled in the simultaneous thrills of novelty and familiarity. Yes, Istanbul was all just as the movies had promised and still so much more.

At a music store somewhere in the triangle formed by the Blue Mosque and the Hagia Sophia and the Grand Bazaar, I continued a personal custom I had started forty years earlier in Lisbon: when in an interesting foreign land, acquire some of the local music. Among the CDs I bought was a red-covered one featuring a portly bearded clarinet player with an earring. I knew nothing about Hüsnü Şenlendirici or the sounds he made, but he looked interesting. I fell in love with his music as soon as I heard it, though. Sinuous, stuttering, constantly shifting rhythm and direction, in God-knew-what scale, and often taking the form of a rapidly-shifting dialogue between his clarinet and a string orchestra, where each would produce a new portion of the melody line in rapid succession.

I later learned that Şenlendirici was Romani, and this unlocked a lot of what I was hearing. As I found upon inquiry, the Romani are a not particularly well-treated minority in Turkey (as in most places), and they have a some-what separate musical culture. Much of their music is heavily dance-oriented (belly dance in particular), relying largely on a so-called Karsilama rhythm (9/8, broken out as 2+2+2+3) and their preferred scale is the Gypsy (also known as Arabic) scale. And all of this was on display in Şenlendirici's CD.

Exotic? Sure, to me at least. I've highlighted the first cut here, *Oyun Havasi* (Dance Mood), because it cuts right to the chase of everything I've been mentioning. As soon as one plays it one confronts all these differences, which I was finding delightful.

The world is so full of the exotic, it's a shame not to reach out for it when it's on offer. And in this part of our travels, it was.

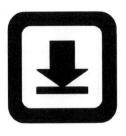

81

IMAGINARY PATHS

ALWAYS STARTING OVER, WRITTEN BY TOM KITT AND BRIAN YORKEY,
PERFORMED BY IDINA MENZEL (2014), ENCOUNTERED 2015

PLAYLIST TRACK No. 114

THE ICONOGRAPHIC IMAGE, effectively the logo, of the musical *If/Then*, to which the album cover is also devoted, is of the character Elizabeth (Idina Menzel), poised at a fork in a park path. She is also, as the story starts, at a fork in her life's path. It would appear that if she chooses one direction her whole life will be different from what it will be like if she chooses the other. However, the audience will be privileged to see the two versions of her life, side by side. Her two paths turn out to be very different, and yet end up in somewhat similar places.

But the musical carries the story of paths a little further forward. We learn that that "One road ends where one begins," and hence, by transitivity, one begins where another ends, and so even the similar places Elizabeth has arrived at are only intermediate destinations on her life's journey. She will still have to go on, knowing as little of the future as she did before that first decision, but perhaps less intimidated by the process or the prospects. Indeed, the musical's signature anthem, *Always Starting Over*, the last number before the finale, has Elizabeth resolving, whatever may come, not only to "start over and over and over somehow," but in the process to "be bold." It's vintage Broadway, valorizing individual lives and individual choices and endowing them with value far greater than they probably deserve in the grand scheme of things. When I saw it in 2015, I adored it, even though I recognized how much ideological hokum lay just below its beautifully-polished surface. And – the reader surely knows now what happened next – I had to download the album. But the use I would put it to might not have been as predictable.

With only a couple of minor breaks, I have been working out at my same gym in downtown Baltimore since about 1981. But at around the time I saw *If/Then*, I was getting more serious about it. I was now eligible for Medicare, gaining weight, and getting old. Countermeasures had to be taken. Late in 2015, I started working with a personal trainer, and I believe it was also at this time that I became a devotee of the Expresso stationary bikes available at the gym.

My ridership on actual bicycles, abandoned when I went to college, had already resumed a decade earlier, on a very occasional basis. Great frequency was impossible. Being an urban dweller, I'd had to keep my bike carefully locked down (behind four locks), and then, after liberating it from its shed, I'd have to decide whether to strap a rack on my car to drive miles to a suburban trail or just ride in the city. And if I did the latter, then I'd have to deal with potholes, the threat of flat tires, the promise of lethal drivers, and the frustration of limited streets on which riding was only remotely safe.

Expresso was the perfect antidote. Unlike every other stationary bike I'd encountered, this one yielded something akin to the experience of a real bike ride, only stripped of the fear of collisions, and unaccompanied by logistical prerequisites. The verisimilitude of the ride owed to four features: a screen that displayed a picture that changed in real time of the territory you were riding through, constant adjustment of the tension of the chain to conform to what was visible on the screen, 30 gears to shift through, and a limited steering functionality. The screen picture wasn't photorealistic, but of decent video-game quality.

There were a couple of unrealistic touches; you couldn't collide with the other cyclists around you; they'd just disappear if you steered into them. And you couldn't actually steer off whatever trail you were riding through. The biggest one, though, was built into the trail and road structure. There was no realism in the way the few nearby roads had almost no visible, and no usable, intersections with the path you had to go. Each route was a circle you couldn't leave, and for the most part, seemed to have entered by no apparent access point.

And yet, despite these drawbacks, there was tremendous imaginative stimulation in riding these roads with their constantly varying landscapes and differing topographies. At present writing, there are 50 courses, many of which take me well over an hour to traverse. In other words, there is a great choice of paths and experiences. Exactly what *If/Then* is all about.

No surprise, then, that the original cast album I'd downloaded was what I would listen to repeatedly as I'd ride the Expresso cycles. The very first thing you'd do when you started a ride was select a course, exactly what Elizabeth does. And then you'd have the anticipation of surprises (there were always surprises because you couldn't remember everything that happened on any of those 50 courses), corresponding to the apprehension and anticipation which informs so many of the songs in the musical. Likewise, the moments that challenged one as a rider echoed the travails that Elizabeth encounters.

To be sure, it takes more than a fortuitous correspondence between the preoccupations of a musical and one's own to make one keep coming back to listen to the musical. Yorkey and Kitt write great melodies and great lyrics, with melody fragments continuingly recycling through successive songs to reinform their meaning and resonance. The four principal voices, particularly Menzel's, are gorgeous, and Menzel in particular has a big voice. When, for instance, she sings the last line of her anthem, she concludes, "My new life starts right now." There's a dramatic pause of two measures before she begins the last word, and then she sustains that "now" through six chord changes and nearly six measures. Not many singers could do that.

Oh, of course I listened to many things as I cycled. But there is no doubt that this album was my most frequent choice. I rode hundreds of miles, and went through at least four sets of headphones and three iPods. But there was always one supreme album.

 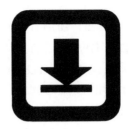

82

RETIREMENT IMAGINED

FOLLOW THE FLOWER, COMPOSED BY CHRISTOPHE BECK
(2003), ENCOUNTERED CA. 2016

DON'T DIE WITH YOUR MUSIC IN YOU, WRITTEN AND
PERFORMED BY BOB SIMA (2007), ENCOUNTERED CA. 2016

PLAYLIST NOS. 115, 116

I CAN VIVIDLY recall that in the first fine flush of rapture at founding my own small law firm described in Chapter 67 I told myself that I would never want to quit such a rewarding way of life, ever. Which goes to prove that you should never say never. There did in fact come a time when I would feel differently.

Let me rush to add that I never lost my love for the law or for the firm I founded; but if you're lucky as you grow older, you will encounter additional things you love as much. And this was happening to me. I had recently tasted deeply of the joys of travel (more deeply than I've detailed in this book), and I was determined to continue. I was doing more writing all the time and wanted to devote still more time to it. I also wanted to work out more often at my gym. And there were other inclinations (not least of which was polishing my harmonica skills) that were at war with the demands of my job. As I was beginning to put it in conversations with friends and relatives, my job was getting in the way of my life.

I had what they call an "aha moment" on a 2016 road trip down the Mississippi River. I had put myself on a tight schedule, and then, as was entirely to be expected doing what I did for a living, my cellphone rang, and I found myself sidelined for half an hour in a trailer park answering the call. That call meant new business for me (what turned out in due course to be my last trial) – and I was grateful for the business. But I was staring at a lovely view of the Mississippi as we spoke, and I felt irked by the interruption. I had tracks to make, and the clock was ticking. Finally, I was putting the feeling into words: I wanted out. And as it happened, I knew I could afford to quit.

I started letting my partners know I was planning to leave. Soon I'd set a date, in 2017, and even advised my clients of it. And then something interfered, and I was unavoidably delayed for ten months.

In the meantime, I began trying to imagine what my retirement would be like. My inspiration came from various sources. One was the movie *Under the Tuscan Sun*, which had been released in 2003, but which I got around to seeing at this point. It's not formally about retirement at all; it's about the return to life of a suddenly and unexpectedly homeless U.S. divorcée who embarks on a tourist trip of Tuscany and finds herself impulsively fashioning a home, an immersion in Italian society, and eventually love and a family from a spur-of-the-moment decision to get off the bus and abandon the tour. It spoke to me, feeding my sense that if I could "get off the bus" of my career, I would be able to achieve some kind of similar immersion in wonder.

Of course I downloaded and loved the original soundtrack album. The music cue which spoke to me most while I was thinking these thoughts was *Follow the Flower*, which plays sometime during the first twenty minutes of the movie. The flower in question is the tour guide's totem to keep his flock with him as the bus passengers debouch for a moment in front of the Florence Cathedral. Then they progress on to the ancient village of Cortona, where life greets them in the form of a street market full of intriguing vegetables and vendors, a mysterious British actress caressing a cat, and (after the music cue ends) a real estate agent's office where a villa that catches our heroine's eye is on offer. Everything seems infinitely beautiful and promising, and all that seems to be required of her to access it is that she reach out and grab it. This may seem formulaic in outline, and what happens next is not hard to guess, but, particularly with the insistent music, the situation and its working out sell themselves.

The music: focused mostly on a variety of plucked instruments adding accents, melody and rhythm, punctuated by bird-calls from woodwinds.

The music picks up and halts, picks up and halts, crescendoing and pulling back, mimicking the pulsations of the divorcée's intrigued encounter with this magical world, and her longing to become part of it, which we know she'll surrender to, because the movie's called *Under the Tuscan Sun*.

As what I was about to do was called retirement. There wasn't much difference between the fantasies.

Of course, notwithstanding the movie, my hopes for retirement did not include living out my days as an expat. But I did hope to be creative, not only with my writing but also with my instrument, the harmonica. A friend invited me to an event at which a number of local musical acts were playing, one of them being the country-music-adjacent Bob Sima. I'd been tipped off to bring my harmonicas, and sure enough Sima encouraged anyone so inclined to jam with him. I asked, and he passed the mike down to me from the stage, and I started blowing, and, even though I'd never heard his songs before, it was several minutes of magical collaboration. Afterwards, I bought all four of his CDs on offer.

One of the songs he sang spoke intimately to where I was in my thinking.

Won't you sing us all your songs, sing us all the songs
Sing us all the songs that you know
Won't you sing us all your songs, sing us all your songs
Sing us all your songs before you go
Don't die with your music, your sweet sweet music
Don't die with your music in you

The fact was, in my sixties, I was still laboring under the burden of the things I hadn't done. Sima's lyric emphasized that one should not acquiesce in not doing them. One should fiercely persist in finishing whatever form of creation he or she might be born to.

And yes, of course that was likely to mean that one had to jettison one's job when the time came. In my case, the time was arriving. True, once upon a time the crafting of a legal brief had deeply satisfied me, for a great brief is a genuine work of art. But I felt I was called now to new things. And if I wanted to get to them, I had to leave the law behind.

Granted, this was all still what I was imagining. Perhaps I would just rot or wilt under the pressures and seductions of retirement. But it was importuning me, and I had to follow.

83

RETIREMENT REALIZED: IN GOING BACK IS MY GOING FORWARD

ONE DAY IN ST. TROPEZ, BY MICHAEL FRANKS (2011), ENCOUNTERED 2019

PLAYLIST NO. 117

SOMETIMES A SONG can be a part of your music collection for years until your mind and your life are in the right place for it to pique your sensibilities. This is about one such song.

By 2017 at the latest, I had downloaded a 2011 album entitled *Time Together*, written and sung by my long-time idol Michael Franks, whom I've already cited twice in these pages. It wasn't until after I retired in 2018, though, that that song really started to speak to me. I believe I running in my gym when it came rising up into my headphones, in a Michael Franks playlist I'd created for myself. When I listened, I could feel my eyes getting wet with some uncategorizable emotion in between sadness and joy.

The song is a samba-fied reminiscence of an extraordinary occasion. I'll start with some of the lyrics.

The year was 1963.
We toured through France,
My thumb and me.
We yankees then

Were seen as friends,
And so I bummed my way
One summer day to St. Tropez.
Outside Toulon an XKE
On some blue highway
Stopped for me.
The driver's seat
Held blonde Brigitte
With whom I parled Français
That summer day in St. Tropez.
And at her villa
I met Marcello
And other distingués
Of Cinema Français.
That poolside star
Noticed my guitar
And my shyness flew away
When she asked me to play.

(This would have been the summer before Franks' 19th birthday and Bardot's 29th, so the tale is plausible.) Even setting aside the enviable experience it chronicles, the languid guitar (courtesy of Romero Lumambo), and Franks' understated delivery, the song works because of the delight Franks evidently takes in the memory, in the process of re-situating himself if only in his imagination, at a memorable occasion. This is an old man's pleasure in remembering himself young – and it should be noted that in his old age Franks has also limned the joys of senior domesticity. He seems to be a man unplagued by regrets, especially over the passage of time. So the song is not a sigh of sorrow that he is no longer young; it simply exults in having once been young.

And that is where I found myself as well, once my retirement took hold. Much of what I'd retired to pursue happened – or at least until COVID came to town. I was reviewing and writing plays, and getting some initial productions and readings. I was improving my harmonica, routinely sitting in with my church choir. I was hitting the gym three times a week. I was socializing with other retirees at my social club. I was traveling a lot. But increasingly I falling under the spell of my past, and that spell was directing my steps, even before

COVID took a commanding role in my daily agenda, adding a separate source of direction to my activities.

Throughout my writing career, I've always been interested in trying to address my past. I'm not sure where the interest comes from. All I can say for sure is that it's more than a response to the practical pressure to write about what one knows. I can speculate endlessly about my own psychology without reaching firm conclusions, but I do know for sure that compulsion enters into it somewhere. I've devoted far more of my retirement than I'd ever anticipated to ordering the approximately 50,000 images and videos in my family's five-generation photo collection. And I've written this book.

In saying that, I do not mean to mislead. Much of this book had been sketched out over more than a decade, in the form of blog postings on one of my two websites, most of them originally written while I was still in the workforce. I've changed every posting I've used, many quite substantially, so this book is not the same thing by any means. But my point is that the creative process has been going on for a long time. It's just that at this juncture I'm bringing it to a head. Being 71 years of age as of this writing, I know it's time for me to begin narrowing my focus to the things that matter most. And for some reason the recreation of earlier days is one of those paramount things. I'm far from single-minded, and there are other ways I need to be creative too, but I know that this effort is imperative.

So, like Michael Franks, I celebrate the past. And I try to understand it. But I do not wish to relive it, even though I would love to find myself blessed with a young man's slimness, health, and potency again. It's just that I never expected I could hang onto those things forever, and so I'm not disappointed. And even with a virus abroad in the here and now, I do not overglamorize the past or undervalue the present. Like Michael Franks, I find much to appreciate in being the age I am.

But still, the past calls out to me. And I must respond.

Thus, for example, Chapter 43, about my lunch with eminent British literati at Bertorelli's in 1974 seems to answer to Michael's evocation of a poolside evening with movie stars eleven years earlier. I was there, I was blessed to have it, I am still blessed. I was blessed to have the glamorous Fiona to write to in my teens (Chapter 12); I am still blessed to exchange letters with her at the holidays. I was blessed to have found (as I wrote above in Chapters 43 and 52) that it was bliss in certain dawns to be alive; I remain blessed to be friends with some of the women who made those dawns special. And most of all, I am blessed with Mary, and with my children and grandchildren. I would not wish to dispense with a one of them. Nor would I disavow one embarrassing jot or painful tittle of my past, of which there were plenty, because I am grateful for my present.

I know that there are now more yesterdays in my life than tomorrows. Oddly, it does not bother me much. A friend of mine who is on the point of dying as I write these words is reported to have said to one he knew would repeat the words that he had no regrets, because he was so grateful for the life he had had. I hope and I expect that whenever that time comes for me, I shall be able to say the same.

But that time has not yet come for me. For me, this is still the moment of the creative itch, the determined drive to the finish line. It is, God willing, still the time for further explorations and discoveries in this world, and fights to make this world a better place for those I shall one day leave behind.

It is just my peculiarity that I seem to need to make much of what I do about myself. I hope, in satisfying that need, I have been entertaining, and perhaps even enlightening for you, the reader.

84

IN THE WORST OF TIMES

OVERTURE TO MERRILY WE ROLL ALONG, COMPOSED BY STEPHEN SONDHEIM, ORCHESTRATION BY JONATHAN TUNICK, PERFORMED BY BROADWAY MUSICIANS, PART OF TAKE ME TO THE WORLD: A SONDHEIM 90TH BIRTHDAY CELEBRATION (2020), ENCOUNTERED 2020

SUBSTITUTE PLAYLIST TRACK NO. 118. LINK TO ACTUAL PERFORMANCE: HTTPS://YOUTU.BE/A92WZIVEUAW

AND SO WE come to the present day as this chapter is being written, what is by common consent one of the darkest times in our history: national, international, economic, ecological, epidemiological, political. Whatever the future may hold, as of this moment most of those who can do so are restricted to quarters to try to avoid being infected with a pandemic virus, while the economy staggers, and demonstrations rage outside, and the planet hurtles towards catastrophe.

There are many musical responses around, mostly attempts to cheer us listeners up. And heaven knows we need them. I'd single out for honorable mention *Rise Up*, performed by Andra Day (a 2015 song repurposed for a justly inspirational commercial implicitly addressing these times), and *Times Like These* (a distant-collaboration effort by a large ad hoc group of British pop stars dubbed Live Lounge Allstars). But I can point to the exact moment I encountered a piece of music that made me begin to feel a little better, and continues to do so every time I replay it.

It will go without saying to any reader who has followed me through these stories that the aspect of the current situation that has made me feel the worst is the absence of theater. As of this writing, theater seems the last thing likely to reopen, and it was the thing I had intended to focus on the most in my retirement. In the midst of this deprivation, there was a virtual benefit concert in celebration of Stephen Sondheim's 90th birthday, viewable here:

The second event in the concert (at 2:23) is an utter tour-de-force: a performance by (according to my count) 20 musicians of the wonderful Overture to *Merrily We Roll Along* – each musician in his or her own space. And unlike other spliced-together-after-the-fact collaborations between artists which have become a commonplace under current circumstances, this appears to be a real-time performance by the entire ensemble. And there is no compromise in quality of either sound or performance that I can hear; it's just an utterly professional Broadway pit orchestra doing its bang-on-time thing, nicely packaged by video experts.

It seems to bring tears to my eyes each time I play it, partly, I suppose, because, whatever the flaws in the show from which it came (only 16 performances in the original 1981 run), there is nothing at all wrong with the Overture, a thoughtful stitching-together of a few very jazzy and tuneful melodies, brilliantly orchestrated by Jonathan Tunick.

But there's a bigger reason too. The spontaneous ensemble effect is something that hitherto I would have said could only have been produced by performers interacting in the same place at the same time. And I would have been wrong. And then, if I was wrong about that kind of limitation, what more might also be attainable while we await whatever kind of normality finally returns? So this number provides a solid little precedent upon which hopefulness can legitimately be built. Maybe we can do more than we think, even under current circumstances.

I have never given in to despair. I have never lost my innate conviction that we as a nation, a people, and a planet will get through somehow. True, we'll never be able to say that we've fully done it. But perhaps we'll be able to lay claim to accomplishing a meaningful chunk of the task. I still think there's a good chance that I'll live to see at least that much, but no one can even tell me that for sure. At this age, I know that my window of opportunity to see better times is far narrower than it was in the years I have mostly written about here. All the more reason, then, that I seize hungrily on any grounds for hopefulness.

And in light of that and other encouragement, I, and we, go on.

AFTERWORD

THE BLOG POSTINGS that were the earliest form of this book were published without any overall plan; my only design in the years I was placing them online was to pair important moments of my life with the music I associated with them. From the moment I started writing my first post to the moment I hit the "publish" button on my last, I never consciously hewed to any more deeply articulated design than that. Even when I started refashioning those posts into a book, I never sat down and identified themes or considered what story arcs I might be building. I worked without any blueprint or guiding philosophy.

When I was done with a later draft, though, I decided to resurvey my work with a reader's eye. What I saw then astounded me. The book did not plot just the trajectory of starting young and going on until I found myself old, which is what you'd expect of a memoir. Rather, it sketched out a very particular trajectory.

That trajectory started with something I'd never really admitted to myself before, but on reading, it's sitting there. I had experienced a primal wound, the breakup of my parents' marriage and the uprooting loss of status, place, even of name. It wasn't the worst such wound anyone had ever sustained, and in many ways it actually left me with advantages of class and education, but it was nonetheless a wound, and it was serious. I'd written once before about the changes in my life during my first, say, seven years, but it was all happy talk, and some of it was unearned.

The heart of it, as I could now glean from the first few chapters of this book, was that I had been taken out of a world where there was one set of expectations and role models, and I'd been set down in another world entirely. In the new world, the wound was compounded by a new continuing one, because my parents, though they loved me, were all so separate from and (in their own minds) above focusing upon the challenges I had to navigate with my peers, that they provided me with next to no clues how to behave. I was given high aspirations but not the commonsense lessons that would best have equipped me to realize them. I turned to popular culture, music especially, for guidance in working it all out, but that provided (as we've seen) unreliable information. In consequence, I proved headstrong at times when I should have been thoughtful and tactful, as I might have been had I been trained by less insular adults

In two pursuits especially, that is, in forming attachments with girls and (later) with women, and in navigating the credentialing and apprenticeship processes that start a career, I fumbled, probably worse than most people would have done with my advantages.

The story of the repeated early romantic failures might seem to the reader to have taken up too much space in this account, and yet, as I read it, the early pain, in retrospect, seems to have fueled a slow learning process, one I needed to chronicle. I finally did get the task right, and in a deliberate way, not solely by dumb luck. But it took many tries and therapy and a failed marriage and an abandonment, for a while, of the principles I had developed early. My therapist, as the reader may recall, had told me I was no psychopath or narcissist, yet I was acting a bit like one for a time. But I could and eventually did stop.

And the tale of how my lack of any sense of how to navigate institutional politics, academic and corporate, cost me my first career and probably damaged my second seems to follow the same pattern: repeated failures, with a too-slow but eventual learning of lessons. I probably could have retold much more in this area, but I lacked the paired songs for it, and so did not go there as thoroughly.

And I suppose I should add that a reader could discern the same kind of trajectory in the chapters on my religious faith.

Whatever the woes of the moment, though, I have always found things to buoy me up: literature, movies, drama, football games, the glamor of the city, travel, writing. And music, most of all – although, as I've made clear, the lessons music has taught me, including those on subjects I needed most urgently to be taught, have sometimes led me astray.

A collection of essays, being by nature episodic, is not the right framework for and cannot constitute a true autobiography. Likewise, a selection of a hundred or so songs cannot give a very complete idea of my musical tastes. Not only were many things I loved left out, but I suspect some readers will feel there was both too much of some other things, like the Beatles or Michael Franks or 60s pop music, and too little of others, especially what's come out in more recent years. Perhaps. But it was never my purpose to be either complete or balanced. I've paired my story with the songs my story called for, let the chips fall where they may. And I can only hope, if I got the pairing right, the chips fall in the right place for the reader, too.

Thank you for sharing this journey. I hope you've found it of interest. And if I was really lucky, some of the things that mattered or happened to me will chime with reminiscences you may have about your life, and that things I see in the music I've written about may prompt answering thoughts in you.

Jack L.B. Gohn
May 2021

ABOUT THE AUTHOR

JACK L.B. GOHN spent his earliest life in London and Vienna, grew up mainly in Ann Arbor, and has spent most of his adult life in Baltimore. His published writings include scholarly books and papers, book criticism, a newspaper column on law and policy, and theater criticism. Other writings have appeared in such diverse places as the website of the Baltimore Symphony Orchestra, the National Catholic Reporter, and the Wall Street Journal. Most recently he has been writing plays. He belongs to the American Theatre Critics Association and the Dramatists Guild.

He has been indirectly writing memoirs all his life. *What I Was Listening To When ...* is a first for him: a memoir without indirection.

Follow him at **JACKGOHN.COM**.

Image courtesy of Sandi Gohn

CPSIA information can be obtained
at www.ICGtesting.com
Printed in the USA
BVHW010308140922
646968BV00004B/26